Lecture Notes in Computer Science   11287

Commenced Publication in 1973
Founding and Former Series Editors:
Gerhard Goos, Juris Hartmanis, and Jan van Leeuwen

More information about this series at http://www.springer.com/series/7410

Feng Liu · Shouhuai Xu
Moti Yung (Eds.)

Science of Cyber Security

First International Conference, SciSec 2018
Beijing, China, August 12–14, 2018
Revised Selected Papers

 Springer

Editors
Feng Liu
Institute of Information Engineering
and School of Cybersecurity
University of Chinese Academy of Sciences
Beijing, China

Moti Yung
Google and Columbia University
New York, NY, USA

Shouhuai Xu
The University of Texas at San Antonio
San Antonio, TX, USA

ISSN 0302-9743   ISSN 1611-3349   (electronic)
Lecture Notes in Computer Science
ISBN 978-3-030-03025-4   ISBN 978-3-030-03026-1   (eBook)
https://doi.org/10.1007/978-3-030-03026-1

Library of Congress Control Number: 2018958768

LNCS Sublibrary: SL4 – Security and Cryptology

This Springer imprint is published by the registered company Springer Nature Switzerland AG
The registered company address is: Gewerbestrasse 11, 6330 Cham, Switzerland

Preface

Welcome to the proceedings of the inaugural edition of The International Conference on Science of Cyber Security (SciSec 2018)! The mission of SciSec is to catalyze the research collaborations between the relevant communities and disciplines that should work together in exploring the scientific aspects behind cyber security. We believe that this collaboration is needed in order to deepen our understanding of, and build a firm foundation for, the emerging science of cyber security. SciSec is unique in appreciating the importance of multidisciplinary and interdisciplinary broad research efforts toward the ultimate goal of a sound science of cyber security.

SciSec 2018 was hosted by the State Key Laboratory of Information Security, Institute of Information Engineering, Chinese Academy of Sciences, and was held at The International Conference Center, University of Chinese Academy of Sciences, Beijing, China, during August 12–14, 2018. The contributions to the conference were selected from 54 submissions from six different countries and areas; the Program Committee selected 21 papers (11 full papers, six short papers, and four IJDCF-session papers) for presentation. The committee further selected one paper for the Student Distinguished Paper Award. The conference organizers also invited two keynote talks: The first one titled "The Case for (and Against) Science of Security" delivered by Dr. Moti Yung, Research Scientist, Google, and Adjunct Research Professor, Computer Science Department, Columbia University, and the second one titled "Redefine Cybersecurity" delivered by Dr. Yuejin Du, Vice President of Technology, Alibaba Group. The conference program also included a two-hour tutorial on "Cybersecurity Dynamics" delivered by Professor Shouhuai Xu, Department of Computer Science, University of Texas at San Antonio. Finally, the conference program provided a two-hour panel discussion on "Study Focus in Science of Cyber Security," where existing and emerging issues were argued and debated about.

We would like to thank all of the authors of submitted papers for their interest in SciSec 2018. We also would like to thank the reviewers, keynote speakers, and participants for their contributions to the success of the conference. Our sincere gratitude further goes to members of the Program Committee, Publicity Committee, Journal Special Issue Chair, External Reviewers, and Organizing Committee members for their hard work and great efforts throughout the entire process of preparing and managing the event. Further, we are grateful for the generous financial support from the State Key Laboratory of Information Security and the Institute of Information Engineering, Chinese Academy of Sciences.

We hope you will enjoy this conference proceedings volume and that it will inspire you in your future research.

August 2018

Feng Liu
Shouhuai Xu
Moti Yung

Organization

General Chair

Dan Meng IIE, Chinese Academy of Sciences, China

Program Committee Chairs

Feng Liu IIE, Chinese Academy of Sciences, China
Shouhuai Xu University of Texas, San Antonio, USA
Moti Yung Snapchat Inc. and Columbia University, USA

Publicity Committee Chairs

Habtamu Abie Norwegian Computing Center, Norway
Hongchao Hu National Digital Switching System Engineering
and Technological R&D Center, China
Wenlian Lu Fudan University, China
Dongbin Wang Beijing University of Posts and Telecommunications, China
Sheng Wen Swinburne University of Technology, Australia
Xiaofan Yang Chongqing University, China
Qingji Zheng Robert Bosch RTC, Pittsburgh, USA

Journal Special Issue Chair

Sheng Wen Swinburne University of Technology, Australia

Program Committee Members

Habtamu Abie Norwegian Computing Centre, Norway
Luca Allodi Eindhoven University of Technology, The Netherlands
Richard R. Brooks Clemson Univresity, USA
Alvaro Cardenas University of Texas at Dallas, USA
Kai Chen Institute of Information Engineering, Chinese Academy
of Sciences, China
Qian Chen University of Texas at San Antonio, USA
JianXi Gao Rensselaer Polytechnic Institute, USA
Dieter Gollmann TU Hamburg-Harburg, Germany
Changzhen Hu Beijing Institute of Technology, China
Hongchao Hu National Digital Switching System Engineering
and Technological R&D Center, China
Qinlong Huang Beijing University of Posts and Telecommunications, China
ZiGang Huang Lanzhou University, China

Guoping Jiang	Nanjing University of Posts and Telecommunications, China
Yier Jin	University of Florida, USA
Zbigniew Kalbarczyk	University of Illinois at Urbana-Champaign, USA
Hui Lu	Chinese Academy of Sciences, China
Wenlian Lu	Fudan University, China
Zhuo Lu	University of South Florida, USA
Xiapu Luo	The Hong Kong Polytechnic University, SAR China
Pratyusa K. Manadhata	Hewlett-Packard Labs, USA
Thomas Moyer	University of North Carolina at Charlotte, USA
Andrew Odlyzko	University of Minnesota, USA
Nitesh Saxena	University of Alabama at Birmingham, USA
Xiaokui Shu	IBM T.J. Watson Research Center, USA
Sean Smith	Dartmouth College, USA
Lipeng Song	North University of China, China
Kun Sun	George Mason University, USA
Dongbin Wang	Beijing University of Posts and Telecommunications, China
Haiyan Wang	Arizona State University, USA
Jingguo Wang	University of Texas at Arlington, USA
Sheng Wen	Swinburne University of Technology, Australia
Chengyi Xia	Tianjin University of Technology, China
Yang Xiang	Swinburne University of Technology, Austrilia
Jie Xu	University of Miami, USA
Maochao Xu	Illinois State University, USA
Xinjian Xu	Shanghai University, China
Fei Yan	Wuhan University, China
Guanhua Yan	Binghamton University, State University of New York, USA
Weiqi Yan	Aucland University of Technology, New Zealand
Xiaofan Yang	Chongqing University, China
Lidong Zhai	Chinese Academy of Sciences, China
Hongyong Zhao	Nanjing University of Aeronautics and Astronautics, China
Sencun Zhu	Penn State University, USA
Changchun Zou	University of Central Florida, USA
Deqing Zou	Huazhong University of Science and Technology, China

Organizing Committee Chair

Feng Liu	IIE, Chinese Academy of Sciences, China

Organizing Committee Members

Dingyu Yan	IIE, Chinese Academy of Sciences, China
Qian Zhao	IIE, Chinese Academy of Sciences, China
Yaqin Zhang	IIE, Chinese Academy of Sciences, China
Kun Jia	IIE, Chinese Academy of Sciences, China

Jiazhi Liu   IIE, Chinese Academy of Sciences, China
Yuantian Zhang   IIE, Chinese Academy of Sciences, China

Additional Reviewers

Pavlo Burda   Bingfei Ren
Yi Chen   Jianhua Sun
Yuxuan Chen   Yao Sun
Jairo Giraldo   Yuanyi Sun
Chunheng Jiang   Junia Valente
Jiazhi Liu   Shengye Wan
Xueming Liu   Lun-Pin Yuan
Zhiqiang Lv   Yushu Zhang

Sponsors

中国科学院信息工程研究所
INSTITUTE OF INFORMATION ENGINEERING, CAS

信息安全国家重点实验室
STATE KEY LABORATORY OF INFORMATION SECURITY

新一代信息技术先导专项
The next generation of information technology of forwarding China

Multimedia Security Expert Committee
Chinese Institute of Electronics

EasyChair
The conference system

Contents

Metrics and Measurements

Practical Metrics for Evaluating Anonymous Networks

Zhi Wang[1,2], Jinli Zhang[1(✉)], Qixu Liu[1,2], Xiang Cui[3],
and Junwei Su[1,2]

[1] Institute of Information Engineering, Chinese Academy of Sciences,
Beijing, China
zhangjinli@iie.ac.cn
[2] School of Cyber Security, University of Chinese Academy of Sciences,
Beijing, China
[3] Cyberspace Institute of Advanced Technology, Guangzhou University,
Guangzhou, China

Abstract. As an application of privacy-enhancing technology, anonymous networks play an important role in protecting the privacy of Internet users. Different user groups have different perspectives on the need for privacy protection, but now there is a lack of a clear evaluation of each anonymous network. Some works evaluated anonymous networks, but only focused on a part of the anonymous networks metrics rather than a comprehensive evaluation that can be of great help in designing and improving anonymous networks and can also be a reference for users' choices. Therefore, this paper proposes a set of anonymous network evaluation metrics from the perspective of developers and users, including anonymity, anti-traceability, anti-blockade, anti-eavesdropping, robustness and usability, which can complete the comprehensive evaluation of anonymous networks. For each metric, we consider different factors and give a quantitative or qualitative method to evaluate it with a score or a level. Then we apply our metrics and methods to the most popular anonymous network Tor for evaluation. Experiments show that the metrics are effective and practical.

Keywords: Anonymous networks · Metrics · Tor · Evaluation

1 Introduction

At present, with the increasing surveillance of online communications, people are paying more attention to personal privacy and privacy-enhancing technologies. Anonymous network hides the true source or destination address of a traffic, preventing the identity of the client or server from being determined or identified. Therefore, more people choose to use anonymous tools to access the Internet. Anonymous network has received much attention since it was put forward in 1981 by Chaum [1]. Since then, a body of researches have concerned about the anonymous network, mostly about building, analyzing, and attacking. However, there are barely measurements of anonymous networks, and some works focus only on specific properties [2–4], which does not help understanding the anonymous network comprehensively.

© Springer Nature Switzerland AG 2018
F. Liu et al. (Eds.): SciSec 2018, LNCS 11287, pp. 3–18, 2018.
https://doi.org/10.1007/978-3-030-03026-1_1

Among the familiar anonymous tools and networks such as Tor [5], I2P [6], Freenet [7], Java Anon Proxy [8], Crowds [9] etc. Tor is almost the sign of anonymous network. By using Tor, users can obtain a non-personalized Internet access. Other anonymous networks have different scenarios. I2P is mainly used in the internal network and has more routers than Tor to communicate anonymously. If there is a set of metrics to evaluate all anonymous networks, users can refer to the need to select the appropriate anonymous tool.

In this paper, we propose a practical set of metrics to evaluate anonymous networks, which are necessary for users and developers. We present almost all properties related to anonymous networks and analyze the significance and necessity of them. For each property, a method is given to evaluate it. To verify that the methods are practicable, the metrics and methods are applied to the popular anonymous network Tor. The contributions of this work are as follows:

1. A set of practical metrics are proposed to evaluate anonymous networks, including anonymity, anti-traceability, anti-blockade, anti-eavesdropping, robustness and usability.
2. For each metric, a quantitative or qualitative method is designed or developed to evaluate it.
3. The metrics and methods are applied to the popular anonymous network Tor to certify the feasibility.

Specifically, we provide an overview on Tor, its hidden service, and the existing metrics of anonymous network in Sect. 2. We next present, in Sect. 3, a set of metrics and the basic methods to evaluate them. In Sect. 4, we apply our metrics and methods to anonymous network Tor. We conclude with our work and future work in Sect. 5.

2   Related Work

2.1   Anonymous Networks

Tor is a circuit-based anonymous communication service. Tor addresses some limitations by adding perfect forward secrecy, congestion control, directory servers, integrity checking, configurable exit policies, and providing location-hidden services. Tor is a free software and an open network that defends against traffic analysis and improves our privacy and security on the Internet [10]. Tor protects senders' location from being monitored through usually three relays provided by volunteers. Tor now has more than 2 million direct-connecting clients requesting from directory authorities or mirrors, and about 7000 running relays [11]. When users choose a path and build a circuit, each of relay nodes only knows its predecessor and successor, and none of them knows all addresses. The next address is wrapped in a fixed-size cell, which is unwrapped only by a symmetric key at each node (like the layer of an onion, so called onion routing). Each node of Tor has a pair of identity key and onion key. The former is used to sign router descriptor and protect onion key, and the latter is used to encrypt the transport content. To avoid delay, Tor builds circuits in advance, and each circuit can be shared by multiple TCP streams to improve efficiency and anonymity.

Tor also provides recipient anonymity through hidden services as a mechanism to anonymously offer services accessible by other users through the Tor network. User can run a web service without revealing identity and location. The domain name of web service is the first 10 bytes of a base32 encoded hash value of public key with an ". onion" ending. This ".onion" hidden service is only accessible through Tor browser.

2.2 Metrics of Anonymous Network

Anonymous network evaluation metrics are related to the availability and integrity of anonymous networks and are of great significance for improving existing anonymous networks and protecting user privacy. There have been some researches on measuring anonymous networks as shown in Table 1.

Table 1. History measurements on anonymous network.

Metrics	Method	Features	Evaluation[a]	Time-author
Anonymity	Information theory	Size of the anonymity set	1	2002_Diaz [12], 2006_Sebastian [13]
	Probabilistic	Actions	2	2005_Bhargava [14] 2005_Halpern [15]
	Bipartite graph	Inputs and Outputs	1	2007_Edman [16]
	Composability theorem	Adversary and challenges	2	2014_Backes [17]
	Information theory	Nodes, bandwidth and path	1	2011_Hamel [18]
Robustness	Probabilistic	Bandwidth, latency, throughput, etc.	1	2015_Fatemeh [3]
	Game-based	Router features	2	2010_Gilles [4]
Unlinkability	Information theory	Set of senders and/or set of messages sent	1	2003_Steinbrecher [19]
	Expected distance	Relations of entities	1	2008_Lars [20]
Unobservability	Information theory	Distribution of packet status	1	2015_Tan [21]
	Attacks	Responses	2	2013_Amir [22]
Usability	Side channel	Latencies	1	2015_Cangialosi [23]
	User usage	Installation and configuration	2	2005_Dingledine [24]
		Guideline violations and Bandwidth	1	2009_Jens [1]
		Configuration	1	2017_Lee [25]
		Latencies	2	2010_Fabian [26]
Anti-traceability	Watermark or penetration	Traffic flow	2	2012_Chen [27]
	Website fingerprinting	Transmission 1 and packet(s) features	2	2014_Tao [28]
		Circuits	2	2015_Kwon [29]
Anti-blockade	Domain-fronting	Domain and protocol	2	2015_Fifield [30]
	IP Spoofing	Protocol	2	2012_Qiyan [31]
	Traffic modulating	Protocol and communication	2	2013_Amir [32]

[a]1 for quantitative and 2 for qualitative.

For measuring anonymity, Reiter et al. [9] quantified the anonymity degree, [16] used a bipartite graph to quantify anonymity, Berthold et al. [33] and Diaz et al. [12] presented quantitative standards of anonymity. There are also some qualitative measurements for anonymity [14, 15, 17]. According to [34], unlinkability represents the inability of the observer to distinguish whether the entities or actions within the system are related or not, which is related to anonymity. [19, 20] quantified the unlinkability from the perspective of entropy. Usability is about the user experience and it is about whether an anonymous system can operate for a long time. [24, 25] evaluated the use of anonymous tools, including their installation and configuration, of which [25] also quantified the usability. [1, 23, 26] qualitatively and quantitatively evaluate usability from the aspect of performance. Robustness is used to guarantee the availability of anonymous networks. [3] evaluates the performance impact of anonymous networks from the standpoint of confrontation. [4] proposed a game-based method for robustness and evaluated in Crowds, Tor, etc. With the development of privacy technology, more work has been done on the tracking of anonymous network entities. Chen [27] reviewed some traceability methods, including stream watermark modulation tracking techniques [1, 36, 37], replay [18] and penetration injection techniques [38]. In recent years, Tao et al. [28, 29] combined machine learning [39, 40] and neural network [41] to analyze traffic data transmission features, packets features, circuits features, etc., and constructed website fingerprints to achieve tracking. Some adversaries or ISPs block anonymous networks through protocols or Deep Packet Inspection (DPI), which has spawned the anti-blockade [30–32] of anonymous networks. Amir et al. [22] and Tan et al. [21] measure the unobservability similar to anti-blockade of anonymous network.

3   Metrics and Methods

We summarize the previous studies and propose a set of metrics for evaluating anonymous communication networks to some extent. We select anonymity, anti-traceability, anti-blockade, anti-eavesdropping, robustness and usability in Fig. 1, and divide them into quantitative and qualitative properties. In this section, we discuss and analysis each property, then propose a quantitative or qualitative method. In the next section, we will give a score or a level to each metric.

3.1   Anonymity

Anonymity is the most essential property in anonymous communication networks. Communication consists of communication object (content of a communication) and communication subject (sender and receiver of a communication). Since communication object is often well protected by security protocols, anonymity mainly focuses on the communication subject. **Anonymity** is a metric that ensures the identity and the relationship of a communication subject not being identified [34].

The evaluation of anonymity is based on a model and is measured quantitatively into different grades. We define the anonymous communication network model as a directed graph $G = <V, E>$. V represents the set of communication nodes. According to the Internet standard, network communication of an application must contain its IP

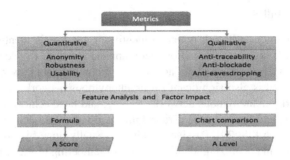

Fig. 1. The structure of metrics for anonymous networks

address. Therefore, the anonymous network usually hides the real IPs through multiple hops. The metric we considered contains the size and other features of the nodes. On the other hand, the path selection of nodes is also important. E represents a set of paths between nodes. Paths cannot be fixed, and the path selection algorithm preferably has a certain randomness, which will make it difficult to determine the communication subject. We also consider other path policies. Each node feature and path policy have a certain weight representing how much contribution to the anonymity. We define the anonymity grade of the anonymous network based on the model, with a range of (1, 10). V and E in the model are equally important, so they each have half the weight.

$$G = \frac{1}{2}v + \sum_i n_i w_i + \frac{1}{2}e + \sum_j p_j w_j \qquad (1)$$

The explanations of the formula are as follows:

- v represents the number of the used nodes and e represents the randomness and importance of the path.
- Both of v and e range from (1, 10). In general, anonymous networks have 2–6 nodes because less than 2 are easy to track, and more than 6 have high latency.
- n represents the node features and p represents the routing policy of the path. The value of n and p are usually 1, and they just represent one option.
- w represents the weight of each condition and ranges from (0.1, 0.5), as they are outside the coefficient 1/2.
- i and j take integer values.

The simplest level is shown in Formula (2) and its grade is 1 when an anonymous network has only one hop and one alternative path without other conditions.

$$G = \frac{1}{2}v + \frac{1}{2}e \qquad (2)$$

3.2 Anti-traceability

Tracking of anonymous network refers to identifying the user's identity or location, including the user's account information, geographical location, etc. **Anti-traceability** is a property that aims at avoiding adversaries from obtaining users' information through tracking and is also significant for an anonymous network. Researchers have done a lot of work on anonymous network tracking, and have achieved rich results on Tor [28], I2P [42] and Freenet [43]. Traceability is divided into active approach [27] and passive approach [28, 29]. Passive tracking is usually done by eavesdropping on activity of the user and analyzing identity instead of tampering traffic which can obtain more tracking information.

We design a passive method to measure the anti-traceability of anonymous network. Our team develop an experimental website [44] that can collect the expect information, including the type of computer operating system, platform, screen resolution, pixel ratio, color depth, host, cookie, canvas, http user agent, time zone, WebGL, user's location information including Intranet IP and Internal IP and a unique fingerprint string derived from the other information, etc. The more information we get, the better for tracking the user. Of course, the ability of this website obtaining information has been verified through several tests.

3.3 Anti-blockade

There are three common approaches in blocking the access to an anonymous network communication: blocking by address, blocking by content and blocking by protocol. Blocking by address is usually blacklisting some definite anonymous communication IP addresses or domain names to disconnect all communications. Blocking by content is based on the contents of the transmitted data to block connection [30]. Blocking by protocol is an active probing. Since the protocol does not consider anti-censorship in the original design, it is easy to be exploited by attackers. **Anti-blockade** is a property that aims at evading censorships from adversaries. There are also a lot of counter-measures. Many anonymous communications come up with protocol camouflage and traffic obfuscation [31, 32], which disguises protocols as normal communication protocols such as HTTP or HTTPS. In recent years, Tor also has shifted its focus from anonymity to anti-censorship [21, 22]. It has launched countermeasures such as obfs2, obfs3, obfs4, FTE, ScrambleSuit and Meek in succession. The effect of their camouflage and whether they can be distinguished are important for anonymous networks.

Anti-blockade of anonymous networks is mainly confusing their own protocols with the existing and unblocked protocols. We distinguish the differences between the target protocol and the simulated protocol by comparing some obvious characteristics, including packet size distribution, throughput, etc. Our method uses different protocols to perform the same operation under the same environment. Finally, we analyze and compare the variance of the protocol characteristic values through graph distribution to show the anti-censorship qualitative performance.

3.4 Anti-eavesdropping

Although the content encryption is the field of cryptography, anonymous network should not only guarantee the anonymity of communication subject, but also ensure the unobservability of communication object. Anonymous network communication object mainly includes communication data content, as well as the node location. **Anti-eavesdropping** of anonymous network is a property that further strengthens and protects the anonymity of communication subject. The anonymous network usually hides location information of nodes through its own encryption algorithms, which can prevent the active and passive attacks from listening to the communication nodes information.

It is well known that HTTPS encrypts communication content and HTTP not. However, anonymous networks may have their own encrypted communication systems, and even content that communicates using HTTP may not be viewed in clear text. To verify that anonymous network has anti-eavesdropping capability, we examine and review the content information of the anonymous communication system through traffic analysis combined with protocol analysis.

3.5 Robustness

Robustness [45] is the property of being strong and healthy in constitution. Robustness of an anonymous network can be thought of the ability to provide an acceptable quality of service performance in face of various faults and other changes without adapting its initial stable configuration. Consider the unexpected attacks, such as denial of service attack [46] or an active attack [3], which would force the path to be rebuilt. It makes sense to measure the robustness in order to provide a good quality of communication.

The approach we take is to simulate attackers whose goal is to reduce the quality of service in an open world or using simulators. The adversary is capable of intercepting some nodes and making the connection interrupted, reducing the service quality. Then we select measurements of the service quality that users concerned about most, including bandwidth, throughput or other attributes. We definite the robustness against adversaries to be:

$$R = Q_{ac}/Q \tag{3}$$

Q_{ac} is the service quality after an adversary attacking the anonymous network; Q is the original service quality. R reflects robustness and the greater the R, the better the robustness.

3.6 Usability

While users are concerned about their privacy increasingly, they mostly focus on the usability when choosing an anonymous tool to protect their privacy. After all, most users are not very professional, and just want to surf the Internet anonymously. Consequently, usability is important to an anonymous network. **Usability** is an attribute that reflects how ease to use of an anonymous network. On the other hand, for most anonymous networks, the large amount of participating users can promote the degree of anonymity and performance of anonymous network to a certain extend. Usability is thus not only a convenience, but also a security requirement.

We discuss the usability in terms of a tool's life cycle and cost, from download, installation, configuration, usage to deployability. First, users should be aware of their download address and familiar with their installation steps. Then, users should configure it and make it work well without some troubles. Moreover, users should know the steps to perform a core task. Besides, users should be aware of deploying a node with a less cost (a balance bandwidth) to participate in the anonymous network. Finally, we give a score of each procedure in Fig. 2.

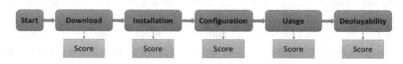

Fig. 2. The method for measuring usability

4   Experimental Evaluation

In this section, we apply our metrics of the anonymous network and the corresponding approaches to Tor to certify that the metrics are feasible and effective.

4.1   Evaluate Anonymity Grade

In order to quantify Tor's anonymity grade, we compare it with another popular anonymous network I2P. All the following values are result from comparison between Tor and I2P, and are given empirically. Generally, Tor has 3 hops ($v = 3$) and I2P has 6 hops in each path. However, Tor and I2P are more than just a simple multi-agent. So far Tor has more than 7,000 total running nodes. Considering that I2P has about 50,000 nodes and Freenet has more than 60,000 nodes, this disadvantage causes Tor to have a lower weight of 0.35 in this feature and a higher weight of I2P. In addition, Tor's nodes are composed of volunteers from all over the world and it is difficult to be tracked. Although it is of high importance, I2P has the same feature and therefore weighs 0.38. Tor has one random path ($e = 1$) and I2P has two paths. Both Tor and I2P's garlic use onion layer encryption that the MITM cannot decipher all IP addresses, so the value is 0.4. Tor can also exclude nodes in insecure countries with a weight of 0.42. In addition, the path of Tor changes every ten minutes, making deanonymization more difficult, with a value of 0.45. I2P has a P2P structure that prevents a single point of failure with a value of 0.35. Finally, the anonymous grade of Tor is 4.0, lower than I2P with 5.53 in Table 2.

There is no absolute anonymity. Although the anonymity grade of Tor is not high theoretically, deanonymization is still very difficult in reality.

Table 2. Anonymity evaluation.

Metrics	Tor	Value	I2P	Value
Hops	$v = 3$	1.5	$v = 6$	3
$n1$	About 7,000 nodes	0.35	About 50,000 nodes	0.4
$n2$	Nodes from all over the world	0.38	Nodes from all over the world	0.38
Paths	$e = 1$	0.5	$e = 2$	1
$p1$	Onion layer encryption	0.4	Onion layer encryption	0.4
$p2$	Exclude insecure nodes	0.42	P2P structure	0.35
$p3$	Changing path	0.45		
Grade		**4.0**		**5.53**

4.2 Measuring for Anti-traceability

We use Tor browser to visit our fingerprint website. We can get some basic information. However, we could not obtain other important features used directly for tracking. In the test, when visiting fingerprint website, we would not obtain any information of the Tor browser because it forbids scripts globally and WebGL<canvas> which gradually replaces cookie to become the mainstream technology of tracking by default and. For experiment, we choose to allow them. Finally, the fingerprint website can obtain cookie, canvas, host, HTTP User Agent, platform, etc., but no Intranet IP address and Internal IP address. As expected, Tor browser builds a set of its own rules, which has a middle-level anti-tracking property as shown in Fig. 3. It cannot be simply identified and also blocks some sensitive messages by default. However, if the user disallows the protective mechanisms accidentally, an attacker still can get some useful information to trace the user indirectly.

Fig. 3. Measuring for anti-traceability

4.3 Measuring for Anti-blockade

Tor itself has some obvious features, such as the fixed 512-byte package, the special TLS fingerprints [47] and the throughout fingerprints [48] and so on. Tor will jump to a configuration window when it detects that the network cannot be connected. It will ask user to configure Tor bridges to avoid censorship. Then user can choose from a set of bridges provided or enter custom bridges. The provided bridges can resist the protocol blockage, and the custom bridges which are unlisted in public can resist the address blocking. The custom bridges can be obtained through the Tor website or the email autoresponder. Next, we will introduce the recommended bridges Meek and obfs4, and analyze anti-blockade of the two methods.

Meek is a pluggable transport, and acks as an obfuscation layer for Tor using "domain fronting" [30] which is a versatile censorship circumvention technique. It uses HTTPS on the outside to request some domain names that permitted by censors in the DNS request and TLS server Name Indication, and hides the real domain names in the HTTP host header on the inside of HTTPS. The censors are unable to distinguish the outside and the inside traffic through a domain name, so they cannot block the domains entirely, which results in gigantic damage.

Obfs4's core designs and features are similar to ScrambleSuit [49] which uses morphing techniques to resist DPI and out-of-band secret exchange to protect against active probing attacks. ScrambleSuit is able to change its flow shape to make it polymorphic, as a result there are no fixed patterns to be distinguished. Obfs4 improves the design on the basis of ScrambleSuit by using high-speed elliptic curve cryptography instead of UniformDH, which is more secure and less cost in exchanging the public key. But whether ScrambleSuit or Obfs4, it still matches a layer of obfuscation for the existing unblocked authenticated protocol like SSH or TLS.

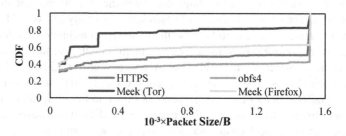

Fig. 4. Four modes of packet size distribution

We measure the anti-blockade of Tor Meek and Tor Obfs4, and compare them with HTTPS protocol. In the experiment, we use the latest Tor browser with Meek and Obfs4 connection modes and Firefox browser respectively performing the same operations under the Windows 7 with the same network environment. The operations include access to the same HTTPS website, search for the same content and browse the same big image file. After obtaining many times of network traffic, we focus on the packet segment size which best reflects the traffic fingerprint [13]. In addition, Tor's Meek traffic is relayed at Meek's agency, so we also capture traffic that Firefox browser is directly accessing Meek-Amazon platform, compared it with Tor's Meek mode. We calculate the cumulative distribution function (CDF) of the packet size from the connection handshake to the end of access over the different modes above. We get the cumulative distribution function of four modes in Fig. 4: Tor's Meek, Tor's Obfs4, Firefox HTTPS and Firefox Meek-Amazon. By observing the distribution, we find that the packet size of Tor's Obfs4 mode is obviously larger than the HTTPS connection overall, whereas the packet size of Tor's Meek mode is relatively concentrated at 92 KB and 284 KB. The amount of 1514 KB-size packets from Firefox browser to Meek-Amazon platform is obviously greater than that of Tor's Meek mode, while 54 KB-size obviously less. It indicates that Tor's Obfs4 and Tor's Meek mode traffic still have a discrimination in packet size characteristic from HTTPS traffic. But they achieve the highest size in 1514. All in all, the anti-blockade of Tor has a middle level.

4.4 Measuring for Anti-eavesdropping

To measure Tor's anti-eavesdropping, we use Tor's Obfs4 mode to connect to Tor network accessing HTTP website that is transmitted in plain text. We also set up our own Obfs4 bridge node, which facilitates traffic capturing between Tor Onion Proxy (OP) and the first hop bridge node and between the bridge node and the next hop node, respectively. In addition, for comparison, we use Firefox and Tor browser to access the same HTTP website. At the client, we find that we can see the packet data under Firefox HTTP request in clear text, including the domain name, cookie, path, etc., while the HTTP packet data under the Tor network is encrypted and unable to be seen. Likewise, we also carry out traffic analysis in Tor's Obfs4 Bridge, and are still unable to see the plaintext. It denotes that the Tor can protect the communication content from being eavesdropped in a high level even if HTTP is used for transmission.

Although Tor has a good anti-eavesdropping compared with regular browsers, we still recommend using HTTPS communication. By analyzing the protocol of Tor, we know that data is transmitted explicitly between Tor's exit node and HTTP website, unlike I2P or Tor hidden service that all communications are encrypted end-to-end. But before data transmitting, Tor constructs circuits incrementally, negotiating a symmetric key through an asymmetric encryption algorithm with each node on the circuit, which ensures the client not being recognized by the exit node or website. HTTPS can enhance Tor's anti-eavesdropping to ensure that all of Tor communication content is encrypted.

4.5 Measuring for Robustness

We use Shadow [50], a Tor simulator, to measure the robustness of anonymous communication networks. In the study of Tor, simulators are widely used, and Shadow is a Distributed Virtual Network (DVN) simulator that runs a Tor network on a single machine. Shadow provides a set of python scripts that allow us to easily generate Tor network topology, parse and draw the virtual network's communication data, such as network throughput, client download statistics, etc.

We install the Shadow simulator and Tor plug-in under the Ubuntu 14.04. Then we download the latest Tor nodes information into the simulator. Considering the bandwidth, we initialize the Tor network with 100 nodes. In order to measure the robustness of Tor anonymous network, we remove 10 nodes, 30 nodes, 50 nodes in turn. Based on the description, we generate four Tor networks with 100 nodes, 90 nodes, 70 nodes and 50 nodes in the same configurations. Finally, we compare the generated communication data and plot into some charts automatically in Fig. 5. We focus on comparing the throughput that results in degraded service quality. From the left Fig. 5 we can see that as the number of nodes decreases, the service quality (throughput) decrease but is not obvious. For a single node, the throughput is basically unaffected in the right of Fig. 5. Table 3 counts the throughput of 100 nodes and 90 nodes network from Fig. 5. We calculate the arithmetic mean of the frequency distribution and get the robustness of

Tor network by removing 10 from 100 nodes. The result is $R = 0.01258$ (MiB/s)/ 0.01512 (MiB/s) $\approx 83\%$ in this small-scale number of nodes, which has a high-level robustness.

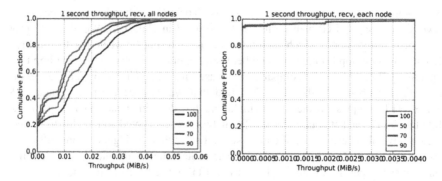

Fig. 5. All nodes and one node received throughput in 1 s

Table 3. Robustness comparison.

Throughput (MiB/s)	0	0–0.01	0.01–0.02	0.02–0.03	0.03–0.04	0.04–0.052/0.045
100 nodes	20%	15%	33%	20%	10%	2%
90 nodes	20%	25%	33%	14%	7%	1%

4.6　Measuring for Usability

Usability of Tor is relatively good. To better explain usability, we compared it with I2P in Windows 7. **Download**: Whether Tor or I2P, the download address is obvious in the official website and users can choose what they need for different operating system. **Installation**: Both their installations are also very simple, just to double-click, but the precondition of I2P is to install Java 1.5 or higher. **Configuration**: After installing, Tor is merely a browser without any configuration and users can surf the web as long as they can connect to Tor's directory server, which is based on the ISP. After installing I2P, it advents three icons in the desktop: Start I2P (no window), start I2P (restartable) and I2P router console. Users double-click "Start I2P (no window)", then the Internet Explorer will open with the "router console" page. The default page is still complex and users need to configure bandwidth, tunnels, nodes and other configurations. Only when connected to about ten active nodes, I2P can work well. **Usage**: Users can visit an Internet website or a hidden service through Tor browser directly as long as they know the URLs. I2P also can visit an eepsite through a browser which has set a proxy through 4444(HTTP) or 4445(HTTPS) port, but to the Internet website users they need to configure an outproxy as I2P is not designed for creating proxies to the outer Internet. **Deoloyability**: Tor can deploy a hidden service and generate an ".onion" site with a few simple steps. I2P can deploy an eepsite and generate an ".i2p" site but with a bit troublesome steps and there are few guidelines found. Table 4 shows the guidance evaluation of usability compared Tor with I2P and takes the decimal grade level.

Table 4. Usability evaluation.

Evaluation	Tor	I2P
Download	9	9
Installation	9	7
Configuration	8	5
Usage	9	8
Deployability	8	6

4.7 Summary and Limitation

In this section, we evaluate the anonymous networks with the proposed metrics. We evaluate Tor and verify the metrics in Table 5. The metrics are measured quantitatively or qualitatively. Although a good measurement standard can be systematically quantified, some of our metrics cannot be quantified well and we measure them qualitatively through other factors. In addition, the numerical selection of some quantitative metrics is empirical and still requires a uniform quantitative method for the evaluation.

Table 5. Evaluation on Tor.

Metrics	Anonymity	Anti-traceability	Anti-blockade	Anti-eavesdropping	Robustness	Usability
Tor	4.0/10	Middle	Middle	High	86%	43/50

5 Conclusion

A set of practical metrics that can comprehensively evaluate anonymous networks is proposed in this paper. Compared to single property measurement previously, we combine properties associated with anonymous networks. Considering the impact for each property, we formulate a quantitative or qualitative measurement, corresponding to a score or level. The metrics are suitable for evaluating an anonymous network or comparing two anonymous networks. In future, we will further refine and clarify the metrics and standardize the quantification. At the same time, different applicable requirements will also be considered to give users more explicit guidance on the choices. This metrics will also be applied to more anonymous networks for horizontal evaluation.

Acknowledgement. This work is supported by Key Laboratory of Network Assessment Technology at Chinese Academy of Sciences and Beijing Key Laboratory of Network Security and Protection Technology, National Key Research and Development Program of China (Nos. 2016YFB0801004, 2016QY08D1602) and Foundation of Key Laboratory of Network Assessment Technology, Chinese Academy of Sciences (CXJJ-17S049).

References

1. Chaum, D.: Untraceable electronic mail, return addresses, and digital pseudonyms. Commun. ACM **24**(2), 84–88 (1981)
2. Jens, S.: Anonymity techniques–usability tests of major anonymity networks. Fakultät Informatik, p. 49 (2009)
3. Fatemeh, S. et al.: Towards measuring resilience in anonymous communication networks. In: Proceedings of ACM Workshop on Privacy in the Electronic Society, pp. 95–99 (2015)
4. Gilles, B. et al.: Robustness guarantees for anonymity. In: Computer Security Foundations Symposium, pp. 91–106 (2010)
5. Dingledine, R., Mathewson, N., Syverson, P.: Tor: the second-generation onion router. J. Frankl. Inst. **239**(2), 135–139 (2004)
6. I2P Anonymous Network. http://www.i2pproject.net. Accessed 15 May 2018
7. Freenet. https://freenetproject.org/. Accessed 15 May 2018
8. JAP. https://anon.inf.tu-dresden.de/index_en.html. Accessed 15 May 2018
9. Reiter, M.K., Rubin, A.D.: Crowds: Anonymity for web transactions. ACM Trans. Inf. Syst. Secur. (TISSEC) **1**(1), 66–92 (1998)
10. Tor Project|Privacy. https://www.torproject.org/. Accessed 23 Nov 2017
11. Welcome to Tor Metrics, https://metrics.torproject.org/. Last accessed 2018/5/13
12. Díaz, C., Seys, S., Claessens, J., Preneel, B.: Towards measuring anonymity. In: Dingledine, R., Syverson, P. (eds.) PET 2002. LNCS, vol. 2482, pp. 54–68. Springer, Heidelberg (2003). https://doi.org/10.1007/3-540-36467-6_5
13. Schiffner, S.: Structuring anonymity metrics. In: ACM Workshop on Digital Identity Management, pp. 55–62. ACM (2006)
14. Bhargava, M., Palamidessi, C.: Probabilistic anonymity. In: Abadi, M., de Alfaro, L. (eds.) CONCUR 2005. LNCS, vol. 3653, pp. 171–185. Springer, Heidelberg (2005). https://doi.org/10.1007/11539452_16
15. Halpern, J.Y., et al.: Anonymity and information hiding in multiagent systems. J. Comput. Secur. **13**(3), 483–514 (2005)
16. Edman, M., Sivrikaya, F., Yener, B.: A combinatorial approach to measuring anonymity. In: Intelligence and Security Informatics, pp. 356–363. IEEE (2007)
17. Backes, M., Kate, A., Meiser S, et al.: (Nothing else) MATor(s): monitoring the anonymity of Tor's path selection. In: ACM CCS, pp. 513–524. ACM (2014)
18. Pries, R., Yu, W., et al.: A new replay attack against anonymous communication networks. In: IEEE International Conference on Communications, pp. 1578–1582. IEEE (2008)
19. Steinbrecher, S., Köpsell, S.: Modelling unlinkability. In: Third International Workshop on Privacy Enhancing Technologies, PET 2003, pp. 32–47. DBLP, Dresden (2003)
20. Lars, F., Stefan, K., et al.: Measuring unlinkability revisited. In: ACM Workshop on Privacy in the Electronic Society, WPES 2008, pp. 105–110. DBLP, Alexandria (2008)
21. Tan, Q., Shi, J., et al.: Towards measuring unobservability in anonymous communication systems. J. Comput. Res. Dev. **52**(10), 2373–2381 (2015)

22. Amir, H., Chad, B., Shmatikov, V.: The Parrot is dead: observing unobservable network communications. In: 2013 IEEE Symposium on Security and Privacy, pp. 65–79 (2013)
23. Cangialosi, F., et al.: Ting: measuring and exploiting latencies between all tor nodes. In: ACM Conference on Internet Measurement Conference, pp. 289–302. ACM (2015)
24. Dingledine, R., Mathewson, N.: Anonymity loves company: usability and the network effect. In: The Workshop on the Economics of Information Security, pp. 610–613 (2006)
25. Lee, L., Fifield, D., Malkin, N., et al.: A usability evaluation of tor launcher. Proc. Priv. Enhancing Technol. **2017**(3), 90–109 (2017)
26. Fabian, B., Goertz, F., Kunz, S., Müller, S., Nitzsche, M.: Privately Waiting – A Usability Analysis of the Tor Anonymity Network. In: Nelson, Matthew L., Shaw, Michael J., Strader, Troy J. (eds.) AMCIS 2010. LNBIP, vol. 58, pp. 63–75. Springer, Heidelberg (2010). https://doi.org/10.1007/978-3-642-15141-5_6
27. Chen, Z., Pu, S., Zhu, S.: Traceback technology for anonymous network. J. Comput. Res. Dev. **49**, 111–117 (2012)
28. Tao, W., Rishab, N., et al.: Effective attacks and provable defenses for website fingerprinting. In: USENIX Security Symposium, pp. 143–157 (2014)
29. Kwon, A., Alsabah, M., et al.: Circuit fingerprinting attacks: passive deanonymization of tor hidden services. In: Usenix Conference on Security Symposium. USENIX, pp. 287–302 (2015)
30. Fifield, D., Lan, C., et al.: Blocking-resistant communication through domain fronting. Proc. Priv. Enhanc. Technol. **2015**(2), 46–64 (2015)
31. Qiyan, W., et al.: CensorSpoofer: asymmetric communication using IP spoofing for censorship-resistant web browsing. Comput. Sci. 121–132 (2012)
32. Amir, H., et al.: I want my voice to be heard: IP over voice-over-IP for unobservable censorship circumvention. In: NDSS (2013)
33. Berthold, et al.: The disadvantages of free MIX routes and how to overcome them. In: International Workshop on Designing Privacy Enhancing Technologies Design Issues in Anonymity & Unobservability, vol. 63 (s164), pp. 30–45 (2001)
34. Pfitzmann, A., Hansen. M.: A terminology for talking about privacy by data minimization: anonymity. Unlinkability, Undetectability, Unobservability, Pseudonymity, and Identity Management, 34 (2010)
35. Wang, X., Chen, S., et al.: Network flow watermarking attack on low-latency anonymous communication systems. In: IEEE Symposium on Security and Privacy, pp. 116–130 (2007)
36. Fu, X., Zhu, Y., Graham, B., et al.: On flow marking attacks in wireless anonymous communication networks. In: IEEE DCS, pp. 493–503. IEEE Computer Society (2005)
37. Houmansadr, A., Kiyavash, N., Borisov, N.: RAINBOW: a robust and invisible non-blind watermark for network flows. In: Network and Distributed System Security Symposium, NDSS 2009. DBLP, San Diego (2009)
38. Christensen, A.: Practical onion hacking: finding the real address of tor clients. http://packetstormsecurity.org/0610-advisories/Practical_Onion_Hacking.pdf
39. Panchenko, A., Lanze, F., Zinnen, A., et al.: Website fingerprinting at internet scale. In: Network and Distributed System Security Symposium (2016)
40. Hayes, J., Danezis, G.: k-fingerprinting: a robust scalable website fingerprinting technique. In: Computer Science (2016)
41. Rimmer, V., Preuveneers, D., Juarez, M., et al.: Automated website fingerprinting through deep learning. In: Network and Distributed System Security Symposium (2018)
42. Crenshaw, A.: Darknets and hidden servers: identifying the true IP/network identity of I2P service hosts. Black Hat DC, 201(1) (2011)
43. Tian, G., Duan, Z., Baumeister, T., Dong, Y., et al.: A traceback attack on freenet. In: IEEE Transactions on Dependable and Secure Computing, p. 1 (2015)

44. Fingerprint collection system. http://fp.bestfp.top/wmg/fw/fp.html. Accessed 14 May 2018
45. Robustness, https://en.wikipedia.org/wiki/Robustness. Last accessed 24 Nov 2017
46. Anupam, D., et al.: Securing anonymous communication channels under the selective DoS attack. In: Conference on Financial Cryptography and Data Security, pp. 362–370 (2013)
47. Mittal, P., Khurshid, A., Juen, J., et al.: Stealthy traffic analysis of low-latency anonymous communication using throughput fingerprinting. In: ACM CCS, pp. 215–226 (2011)
48. He, G., Yang, M., Luo, J., Zhang, L.: Online identification of Tor anonymous communication traffic. J. Softw. **24**(3), 540–546 (2013)
49. Philipp, W., Pulls, T., et al: A polymorphic network protocol to circumvent censorship. In: ACM Workshop on Privacy in the Electronic Society, pp. 213–224 (2013)
50. Fatemeh, S., Goehring, M., Diaz, C.: Tor experimentation tools. In: 2015 IEEE Security and Privacy Workshops (SPW), pp. 206–213 (2015)

Influence of Clustering on Network Robustness Against Epidemic Propagation

Yin-Wei Li[1], Zhen-Hao Zhang[1], Dongmei Fan[2], Yu-Rong Song[2(⊠)], and Guo-Ping Jiang[2]

[1] School of Computer Science, Nanjing University of Posts and Telecommunications, Nanjing 210003, China
[2] School of Automation, Nanjing University of Posts and Telecommunications, Nanjing 210003, China
songyr@njupt.edu.cn

Abstract. How clustering affects network robustness against epidemic propagation is investigated in this paper. The epidemic threshold, the fraction of infected nodes at steady state and epidemic velocity are adopted as the network robustness index. With the help of the networks generated by the 1K null model algorithm (with identical degree distribution), we use three network propagation models (*SIS*, *SIR*, and *SI*) to investigate the influence of clustering against epidemic propagation. The results of simulation show that the clustering of heterogeneous networks has little influence on the network robustness. In homogeneous networks, there is limited increase in epidemic threshold by increasing clustering. However, the fraction of infected nodes at steady state and epidemic velocity evidently decrease with the increase of clustering. By virtue of the generated null models, we further study the relationship between clustering and global efficiency. We find that the global efficiency of networks decreases monotonically with the increase of clustering. This result suggests that we can decrease the epidemic velocity by increasing network clustering.

Keywords: Clustering · Global efficiency · Network robustness
Epidemic propagation

1 Introduction

There are kinds of propagation phenomena in complex networks, such as epidemic spreading through population, computer virus diffusion in the Internet, rumors in the online social networks and cascading failures in power grids. These incidents and disasters seriously affect people's life and threaten the stability of modern society [1–5]. Therefore, the research on restraining propagation phenomena by optimizing network structure is a topic of practical concern.

With the discovery of small-world and scale-free characteristics of complex networks [6, 7], how the network structure influences the spreading dynamics has been widely studied [8–14]. Many scholars measure the network robustness of defense against epidemics by the Epidemic Threshold ("E-*Threshold*" for short). The standard *SIS* epidemic model [15] can be used to study the relation between network structure

© Springer Nature Switzerland AG 2018
F. Liu et al. (Eds.): SciSec 2018, LNCS 11287, pp. 19–33, 2018.
https://doi.org/10.1007/978-3-030-03026-1_2

and spreading process [16]. Based on the homogeneous mixing hypothesis, Ref. [17] found that the E-*Threshold* of homogenous networks is positively related to the reciprocal of the average degree of the network. Pastor and Vespignani [18] studied the outbreak of viruses under heterogeneous networks. They found that the E-*Threshold* for finite size heterogeneous networks is related to degree distribution, and the E-*Threshold* for infinite size heterogeneous networks is zero. Another assessment index for network robustness against epidemic propagation is the fraction of infected nodes at steady state ("E-*fraction*" for short) during the spreading process. Song et al. [19] found that the E-*fraction* of small-world network is larger than that of random networks under the identical threshold conditions. It is not adequate to assess the network robustness by considering the E-*Threshold* simply. Youssef et al. [20] proposed a novel measurement to assess network robustness with the help of *SIS* epidemics model by considering the E-*Threshold* and the E-*fraction* simultaneously. The velocity of epidemic propagation ("E-*Velocity*" for short) in the network is also a criterion for network robustness. In reality, the E-*Velocity* affects the timely control measures. In Ref. [21], the authors found that the time scale of outbreaks is inversely proportional to the network degree fluctuations. Gang et al. [22] investigated the spreading velocity in weighted scale-free networks. Compared with the propagation velocity on un-weighted scale-free networks, the velocity on weighted scale-free networks is smaller.

In summary, the robustness of the network can be assessed by E-*Threshold*, E-*fraction* and E-*Velocity*. Then, are there certain network structures with larger E-*Threshold*, smaller E-*fraction* and slower E-*Velocity*? The study of this problem is of theoretical significance and is beneficial to improve the network robustness against epidemic propagation.

The influence of clustering [6] against epidemic propagation has attracted the attention of scholars. Gleeson et al. [23] used highly clustered networks to analytically study the bond percolation threshold. They found that the increase of clustering in these model networks is shown to bring about a larger bond percolation threshold, namely, clustering increases the epidemic threshold. Newman [24] presented a solvable model of a network and used it to demonstrate that increase of clustering decreases E-*fraction* for an epidemic process on the network and decreases the E-*Threshold*. Coupechoux and Lelarge [25] found that clustering inhibits the propagation in a low connectivity regime of network, while in a high connectivity regime of network, clustering promotes the outbreak of the virus but reduces its E-*fraction*. Kiss and Green [26] have shown that in the models presented in Ref. [24], the degree distribution changes with the change of clustering. So, the lower E-*Threshold* of the networks generated by this model is not attributed to clustering only.

Inspired by the above researches, we can deduce that the influence of clustering against network robustness is related to network structures. In real-world scenarios, it is of practical significance to maintain the node degrees unchanged while probing the influence of clustering against network robustness. To change nodes degree is much more difficult than to change their connections. For example, we can easily adjust the airline, but difficultly increase the capacity of the airport. Up to now, under the condition of constant degree distribution, investigating the network robustness by considering the above three criteria simultaneously is still insufficient. In this paper, we focus on the robustness of networks against epidemic propagation in heterogeneous and homogeneous networks. We use 1K null model algorithm based on the clustering coefficient to generate a large number of null models for homogeneous and hetero-geneous networks respectively. Furthermore, we find that increasing the clustering can decrease the global efficiency through the generated null models with identical degree distribution. With the help of classic epidemic models (*SIS*, *SI* and *SIR*), we investigate the influence of clustering on the network robustness assessed by the above three criteria. We find that the clustering of heterogeneous networks is almost irrelevant to the robustness. But in the homogeneous networks, increasing clustering can effectively improve the robustness.

The rest of the paper is arranged as follows: In Sect. 2, we give a detailed intro-duction to three criteria of network robustness. In Sect. 3, we use the 1K null model algorithm to generate a set of null models from the initial homogeneous and hetero-geneous network respectively, and the Monte Carlo simulations are performed on eight networks picked form the null models. The influences of clustering on network robustness are analyzed for homogeneous and heterogeneous networks. We further analyze the relation between clustering and global efficiency. The conclusions are given in Sect. 4.

2 Network Robustness Index

According to the type of network attack, we can formulate some evaluation index of network robustness. When the network is attacked by a virus, we first hope that the virus will die out quickly and not spread to the entire network. If the virus breaks out in the network, we wish that the fraction of infected nodes at steady state and the sum of the number of individuals that have been infected in the networks are small as much as possible. During the outbreak of the virus, the small velocity of the spreading will leave us more time to deploy the immunization resources to control virus transmission. In this section, we will review the three criteria of the network robustness, namely, E-*Threshold*, E-*fraction* and *E-Velocity*.

2.1 E-*Threshold*

The standard *SIS* model is used to study the E-*Threshold* of the networks by many scholars. First, we briefly review the standard *SIS* model. In *SIS* model, each node in the network represents an individual and links represent the connection among the nodes. There are two states, "susceptible" or "infected". Infected nodes can infect any susceptible nodes which have connections with them with infection rate β per unit time. At the same time, infected nodes are cured and become susceptible again with cure rate δ. The ratio between β and δ is defined the effective spreading rate $\tau = \beta/\delta$.

In homogeneous networks, the E-*Threshold* is derived as

$$\tau_c = 1/\langle k \rangle \tag{1}$$

where $\langle k \rangle$ is the average degree of the network [17].

In heterogeneous networks, Ref. [18] found that the E-*Threshold* for heterogeneous networks is

$$\tau_c = \langle k \rangle / \langle k^2 \rangle \tag{2}$$

where $\langle k^2 \rangle$ is the two order moment of degree.

When the effective spreading rate τ above the E-*Threshold* τ_c, the virus will break out and spread to the entire network. Instead, if the τ below the τ_c, the virus die out exponentially fast. According to Eqs. (1) and (2), the E-*Threshold* is related to $\langle k \rangle$ and $\langle k^2 \rangle$ only. In other words, the E-*Threshold* is mainly determined by the network degree distribution. We verify the conclusion by Monte Carlo simulations in Sect. 3.

2.2   E-*fraction*

When epidemic propagation takes place in the network, it is of practical significance to study the fraction of infected nodes at steady state. In *SIS* model, there is a persistent fraction of infected nodes exists at the steady state. In homogeneous networks, Ref. [27] used *SIS* model to investigate the E-*fraction* and concluded that the E-*fraction* mainly depends on the effective spreading rate τ and the epidemic threshold τ_c. As follow,

$$i(\infty) \sim \tau - \tau_c \tag{3}$$

where $i(\infty)$ is the fraction of infected nodes at steady state. While in the heterogeneous networks, the E-*fraction* is related to τ only, as follow,

$$i(\infty) \sim e^{-C/\tau} \tag{4}$$

where C is a constant.

In addition to the *SIS* model, the *SIR* model is also used to study the E-*fraction*. In *SIR* model, nodes exist in three discrete states, "susceptible", "infected" and "removed". The infected nodes can be cured with removed rate γ and become removed. When the nodes become removed, they will no longer be infected by other infected nodes. So, in *SIR* model, when the propagation is over (at steady state), there are only susceptible and removed nodes in the network, and the sum of the number of nodes that have been infected in the networks is equal to the final removed size. Therefore, we can use the final removed size as the E-*fraction* to evaluate the network robustness. Reference [28] studied the final removed size in homogeneous and heterogeneous networks and obtained the similar results to the *SIS* model. As follow,

$$R(\infty) \sim \tau - \tau_c, \quad \text{homogeneous networks} \tag{5}$$

$$R(\infty) \sim e^{-C/\tau}, \quad \text{heterogeneous networks} \tag{6}$$

where $R(\infty)$ is the fraction of removed nodes at steady state.

According to the above conclusion, E-*fraction* is related to effective spreading rate τ and E-*Threshold* τ_c in homogeneous networks. However, in Sect. 3, we will find that the clustering can change obviously the E-*fraction* of homogeneous networks while keeping the degree distribution fixed.

2.3   E-*Velocity*

When viruses break out in the network, we need more time to control the epidemic propagation. Then, under the same conditions (for example, identical effective spreading rate), the smaller the E-*Velocity* is, the larger the network robustness is. The *SI* model can be used to study E-*Velocity*, in which the infected nodes remain always infective. So, when the propagation is over (at steady state), there is only infected nodes in the networks. Reference [21] obtained the time scale t_h that governs the growth of the infection in the homogeneous and heterogeneous network. The time scale t_h represent the time when the fraction of infected nodes reaches steady state. The greater the t_h is, the smaller the velocity of epidemic propagation is. The results are as follow

$$t_h \sim 1/(\tau\langle k\rangle), \quad \text{homogeneous networks} \tag{7}$$

$$t_h \sim \langle k\rangle/\tau(\langle k^2\rangle - \langle k\rangle), \quad \text{heterogeneous networks} \tag{8}$$

In Ref. [22], the E-*Velocity* can be defined the slope of the density of the infected nodes as

$$V(t) = di(t)/dt \tag{9}$$

where $i(t)$ is the fraction of infected nodes at time t.

From (7), we can see that the velocity of epidemic propagation is proportional to the effective spreading rate and the average degree in the homogeneous network. From (8), we can obtain that if the two order moment of degree is far greater than average degree, epidemics spread almost instantaneously in heterogeneous networks.

When the degree distribution and the effective spreading rate remain unchanged, is the E-*Velocity* related to other characteristic of the networks? It is easy to think that the shorter the average of the shortest path lengths (L) of the network is, the faster the virus spreading is. The definition of the average of the shortest path lengths is as follows,

$$L(G) = \frac{1}{N * (N-1)} \sum_{i \neq j \in G} d_{ij} \tag{10}$$

where the network is defined as G with N nodes, d_{ij} is the shortest path between node i and node j. According to (10), isolated nodes make the average of the shortest path lengths of the network large infinitely. To avoid the shortcoming, Latora et al. [29] used global efficiency (E) as a measure of how efficiently it influences information propagation. The definition of global efficiency is as follows

$$E(G) = \frac{1}{N * (N-1)} \sum_{i \neq j \in G} 1/d_{ij} \tag{11}$$

Similarly, we can use the global efficiency to evaluate the E-*Velocity* of the networks. The global efficiency is proportional to E-*Velocity*. From Eq. (11), we can see that global efficiency is global parameter of network and it is difficult to adjust it for large networks.

3 Numerical Simulations and Analysis

Reference [6] employed the clustering coefficient as the characteristic parameter of the network. Suppose node i has k_i neighbors, E_i denotes the number of existing edges among the k_i neighbors. The clustering coefficient C_i of node i can be defined as follow.

$$C_i = 2k_i/k_i(k_i - 1) \tag{12}$$

The clustering of the network is defined the average over the clustering coefficients of its nodes. From Eq. (12), we can see that the clustering is local parameter of network and it is easy to adjust it for large networks. In this section, with the help of classic epidemic models (*SIS, SI* and *SIR*), we will investigate the impact of clustering on network robustness.

3.1 Experimental Data

The randomized networks generated by random rewiring algorithm [30] have the identical number of nodes and some similar characteristics with the initial network. When the degree distribution of randomized networks is the same as the initial network, we call them the 1K null models [31]. If the generated 1K null models have different clustering, we can use them to analyze the impact of clustering on network robustness. To this end, we can use the random rewiring algorithm to obtain 1K null models with different clustering coefficient. Let initial network be an unweighted and undirected simple network. The procedures of the algorithm are briefly described as follows:

Rewiring the initial network at each time step with the degree-preserving method is shown in Fig. 1. Only if the clustering of the rewired network is improved and the rewired network is still connected, the rewiring is accepted and the rewired network is stored. Taking the rewired network as an new initial network, repeating the above rewiring process until the final time reaches the preset time value.

According to the degree distribution, networks can be divided into homogeneous networks and heterogeneous networks. In this section, the simulations are carried out in the two kinds of networks. We first generate the initial heterogeneous network with scale-free network model [7] and the initial homogeneous network with small-world network model [6]. The average degree of the initial networks is six, and the size of the initial networks is 500. Then, a large number of null models of each network with different clustering are generated.

Homogeneous networks: There are 1432 null models with identical average degree $\langle k \rangle = 6$ which are generated from the initial homogeneous network. We pick eight null models from the set of null networks according to their clustering (see Table 1).

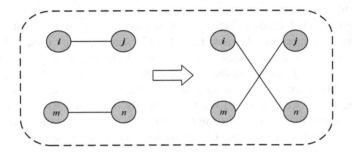

Fig. 1. Randomly rewiring process for preserving node degrees.

Table 1. The structure parameters of selected null models

	heter1	heter2	heter3	heter4	heter5	heter6	heter7	heter8
N	500	500	500	500	500	500	500	500
$\langle k \rangle$	6	6	6	6	6	6	6	6
$\langle k^2 \rangle$	79.26	79.26	79.26	79.26	79.26	79.26	79.26	79.26
C	0.0011	0.0906	0.1804	0.2713	0.3612	0.4512	0.5412	0.6313
E	0.3351	0.3301	0.3263	0.3235	0.3193	0.3168	0.3129	0.3091

Heterogeneous networks: There are 2208 null models with identical average degree $\langle k \rangle = 6$ which are generated from the initial heterogeneous network. Eight null models are picked from the set of null networks according to their clustering (see Table 2).

Table 2. The structure parameters of selected null models

	homo1	homo2	homo3	homo4	homo5	homo6	homo7	homo8
N	500	500	500	500	500	500	500	500
$\langle k \rangle$	6	6	6	6	6	6	6	6
$\langle k^2 \rangle$	37.05	37.05	37.05	37.05	37.05	37.05	37.05	37.05
C	0.0080	0.0983	0.1881	0.2780	0.3680	0.4582	0.5481	0.6382
E	0.2877	0.2774	0.2654	0.2514	0.2377	0.2233	0.2072	0.1895

3.2   *SIS* Model

There is a non-zero epidemic threshold τ_c in the *SIS* model when the size of networks is finite. If $\tau > \tau_c$, the virus outbreaks. Otherwise, the epidemic process will cease fast. As the threshold grows, the network becomes more robust. When virus breaks out in the network, the fraction of infected nodes will finally reach a stable state. Obviously, we can deem that the network robustness is better if the fraction of steady infection is smaller. The simulations performed on each null model are over 3000 runs, the effective spreading rate τ is 0.4, and the initial infected node is chosen randomly.

Figure 2 shows the evolution of epidemic propagation in the two types of networks. The $i(t)$ denotes the fraction of infected nodes at time t. From Fig. 2(a), we can see that the ultimate fraction of steady infection are almost the same. These eight networks also reach the steady state nearly the same time (t = 17). Consequently, these indicate that the E-*fraction*, that is $i(\infty)$, is basically irrelevant to the clustering in heterogeneous networks. Figure 2(b) shows that the E-*fraction* becomes smaller with the increase of clustering in homogeneous networks. Noting the time step that network reaches the steady state, we can see that homo1 reaches the steady state more quickly than homo8, which indicate that increasing clustering can effectively increase the time that networks reach the steady states. Namely, the E-*Velocity* will reduce as the increase of clustering in homogeneous networks.

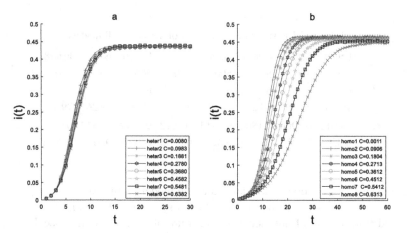

Fig. 2. The evolution of epidemic propagation in the two types of networks. The fraction of infected nodes $i(t)$ is shown as a function of t.

Figure 3 shows the relation between the E-*fraction* and the effective spreading rate τ. The E-*Threshold* of each network are also shown in Fig. 3. Figure 3a shows that the E-*Threshold*s of eight networks are almost the same, which indicating that E-*Threshold* of heterogeneous networks is hardly relevant to clustering. From Fig. 3b, we can see that as the increase of clustering, E-*Threshold* of the homogeneous network become slightly larger. So, our simulation verify the conclusion proposed in Eqs. (1) and (2), namely, the E-*Threshold* is determined mainly by the degree distribution of the network.

In Fig. 4, E-*Velocity* is shown as a function of the t by the Eq. (9). From Fig. 4a, we find that the peak velocity values of heterogeneous networks are almost identical,

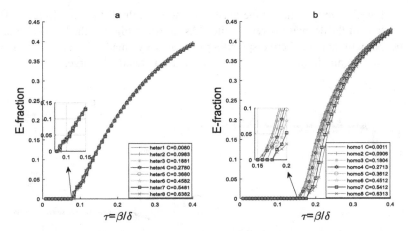

Fig. 3. The fraction of infected nodes at steady state, E-*fraction* is shown as a function of the effective spreading rate τ for different networks.

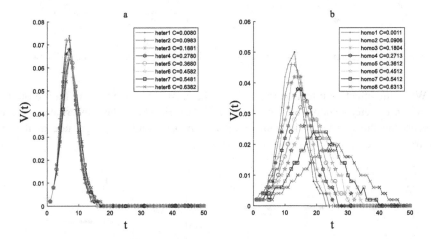

Fig. 4. Epidemic velocity is shown as a function of the *t*.

and the E-*Velocity* reaches the peak values almost at the same time. Whereas in homogeneous networks shown in Fig. 4b, we can see that the smaller the clustering is, the larger the E-*Velocity* is. Moreover, the time when the E-*Velocity* of high clustering networks reaches the peak value is lag far behind that of low clustering networks.

3.3 *SIR* Model

In this section, the simulations are performed on each null model with two effective spreading rate and the initial infected node for each simulation is chosen randomly. Results are averaged over 3000 independent simulation runs.

From Fig. 5a, we find that as the clustering increase, the E-*fraction* decrease. But, the magnitude of the decrease is very limited. As shown in Fig. 5b, the E-*fraction* of all the networks with small effective spreading rate are very small. And as the clustering increase, the magnitude of the E-*fraction*'s decrease is relatively large.

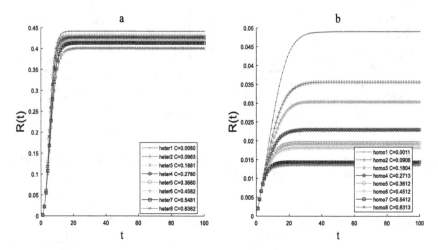

Fig. 5. The evolution of epidemic propagation with $\tau = 0.2$ in the two types of networks.

When the effective infection rate is high, the clustering have little influence on the E-*fraction* in heterogeneous networks (see Fig. 6a). However, the clustering has great influence on the E-*fraction* in homogeneous networks, and the magnitude of the E-*fraction*'s decrease is very large (see Fig. 6b).

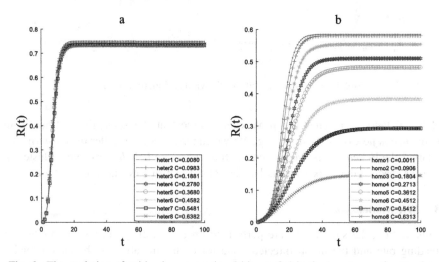

Fig. 6. The evolution of epidemic propagation with $\tau = 0.4$ in the two types of networks.

3.4 *SI* Model

Unlike *SIS* model, infected nodes in *SI* model will not transfer to susceptible nodes, thus there is no epidemic threshold in *SI* model. As there is no transfer from infection to susceptibility, *SI* model has its own advantage in studying the E-*Velocity*. The simulations performed on each null model are over 3000 runs, the infected rate is 0.2, and the initial infected node is chosen randomly.

Figure 7 shows the evolution of epidemic propagation. In Fig. 7a, these eight networks also reach the steady state nearly same time (t = 15). In Fig. 7b, we can see that the time when the E-*fraction* of high clustering networks reaches the stable state (t = 30) is lag far behind that of low clustering networks (t = 15).

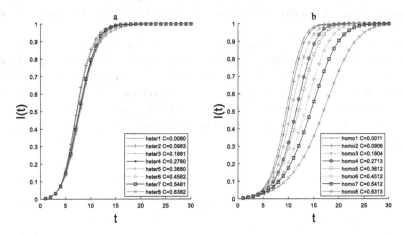

Fig. 7. The evolution of epidemic propagation in the two types of networks. The fraction of infected nodes is shown as a function of t.

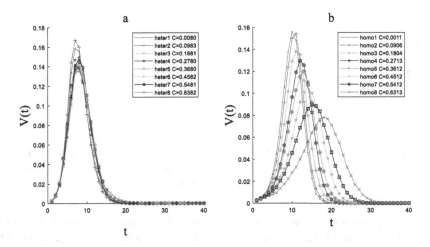

Fig. 8. Epidemic velocity is shown as a function of the t.

The evolution of velocity is showed in Fig. 8. The peak velocity values of heterogeneous networks are little different (see Fig. 8a). And the E-*Velocity* reaches the peak values almost at the same time. As shown in Fig. 8b, the peak velocity value of network with high clustering is far larger than that of network with low clustering, and the time that network with lower clustering reaches the peak value of velocity evidently precedes, and the time when the E-*Velocity* of high clustering networks reaches the peak value is lag far behind that of low clustering networks.

3.5   The Relation Between Clustering and Global Efficiency

From Sect. 3.4, we obtain that the E-*Velocity* is related to the clustering. To investigate the essential reason, we calculate the clustering and global efficiency of all null models generated in Sect. 3.1 and plot the relationship graph according to their clustering value respectively.

In Fig. 9, the black curve shows the relation between clustering and global efficiency of the null models in heterogeneous networks. We find that relative to the range of the clustering, the range of global efficiency reduction is very small. The blue curve shows the relation between clustering and the peak velocity value of epidemic propagation of the eight networks which picked from heterogeneous null models. We can see that as the increase of network clustering, the peak velocity value of epidemic propagation little decreases.

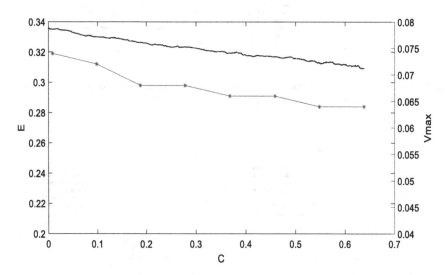

Fig. 9. The black curve shows the relation between clustering and global efficiency of the null models in heterogeneous networks. The blue curve shows the relation between clustering and the peak velocity value of epidemic propagation. (Color figure online)

In Fig. 10, we find that as the increase of network clustering, the global efficiency of network decreases obviously. With the same clustering optimization scope, the range of global efficiency in homogeneous network is far larger than that in heterogeneous network (see Fig. 9). Similarly, the range of the peak velocity value in homogeneous network is far larger than that in heterogeneous network.

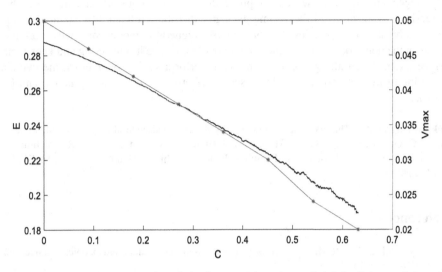

Fig. 10. The black curve shows the relation between clustering and global efficiency of the null models in homogeneous networks. The blue curve shows the relation between clustering and the peak velocity value of epidemic propagation. (Color figure online)

Based on the above findings, we argue that under the identical degree distribution the greater clustering of the homogeneous networks is, the smaller the E-*Velocity* is. Namely, with the increase of clustering, global efficiency reduces, thus causing the decrease of E-*Velocity*. That means, the clustering changes the global efficiency, and subsequently E-*Velocity* is changed. Therefore, to decrease the E-*Velocity*, we can increase the clustering rather than decreasing global efficiency, for the reason that it is difficult to change the global efficiency in large homogeneous networks.

4 Conclusion

This paper has investigated how clustering coefficient affects the networks robustness against epidemic propagation. We have used the 1K null model algorithm to generate a set of null models from the initial homogeneous and heterogeneous networks respectively. With the help of null models, we have used three network models (*SIS*, *SIR*, and *SI*) to verify the influences of clustering against epidemic propagation. The Monte Carlo simulations are performed on eight networks picked form the null models. Simulations results have shown that the clustering of heterogeneous networks has very little influence on the robustness. In homogeneous networks, there is limited increase in epidemic threshold by increasing clustering. However, with the increase of clustering coefficient, the fraction of steady infection and epidemic velocity decline evidently.

Furthermore, we have investigated the relation between clustering and global efficiency. We have found that as the increase of clustering in homogeneous networks, the global efficiency of network decreases obviously. Therefore, when the virus spreads in a homogeneous network, we can improve the network robustness against virus by increasing its clustering while keeping its degree distribution fixed. For example, when the virus breaks out in wireless sensor networks (general homogeneous networks), the agents in the network can rewire their neighbors to improve its clustering and keep their degree fixed. When all agents in the network perform similar operations, the overall clustering of the network will be increased to effectively reduce the E-*fraction* and E-*Velocity*.

Acknowledgments. This work was supported by the National Natural Science Foundation of China (Grant Nos. 61672298, 61373136, 61374180), the Ministry of Education Research in the Humanities and Social Sciences Planning Fund of China (Grant Nos. 17YJAZH071, 15YJAZH016).

References

1. Lloyd, A.L., May, R.M.: How viruses spread among computers and people. Science **292** (5520), 1316–1317 (2001)
2. Motter, A.E., Lai, Y.C.: Cascade-based attacks on complex networks. Phys. Rev. E **66**(2), 065102 (2002)
3. Pastorsatorras, R., Castellano, C., Mieghem, P.V., et al.: Epidemic processes in complex networks. Rev. Mod. Phys. **87**(3), 120–131 (2014)
4. Garas, A., Argyrakis, P., Rozenblat, C., et al.: Worldwide spreading of economic crisis. N. J. Phys. **12**(2), 185–188 (2010)
5. Castellano, C., Fortunato, S., Loreto, V.: Statistical physics of social dynamics. Rev. Mod. Phys. **81**(2), 591–646 (2009)
6. Watts, D.J., Strogatz, S.H.: Collective dynamics of 'small-world' networks. Nature **393** (6684), 440 (1998)
7. Barabási, A.L., Albert, R.: Emergence of scaling in random networks. Science **286**(5439), 509–512 (1999)
8. Karsai, M., Kivelä, M., Pan, R.K., et al.: Small but slow world: How network topology and burstiness slow down spreading. Phys. Rev. E **83**(2), 025102 (2011)
9. Moore, C., Newman, M.E.J.: Exact solution of site and bond percolation on small-world networks. Phys. Rev. E **62**(5), 7059 (2000)
10. Boguná, M., Pastor-Satorras, R.: Epidemic spreading in correlated complex networks. Phys. Rev. E **66**(4), 047104 (2002)
11. Ganesh, A., Massoulie, L., Towsley, D.: The effect of network topology on the spread of epidemics. In: Proceedings IEEE 24th Annual Joint Conference of the IEEE Computer and Communications Societies, pp. 1455–1466. IEEE, Miami (2005)
12. Smilkov, D., Kocarev, L.: Influence of the network topology on epidemic spreading. Phys. Rev. E **85**(2), 016114 (2012)
13. Yang, Y., Nishikawa, T., Motter, A.E.: Small vulnerable sets determine large network cascades in power grids. Science **358**(6365), eaan3184 (2017)
14. Saumell-Mendiola, A., Serrano, M.Á., Boguná, M.: Epidemic spreading on interconnected networks. Phys. Rev. E **86**(2), 026106 (2012)

15. Anderson, R.M., May, R.M.: Infectious Diseases in Humans. Oxford University Press, Oxford (1992)
16. Hethcote, H.W.: The mathematics of infectious diseases. SIAM Rev. **42**(4), 599–653 (2000)
17. Kephart, J.O., White, S.R., Chess, D.M.: Computers and epidemiology. IEEE Spectr. **30**(5), 20–26 (1993)
18. Pastor-Satorras, R., Vespignani, A.: Epidemic spreading in scale-free networks. Phys. Rev. Lett. **86**(14), 3200–3203 (2001)
19. Song, Y.R., Jiang, G.-P.: Research of malware propagation in complex networks based on 1-d cellular automata. Acta Phys. Sin. **58**(9), 5911–5918 (2009)
20. Youssef, M., Kooij, R., Scoglio, C.: Viral conductance: quantifying the robustness of networks with respect to spread of epidemics. J. Comput. Sci. **2**(3), 286–298 (2011)
21. Barthélemy, M., Barrat, A., Pastor-Satorras, R., et al.: Velocity and hierarchical spread of epidemic outbreaks in scale-free networks. Phys. Rev. Lett. **92**(17), 178701 (2004)
22. Gang, Y., Tao, Z., Jie, W., et al.: Epidemic spread in weighted scale-free networks. Chin. Phys. Lett. **22**(2), 510 (2005)
23. Gleeson, J.P., Melnik, S., Hackett, A.: How clustering affects the bond percolation threshold in complex networks. Phys. Rev. E **81**(2), 066114 (2010)
24. Newman, M.E.J.: Properties of highly clustered. Phys. Rev. E **68**(2), 026121 (2003)
25. Coupechoux, E., Lelarge, M.: How clustering affects epidemics in random networks. Adv. Appl. Probab. **46**(4), 985–1008 (2014)
26. Kiss, I.Z., Green, D.M.: Comment on "properties of highly clustered networks". Phys. Rev. E **78**(4 Pt 2), 048101 (2008)
27. Pastor-Satorras, R., Vespignani, A.: Epidemic dynamics and endemic states in complex networks. Phys. Rev. E **63**(6), 066117 (2001)
28. Moreno, Y., Pastor-Satorras, R., Vespignani, A.: Epidemic outbreaks in complex heterogeneous networks. Eur. Phys. J. B **26**(4), 521–529 (2002)
29. Latora, V., Marchiori, M.: Efficient behavior of small-world networks. Phys. Rev. Lett. **87**(19), 198701 (2001)
30. Sergei, M., Kim, S., Alexei, Z.: Detection of topological patterns in complex networks: correlation profile of the internet. Phys. A Stat. Mech. Appl. **333**(1), 529–540 (2004)
31. Strong, D.R., Daniel, S., Abele, L.G., et al.: Ecological Communities. Princeton University Press, Princeton (1984)

An Attack Graph Generation Method Based on Parallel Computing

Ningyuan Cao[✉], Kun Lv, and Changzhen Hu

School of Computer Science and Technology, Beijing Institute of Technology,
Beijing, China
jcrosmith9527@gmail.com, kunlv@bit.edu.cn

Abstract. Attack graph is used as a model that enumerates all possible attack paths based on a comprehensive analysis of multiple network configurations and vulnerability information. An attack graph generation method based on parallel computing is therefore proposed to solve the thorny problem of calculations as the network scale continues to expand. We utilize multilevel k-way partition algorithm to divide network topology into parts in efficiency of parallel computing and introduce Spark into the attack graph generation as a parallel computing platform. After the generation, we have a tool named Monitor to regenerate the attack graph of the changed target network. The method can improve the speed of calculations to solve large and complex computational problems and save time of generating the whole attack graph when the network changed. The experiments which had been done show that the algorithm proposed to this paper is more efficient benefiting from smaller communication overhead and better load balance.

Keywords: Attack graph · Vulnerability · Exploit
Multilevel k-way partition · Parallel computing

1 Introduction

The traditional vulnerability scanning technique is a rule-based vulnerability assessment method that analyzes the vulnerabilities existing in the target network in isolation and fails to evaluate the potential threats resulted from these vulnerability interactions. An attack graph is a model-based vulnerability assessment method that enumerates all possible attack paths based on a comprehensive analysis of multiple network configurations and vulnerability information from an attacker's perspective to help defenders visually understand the relationships among vulnerabilities within the target network, the relationship between vulnerabilities and cybersecurity configurations, and potential threats.

The attack graph was proposed by Cuningham et al. in 1985, and they believe that it is composed of a variety of physical or logical components connected to

This work is supported by funding from Basic Scientific Research Program of Chinese Ministry of Industry and Information Technology (Grant No. JCKY2016602B001).

© Springer Nature Switzerland AG 2018
F. Liu et al. (Eds.): SciSec 2018, LNCS 11287, pp. 34–48, 2018.
https://doi.org/10.1007/978-3-030-03026-1_3

each other. A typical attack graph consists of nodes which are the state of the network and the directed edges of connected nodes which represent the transition between network states.

Attack graph has been extensively used to analyse network security and evaluate research. From the safety life cycle PDR (protection, detection, response) point of view, attack graph can be implemented to network security design, network security and vulnerability management, intrusion detection system and intrusion response. From the field of application, it can be applied not only to the common Internet but also to wireless networks, industrial control networks, especially power networks and other industries or fields that have very high dependence on networks. From an application perspective, the attack graph can be applied to network penetration testing, network security defense and network attack simulation.

Owing to the enormous amount of devices and complex connection between these terminals in the large-scale network, it brings great difficulty to generate attack graph. There are some problems for attack graph generation such as the state space explosion, the high complexity of algorithms, difficulty of graphical demonstration, and so on.

One feasible approach to cope with this trouble is to introduce parallel computing into attack graph generation. Parallel computing can save time and costs and solve larger and more complex issues. The basic idea of the attack graph generation by parallel computing is using multiple processors to solve the same problem collaboratively. Each part which the problem to be resolved is divided into is parallelized by an independent processor. Therefore, it is also a need to partition the network topology considering the large amount of network hosts and efficiency of parallel computing.

We believe that the generation of attack graphs should be divided into these major parts: Target Network Modeling, Attack Graph Modeling, Graph Partition and Parallel Computing.

Target Network Model describes the network topology structure that includes configurations of hosts which generally contain the network topology, the software applications running on the each host, and the vulnerabilities that can be exploited and host reachability relationship. Attack Graph Model indicates all possible attack paths based on a comprehensive analysis of multiple network configurations and vulnerability information. Nodes of attack graph are the information which had been exploited and the edges are the attack paths between hosts.

For convenience and efficiency of parallel computing, network topology needs to be divided into subgraphs. Multilevel k-way partition algorithm is proposed to solve the problem for network topology partition according to its fast speed and high quality. Spark is introduced into the method of attack graph generation to perform parallel computing in order to achieve rapid processing of large-scale and complex network structures.

After the generation, we have a tool named Monitor which can scan the target network and regenerate the attack graph of the changed parts of the target network if the current network is different from the previous one.

2   Related Work

Network topology that refers to the physical layout of interconnecting various devices with transmission media can be transformed into the graph structure. Since graph partition is totally an NP complete problem that mentioned by Garey [1] in 1976, it's hard to figure out the best strategy for graph partition. Searching for all the solution space has very low efficiency and with the scale of size of graph continues to grow, it will be almost impossible to turn up the best solution.

Rao and Leighton have proposed an algorithm landmark in 1999 [2]. The algorithm can find the approximate solution that is very close to the optimal solution in the time of O(logN), and N in the time complexity represents the number of vertices in the graph.

According to the good performance that heuristic algorithms produce close to the optimal solution in a tolerable time, heuristic algorithms are widely used to solve NP-complete problems.

MulVAL is an end-to-end framework and reasoning system that can perform multi-host, multi-stage vulnerability analysis on the network, automatically integrate formal vulnerability specifications from the vulnerability reporting community, and extend it to a network with thousands of computers [3].

NetSPA (Network Security Plan Architecture) was proposed by MIT in 2016 [4]. In the experiment, the experimenter uses an attack graph to simulate the effects of opponents and simple countermeasures. It uses firewall rules and network vulnerability scanning tools to create a model of the organization's network. Then, it uses this model to calculate Network Reachability and Multiple-Prerequisite Attack Graph to represent the potential path that an adversary uses to launch a known attack. This will find all hosts where the attacker started from one or more locations and eventually invaded.

Kaynar et al. [5]reported on their research on the generation of distributed attack graphs and introduced a parallel and distributed algorithm based on memory that generates attack graphs on distributed multi-agent platforms.

3   Modeling

3.1   Target Network Modeling

As target network is a topology structure like Fig. 1 as follows, the graph structure to represent it with this three-tuples ⟨Host, Adjacency, Weight⟩ should be a wise decision. Each node of the graph donates the corresponding host in the target network which contains the network topology and the host configuration

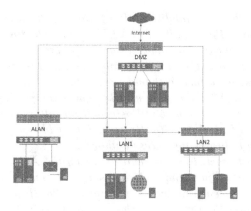

Fig. 1. Network topology.

and each edge of the graph indicates whether the two hosts can connect to each other. The network model is illustrated in Fig. 2, and formally defined next.

Definition. *Host is a list that contains all hosts of the target network which is represented by a three-tuples ⟨Hostname, IPAddress, SoftwareApplication⟩. Hostname is the unique identification of each host in the target network. IPAddress donates the IP address associated with the network interface.*

SoftwareApplication is the software installed on each host which contains SoftwareApplicationName, Port, Vulnerability. SoftwareApplicationName is the name of software application installed or running on the host. Port denotes the port on which it is serving.

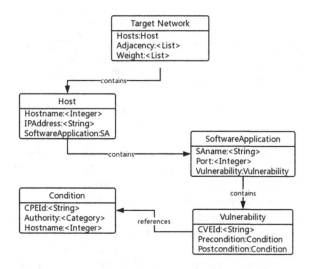

Fig. 2. Target network model.

Vulnerability is the vulnerabilities of software application and it includes CVEId, Precondition, Postcondition. CVEId is the identification of publicly known information-security vulnerabilities and exposures that the Common Vulnerabilities and Exposures (CVE) system provides. In order to access the target host in the network, an attacker should satisfy the authority that is stored in the list Preconditions. After that, the attacker gains the privileges stored in the list Postconditions. Preconditions and Postconditions all inherit condition which generally includes CPEId, Authority, Hostname. CPEId is an identifier for software and Authority indicates the access authority.

Definition. *Host reachability is represented by the Adjacency and Weight. Adjacency is a total of n lines, and each line is a point number connected to point i. Each row of the adjacency matrix corresponds to the Hostname of connected hosts. Weight indicates the weight of each edge and represents the importance of connections between hosts.*

3.2 Attack Graph Modeling

Attack graph generated by the target network ultimately is defined as a two-tuples ⟨*AttackGraphNode, AttackGraphEdge*⟩. AttackGraphNode is the node of the attack graph that contains the information of exploited hosts and Attack-GraphEdge is the edge that indicates those nodes are connected. The attack graph model is proposed in Fig. 3, and the final attack graph generated is illustrated in Fig. 4.

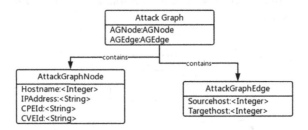

Fig. 3. Attack graph model.

Definition. *AttackGraphNode in the attack graph is represented by a five-tuples ⟨HostName, IPAddress, CPEId, CVEId⟩. Hostname is the code name to identify each host in the target network. IPAddress is the Ip address associated with the network interface. CPEId is an identifier for software. CVEId is the identification of publicly known information-security vulnerabilities and exposures that the Common Vulnerabilities and Exposures (CVE) system provides.*

Definition. *AttackGraphEdge in the attack graph is defined as a two-tuples ⟨SourceNode, TargetNode⟩. SourceNode and TargetNode represent the relationship whether two nodes of the attack graph are associated. And the source node is the attack node and the target node is the victim node.*

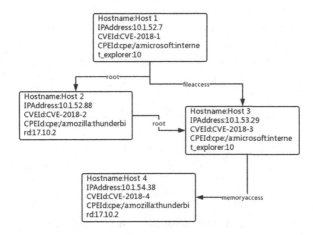

Fig. 4. Attack graph example.

4 Graph Partition of Network Topology

With the continuous increase in the scale of the network and the number of hosts, storage overhead structure of the target network will continue to grow and it will definitely bring problems that network structure wastes quantities of memory for storage and accessing the memory by each agent brings great communication overhead. If we choose to divide the network structure into many subgraphs and send it to the parallel computing program, it will reduce the communication overhead substantially and achieve a great load balance to improve the computational efficiency ultimately.

Currently, mainstream graph partition algorithm is a multilevel k-way partition algorithm and it was proposed to solve the problem for network topology partition according to its fast speed and high quality in the past few years. Multilevel k-way partition generally contains three phases: coarsening phase, initial partitioning phase and uncoarsening phase. The phases of multilevel k-way partition are illustrated in Fig. 5.

During the coarsening phase, a series of smaller graphs $G_i = \langle V_i, E_i \rangle$ are constructed from the original graph $G_0 = \langle V_0, E_0 \rangle$, requesting $|V_i| < |V_{i-1}|$. Several vertices in G_i are combined into one vertex in G_{i+1} based on the method of matching that generally includes random matching and heavy-edge matching.

In initial partitioning phase, graph partition is performed by dichotomy usually which makes that each sub-domain after subdivision contains approximately the same number of vertices or vertex weight and has the smallest cut edge.

The coarsening graph G_m is mapped back to original graph G_0 in the uncoarsening phase through each partition P_m of the coarsening graph G_m.

METIS is a powerful multilevel k-way partition graph segmentation software package developed by Karypis Lab [6]. METIS has a high-quality segmentation result that is said to be 10%–50% more accurate than the usual spectral clustering. Besides, METIS is highly efficient and is 1–2 orders of magnitude faster

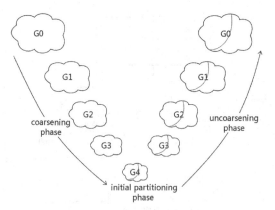

Fig. 5. Multilevel k-way partition.

than the usual division method. Therefore, it is a brilliant concept of combining METIS into the attack graph generation.

5   Parallel Computing of Attack Graph Generation

Spark is an open-source cluster-computing framework developed at the University of California, Berkeley's AMPLab [17]. In simple terms, a cluster is a group of computers that provide a group of network resources to users as a whole. Spark provides a comprehensive, unified framework for managing large data processing needs for data sets and data sources (batch data or real-time streaming data) with different properties (text data, chart data, etc.). Each Application acquires a dedicated executor process, which has been resident during Application and runs Tasks in a multi-threaded manner. The operation chart of attack graph generation algorithm by Spark is shown in Fig. 6 as follows.

The attack graph generation algorithm performed on each executor is explained next in detail. Adjacency matrix is divided into partial adjacency matrix by the *Divide()* function as shown in Algorithm 1 according to the results of graph partition firstly. Then, we call the *parallelize()* function of SparkContext to create a RDD (Resilient Distributed Datasets) that can be operated by Spark and the *broadcast()* function to broadcast the network hosts for maintaining a read-only cache variable on each machine, instead of sending a copy of the variable to the tasks. *Map()* is to utilize a function which is proposed to depth-first search the partial adjacency matrix with *DepthSearch()* as shown in Algorithm 2 and to find the privileges of each host in the target network and exploit the host for each element with *Exploit()* as shown in Algorithm 3 in the RDD and construct a new RDD with the return value until no more found privileges. At last, partial attack graphs returned are merged into the final attack graph with the function *Mergepartialgraph()* as shown in Algorithm 4. The schematic diagram of the attack graph generation is shown in Fig. 7 as follows.

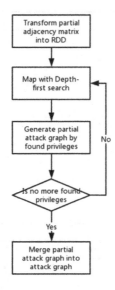

Fig. 6. Flow chart of attack graph generation.

The *DepethSearch()* function performed in each task is to depth-first search and exploit the hosts to gain the privileges from the initial privileges. If the reachable target host has not been visited yet, the algorithm will scan the host and exploit it to get privileges and then the other reachable hosts from the this host will be executed the *DepethSearch()* function. The *Exploit()* function is to transform the information of hosts into the types of attack graph nodes and add the attackers which are the source node and victims which are the target node into the types of attack graph edges. The *Mergepartialgraph()* function is to merge partial graphs which are returned by each task after all attack graph generation tasks finished. If a privilege or attack path exists in more than one partial attack graph, the attack graph can only contain one instance of it. After eliminating duplicate privilege or attack path in the resulting attack graph, we will get the final generated attack graph.

6   Monitor

The target network would not be immutable in reality. Once the network changes, the generated attack graph must be modified according to the changed parts. Considering whether it is a waste of time or a waste of resources, it is obviously unwise to generate a brand new attack graph when a small part of the large scale of network changes. It is easy to think of a method to regenerate partial attack graph for partitions that have changed parts based on the above strategy for dividing the network.

The *Monitor()* function is set to scan the target network regularly and send signal to *Regeneration()* function in Algorithm 5 to regenerate the partial attack

---

Algorithm 1. Divide function

Require: aj, $parts$, k
Ensure: paj
1: **if** $parts$ not exist **then**
2:    **return** new partialadjacency()
3: **end if**
4: **for** i in k **do**
5:    **for** j in (0 to len($parts$)) **do**
6:       **if** $parts[j]$ equal i **then**
7:          paj.append($aj[j]$)
8:       **end if**
9:    **end for**
10: **end for**
11: **return** paj

Algorithm 2. DepthSearch function

Require: paj, $visited$, fps
Ensure: $pags$
1: **for all** fps **do**
2:    **if** $attacker$ not in $visited$ **then**
3:       $visited$.append($attacker$)
4:       $attackgraphnode \leftarrow$ Exploit(fps, $attacker$)
5:       **if** $paj[attacker][viticm]$ is TRUE **then**
6:          $attackgraphedge \leftarrow (attacker, viticm)$
7:          fps.remove($attacker$)
8:          fps.append($viticm$)
9:          DepthSearch($viticm$)
10:      **end if**
11:   **end if**
12: **end for**

---

graphs of the changed parts of the target network if the current network and the duplication of previous network are different. The types of network change can generally contains the hosts change which means that the software application installed or running on the host changes or the information of the host changes and the topology change which means that there are host additions or deletions in the target network or the communication between hosts changes.

In terms of host changes, the process of regeneration is to use network partitions with host changes as input for the algorithm of attack graph generation mentioned in Sect. 5. Then the result after the process of regeneration would be used as input for *Mergepartialgraph()* function with the partial attack graphs of other partitions which had been generated before. Finally, the new attack graph of the target network which has several host configurations changed will be obtained.

In terms of topology changes, it needs to be divided into several situations to discuss. The first case is that the target network adds a new host connected

---

Algorithm 3. Exploit function

Require: *fps*, *host*
Ensure: *node*
1: **if** *host* not exist **then**
2:   **return** new attackgraphnode()
3: **end if**
4: *node.Hostname* ← *host.Hostname*
5: *node.IPAddress* ← *host.IPAddress*
6: **for all** *fps* **do**
7:   **if** *fp.IPAddress* equal *host.IPAddress* **then**
8:     **if** *fp.authority* equal *Precondition.authority* **then**
9:       *node.CVEId* ← *Vulnerability.CVEId*
10:       *node.CPEId* ← *Precondition.CPEId*
11:       *viticm* ← *Postcondition.Hostname*
12:     **end if**
13:   **end if**
14: **end for**
15: **return** *node*

---

with previous hosts. Each partition with hosts which can attack the newly added host would be executed the process of regeneration. The second situation is that there is a host deletion in the target network. Each partition with hosts which are the attacker or victim to the deleted host would be regenerated. The third case is that a host in the target network changes its original connection. Another way to describe this case is that the host move from its original location to a new location. This is a combination of two cases above and all partitions involved should be executed the process of regeneration according to the above two principles. Topology changes may have a mixture of conditions above. According to the different situations, all corresponding graph partitions will be used as input for the algorithm of attack graph generation mentioned in Sect. 5. Next steps are as same as host changes shown above and the final attack graph which makes correspond adjustments will be obtained.

The Monitor will be set to start on time to scan the target network and compare the scanned network with the previous network. On the basis of different type of network change, the Monitor will restart the attack graph generation of the corresponding graph partitions with changes and obtain the attack graph with corresponding adjustments by merging the new partial attack graphs of graph partitions with changes with the previous partial attack graphs of unaltered graph partitions.

7 Experiment

The experiments are used to evaluate the performance of the proposed attack graph generation algorithm comparing to the distributed attack graph generation had done before.

Algorithm 4. Mergepartialgraphs function

Require: *pags*
Ensure: *ag*
 1: **if** *pags.size* == 0 **then**
 2:     **return** new attackgraph()
 3: **end if**
 4: **for** *pag* in *pags* **do**
 5:     **if** *pag.node* not in *ag.node* **then**
 6:         *ag.node*.append(*pag.node*)
 7:     **end if**
 8:     **for all** *pag.edge* **do**
 9:         **if** *TargetNode* not in *ag.edge*[*SourceNode*] **then**
10:             *ag.edge*[*SourceNode*].append(*TargetNode*)
11:         **end if**
12:     **end for**
13: **end for**

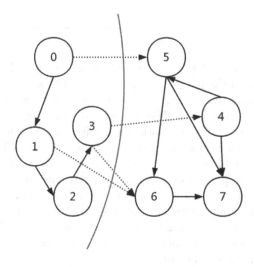

Fig. 7. Partition example of network topology.

Each host in the LANs may contain the following applications: Microsoft Windows 10, Microsoft Outlook 2013, Microsoft Office 2013 and Microsoft Internet Explorer 10. Each web server includes Apache HTTP Server 2.4.3 or Microsoft IIS Server 6.0 and each sql server contains MySQL Database Server or Microsoft SQL Server. All hosts have several vulnerabilities that can be exploited and accessed to other hosts by authority which includes root, file access and memory access. In order to perform experiments with large sizes of network, we add more hosts in LANs or LANs in the target network.

After the target network is generated, we put the number of groups, adjacency matrix and weight of the target network as input data into METIS and then get the partition results to facilitate parallel attack graph generation without

Algorithm 5. Regeneration

Require: *pags tn ntn parts*
Ensure: *ag*
1: **if** *ntn.hosts.info* not equal *tn.hosts.info* **then**
2:    **if** *ntn.aj* equal *tn.aj* **then**
3:       *pntn* ← *host.existInNtn*
4:       *regs*.append(*pntn*)
5:    **end if**
6: **end if**
7: **if** *ntn.hosts* equal *tn.hosts* **then**
8:    **if** *ntn.aj* not equal *tn.aj* **then**
9:       *pntn* ← *host.existInTn*
10:       *pntn* ← *host.formerPart*
11:       *pntn* ← *host.nextPart*
12:       *regs*.append(*pntn*)
13:    **end if**
14: **end if**
15: **for** *ptn* in *ptns* **do**
16:    **for** *pntn* in *pntns* **do**
17:       **if** *pntn* < *ptn* **then**
18:          *regs*.append(*pntn*)
19:       **end if**
20:    **end for**
21: **end for**
22: **for** *host* in *ntn.host* **do**
23:    **if** *host* not exist in *pntns.host* **then**
24:       *pntn* ← *host.formerPart*
25:       *pntn* ← *host.nextPart*
26:       *regs*.append(*pntn*)
27:    **end if**
28: **end for**
29: **return** AGgeneration(*regs*)

considering the specific process. A partition example of network topology which has eight nodes and is divided into two parts is illustrated in Fig. 7. When the number of hosts gradually increases, the number of groups of splitting graphs is adjusted in time according to the task memory of the spark.

The comparative experiment is a multi-process implementation of distributed computing for multiple hosts with similar model and algorithm. And it utilizes multiprocessing package that supports spawning processes using an API similar to the threading module, shared virtual memory and Queue package which have two methods of *get()* and *put()* to implement communication between experimental computers.

The experiments are performed by two computers with 64-bit and 8 G RAM and the running time of generation of the attack graph is as Table 1. The first row of Table 1 is the growing number of hosts of target network. The second row

Table 1. Running time of attack graph generation by spark and comparative experiment

Host number	Spark (s)	Dist (s)
18	2.26	5.95
36	2.40	7.71
90	6.00	13.09
126	9.01	21.21
198	10.27	38.69
243	11.16	62.65
288	12.84	86.32
333	14.00	102.63
495	20.00	261.82

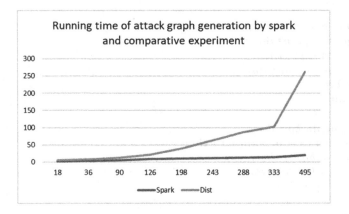

Fig. 8. Line chart of running time.

is the running time of algorithm proposed in this paper and the third row is the running time of the comparative experiment.

After the generation of the target network, we illustrate the effectiveness of the Monitor with a target network of 495 hosts. A local change in the target network moves a partition's host to another partition, and we all need to regenerate these two partitions. Time-consuming regeneration of attack graphs for two partitions is 5.92 s and the time of generating the whole target network is 20.00 s as shown in Table 1.

From the result data of running time, we can find out the algorithm by spark has more efficiency than the comparative experiment obviously which benefits from smaller communication overhead and better load balance. With the number of hosts keeps growing, the running time of spark has substantial growth but also better than the comparative experiment (Fig. 8).

8   Conclusion and Future Work

In this paper, a parallel computing algorithm is introduced for full attack graph generation which is based on Spark and multilevel k-way partition. The results of experiments demonstrate that the algorithm by spark has more efficiency which benefits from smaller communication overhead and better load balance and can be applied to calculate large scale network for attack graph generation. The function of the Monitor has a good performance in large target networks. Monitor is advantageous as long as Monitor generates a partial partitioned attack graph for less than the calculated total time.

One of the possible future work may utilize shared memory to overcome the dilemma that executors are unable to communication between each other due to the architecture of Spark which causes that the algorithm takes more loops to complete the mission. When generating attack graph, it brings an issue with spark's features that some tasks may need the found privileges after a certain task. Each ShuffleDependency which Spark's DAGScheduler builds Stages based on maps to a stage of the spark's job and then causes a shuffle process. Another possible future work can be a purposeful graph partition based on the network topology. The local optimization of METIS makes the number of subgraphs not reduced sufficiently. Better partition strategy may improve the efficiency of parallel computing algorithm of attack graph generation.

References

1. Garey, M.R., Johnson, D.S., Stockmeyer, L.: Some simplified NP-complete graph problems. Theor. Comput. Sci. **1**(3), 237–267 (1976)
2. Leighton, T., Rao, S.: Multi-commodity max-flow min-cut theorems and their use in designing approximation algorithms. JACM **46**(6), 787–832 (1999)
3. Ou, X., Govindavajhala, S., Appel, A.W.: MulVAL: a logic-based network security analyzer. In: Usenix Security Symposium, vol. 8 (2005)
4. Artz, M.L.: NetSPA : a Network Security Planning Architecture (2002)
5. Kaynar, K., Sivrikaya, F.: Distributed attack graph generation. IEEE Trans. Dependable Secur. Comput. **13**(5), 519–532 (2016)
6. Karypis, G., Kumar, V.: METIS: a software package for partitioning unstructured graphs. Int. Cryog. Monogr. 121–124 (1998)
7. Man, D., Zhang, B., Yang, W., Jin, W., Yang, Y.: A method for global attack graph generation. In: 2008 IEEE International Conference on Networking, Sensing and Control, Sanya, pp. 236–241 (2008)
8. Ou, X., Boyer, W.F., McQueen, M.A.: A scalable approach to attack graph generation. In: Proceedings of the 13th ACM Conference on Computer and Communications Security (2006)
9. Keramati, M.: An attack graph based procedure for risk estimation of zero-day attacks. In: 8th International Symposium on Telecommunications (IST), Tehran, pp. 723–728 (2016)
10. Wang, S., Tang, G., Kou, G., Chao, Y.: An attack graph generation method based on heuristic searching strategy. In: 2016 2nd IEEE International Conference on Computer and Communications (ICCC), Chengdu, pp. 1180–1185 (2016)

11. Yi, S., et al.: Overview on attack graph generation and visualization technology. In: 2013 International Conference on Anti-Counterfeiting, Security and Identification (ASID), Shanghai, pp. 1–6 (2013)
12. Ingols, K., Lippmann, R., Piwowarski, K.: Practical attack graph generation for network defense. In: 22nd Annual Computer Security Applications Conference (ACSAC 2006), Miami Beach, FL, pp. 121–130 (2006)
13. Li, K., Hudak, P.: Memory coherence in shared virtual memory systems. ACM Trans. Comput. Syst. **7**(4), 321–359 (1989)
14. Johnson, P., Vernotte, A., Ekstedt, M., Lagerstrom, R.: pwnPr3d: an attack-graph-driven probabilistic threat-modeling approach. In: 2016 11th International Conference on Availability, Reliability and Security (ARES), Salzburg, pp. 278–283 (2016)
15. Cheng, Q., Kwiat, K., Kamhoua, C.A., Njilla, L.: Attack graph based network risk assessment: exact inference vs region-based approximation. In: IEEE 18th International Symposium on High Assurance Systems Engineering (HASE), Singapore, pp. 84–87 (2017)
16. Karypis, G., Kumar, V.: Multilevel k-way hypergraph partitioning. In: Proceedings: Design Automation Conference (Cat. No. 99CH36361), New Orleans, LA, pp. 343–348 (1999)
17. Zaharia, M., Chowdhury, M., Franklin, M.J., et al.: Spark: cluster computing with working sets. HotCloud **10**(10–10), 95 (2010)

Cybersecurity Dynamics

A Note on Dependence of Epidemic Threshold on State Transition Diagram in the SEIC Cybersecurity Dynamical System Model

Hao Qiang[1](✉) and Wenlian Lu[1,2]

[1] School of Mathematical Sciences, Fudan University, Shanghai 200433, China
hqiang14@fudan.edu.cn
[2] State Key Laboratory of Information Security, Institute of Information
Engineering, Chinese Academy of Sciences, Beijing 100093, China

Abstract. Cybersecurity dynamical system model is a promising tool to describe and understand virus spreading in networks. The modelling comprises of two issues: the state transition diagram and the infection graph. Most works focus on proposing models (the state transition diagram) and studying the relationship between dynamics and the infection graph topology. In this paper, We propose the SEIC model and illustrate how the model transition diagram influence the dynamics, in particular, the epidemic threshold by calculating and comparing their thresholds in a class of Secure-Exposed-Infectious-Cured (SEIC) models. We show that as a new state enters the state transition diagram in the fashion of the SEIC model, the epidemic threshold increases, which implies that the model has a larger region of parameters to be stabilized. Numerical examples are presented to verify the theoretical results.

Keywords: Epidemic threshold
Cybersecurity dynamical system model · State transition diagram
SEIC

1 Introduction

With the rapid development of the Internet, computer viruses have been a persistent threat to security of networks. As an important part to secure the networks, theoretical modeling of the spreading of computer virus in networks has attracted many studies and been extensively investigated. Since there have been similarities between the spreading of infectious diseases and computer viruses, it is naturally to apply mathematical techniques which have been developed for the

This work is jointly supported by the National Natural Sciences Foundation of China under Grant No. 61673119.

study of the spreading of infectious diseases to the study of the spreading of computer viruses. In 1920's and 30', [15] established the pioneer Secure-Infectious-Rescued model (the SIRS model) and gave threshold theorem of the spreading of infectious diseases as well as the Secure-Infectious-Secure model (the SIS model) [16].

Inspired by that, [8] have first presented the epidemiology model (SIRS) by adapting mathematical epidemiology to the spread of the computer viruses and a qualitative understanding of computer viruses spreading. In the mean time, [10] employed the SIRS model to simulate the computer viruses spreading. Beside these two typical models, there are a lot of study under different situations and different modelling. The main issue of modelling is presenting the state set and the corresponding specific state transition diagram [5,7].

1.1   Our Contribution

In the present paper, we illustrate the influence of the state transition diagram on the epidemic threshold by investigating a Secure-Exposed-Infectious-Cured (SEIC) model in networks. By extracting the sufficient condition for local stability of the dying-out equilibrium, namely, the equilibrium with all virus infection probabilities equal to zeros, we gave the epidemic threshold τ in form of the parameters of the state transition diagram. We investigate how the threshold changes by removing/adding each state by analytically calculating the largest real parts of the eigenvalues of the Jacobian matrices under different state transition diagrams. This phenomenon can be proved to able to be generally extended to a class of iterative operations on the transition schedule.

1.2   Related Work

The study of epidemic spreading dynamics on complex networks has become a hot topic. Many of these papers were concerned with the problem of epidemic threshold that presents a critical value of parameters intersecting the parameter region of virus dying-out (the infection probability going to zero) and breaking-out (the infection probability going to nonzero). This threshold condition was always formulated by two issues: the *algebraic quantity* that describes the influence of the network topology and the *physical quantity* that is determined by the state transition diagram. [2] developed a nonlinear dynamical system (NLDS) to model viral propagation in any arbitrary network and propose a epidemic threshold for the NLDS system to bound the largest eigenvalue of the adjacency matrix, i.e., $\lambda_1 < \tau$, where τ is the physical quantity of the model. [19] specified this quantity by $\tau = \beta/\gamma$ in a non-homogeneous network SIS model, where β is the cure capability of one node and γ is the edge infection rate. [18] presented a general sufficient condition (epidemic threshold) under which the push- and pull-based epidemic spreading will become stable. However, in a different model of the infection graph, as [4] presented, the algebraic quantity can have different form. For more works on this topic, see [13,14,17,20] and the reference therein.

2   Model Description

A typical cybersecurity dynamical system model on network is twofold. First, we model the infection relationship as a graph. Consider a finite graph $G = (V, E)$ which describes the graph topology of a network, where V is the set of computer nodes in the network and the edge $(u, v) \in E$ means that the node u can directly attack the node v. Let $A = (a_{vu})_{n \times n}$ be the adjacency matrix of the graph G, where $n = |V|$ means the number of nodes and $a_{vu} = 1$ if and only if $(u, v) \in E$ especially $a_{vv} = 0$. In this paper, we focus on the undirected network topology which means $a_{uv} = a_{vu}$.

Second, on each node of the network, a state transition schedule is defined. In this paper, at time t, each node $v \in V$ should be in one of the following four states:

- S: the node is secure.
- E: the node including its vulnerability is exposed to the attacker.
- I: the node is infected by the virus.
- C: the node is cured which means that the infection is cleaned up.

The state transition diagram is shown by Fig. 1. From this diagram, the secure node can be transferred to exposed nodes by some computer viruses such as worms or Trojan Horses. The infectious node may attack their neighbours which are exposed. Also the exposed nodes can be secured again, while the infectious nodes is secured, cleaned up or unexposed by the defense of the network. These transitions occurs as dynamical processes.

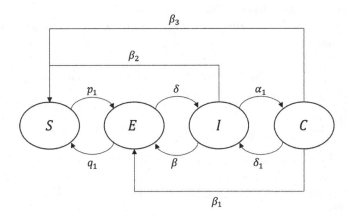

Fig. 1. The state transition diagram of the SEIC model.

We assume that the model is homogeneous. Let $s_v(t)$, $e_v(t)$, $i_v(t)$ and $c_v(t)$ represent the probabilities the node $v \in V$ in state S, E, I and C respectively at time t. The parameters of the transition diagram are: p_1, q_1, $\delta_v(t)$, β, β_1, β_2, β_3, α_1, δ_1, γ. The physical meanings of the parameters are shown in Table 1.

Table 1. The parameters list.

p_1	The probability a secure node v becomes exposed
q_1	The probability an exposed node v becomes secure
$\delta_v(t)$	The probability an exposed node v becomes infected at time t
β	The probability an infectious node v becomes exposed
α_1	The probability an infectious node v becomes cured
δ_1	The probability a secure node v becomes exposed
β_1	The probability a cured node v becomes exposed
β_2	The probability an infectious node v becomes secure
β_3	The probability a cured node v becomes secure
γ	The probability an infectious node u successfully infects an exposed node v over edge $(u, v) \in E$
$A = (a_{vu})_{n \times n}$	The adjacency matrix of the graph G
λ_1	The largest eigenvalue of matrix A

Especially, the parameter $\delta_v(t)$ of the probability that an exposed node v becomes infected at time t is formulated by the infection from the node's neighborhood, following the arguments in [19] as follows.

$$\delta_v(t) = 1 - \prod_{(u,v) \in E(t)} \left[1 - \gamma \cdot i_u(t) \right] = 1 - \prod_{u \in V} \left[1 - a_{vu} \gamma \cdot i_u(t) \right]. \qquad (1)$$

where γ stands for the infection rate.

To sum up, according to the state transition diagram, the master equation of this SEIC model is:

$$\begin{cases} \dfrac{ds_v(t)}{dt} = -p_1 s_v(t) + q_1 e_v(t) + \beta_2 i_v(t) + \beta_3 c_v(t), \\ \dfrac{de_v(t)}{dt} = p_1 s_v(t) + \left(-\delta_v(t) - q_1 \right) e_v(t) + \beta i_v(t) + \beta_1 c_v(t), \\ \dfrac{di_v(t)}{dt} = \delta_v(t) e_v(t) + \left(-\beta - \alpha_1 - \beta_2 \right) i_v(t) + \delta_1 c_v(t), \\ \dfrac{dc_v(t)}{dt} = \alpha_1 i_v(t) + \left(-\delta_1 - \beta_3 - \beta_1 \right) c_v(t). \end{cases} \qquad (2)$$

Noting that $s_v(t) + e_v(t) + i_v(t) + c_v(t) = 1$ holds for all $v \in V$ at any time t if the initial values hold.

3 Epidemic Threshold Analysis

In this section we present a sufficient condition under which the virus spreading will die out.

Let us consider system (2). Because of $s_v(t) + e_v(t) + i_v(t) + c_v(t) = 1$, we can replace $e_v(t)$ by $1 - s_v(t) - i_v(t) - c_v(t)$ as follows:

$$\begin{cases} \dfrac{\mathrm{d}s_v(t)}{\mathrm{d}t} = -p_1 s_v(t) + q_1(1 - s_v(t) - i_v(t) - c_v(t)) + \beta_2 i_v(t) + \beta_3 c_v(t), \\[2mm] \dfrac{\mathrm{d}i_v(t)}{\mathrm{d}t} = \delta_v(t)(1 - s_v(t) - i_v(t) - c_v(t)) + \left(-\beta - \alpha_1 - \beta_2\right) i_v(t) + \delta_1 c_v(t), \\[2mm] \dfrac{\mathrm{d}c_v(t)}{\mathrm{d}t} = \alpha_1 i_v(t) + \left(-\delta_1 - \beta_3 - \beta_1\right) c_v(t). \end{cases}$$

$$(3)$$

Let $s(t) = \left(s_1(t), \cdots, s_n(t)\right)^\top$, $i(t) = \left(i_1(t), \cdots, i_n(t)\right)^\top$, $c(t) = \left(c_1(t), \cdots, c_n(t)\right)^\top$. Our goal is to guarantee security of the network, i.e. $i_v(t) = 0$ and $c_v(t) = 0$ for all node v. Obviously, with fixing $i_v = c_v = 0$ for all $v \in V$, there exists a unique equilibrium $(s_v^*, i_v^*, c_v^*) = (\dfrac{q_1}{p_1 + q_1}, 0, 0)$ $(v = 1, \cdots, n)$. This is the *dying-out equilibrium*.

For a class of cybersecurity dynamical system model in networks, we present the following definition.

Definition 1. *(The epidemic threshold) A epidemic threshold is a value τ such that the dying-out equilibrium is stable if $\lambda_1 < \tau$ and unstable if $\lambda_1 > \tau$, where λ_1 is the largest eigenvalue of the adjustment matrix A of the underlying graph G.*

To specify it, [19] showed us that in a non-homogeneous network SIS model, the epidemic threshold gives $\tau = \beta/\gamma$ which means that if $\lambda_1 < \beta/\gamma$, the virus spreading will die out.

Consider a general nonlinear dynamical system as follows

$$\frac{\mathrm{d}x}{\mathrm{d}t} = f(x) \tag{4}$$

with $x \in R^n$ and a differentiable map $f : R^n \to R^n$. Assume $f(0) = 0$. It is well known that if all the real parts of the eigenvalues of the Jacobian matrix $\dfrac{\mathrm{d}f}{\mathrm{d}x}$ at the origin are negative, then the origin equilibrium is stable; otherwise if one of the real of the eigenvalues of the Jacobian is positive, this origin equilibrium is unstable. Thus we present the sufficient condition.

Theorem 1. *The epidemic threshold of the SEIC model gives*

$$\tau_{SEIC} = \frac{\beta + \alpha_1 + \beta_2 - \frac{\delta_1 \alpha_1}{\delta_1 + \beta_3 + \beta_1}}{\gamma \cdot \frac{p_1}{p_1 + q_1}}. \tag{5}$$

Proof. The linearization gives the Jacobian matrix of system (3) at the dying-out equilibrium as follows:

$$D = \begin{pmatrix} -(p_1 + q_1)I_n & (\beta_2 - q_1)I_n & (\beta_3 - q_1)I_n \\ 0 & e^*\gamma A - (\alpha_1 + \beta + \beta_2)I_n & \delta_1 I_n \\ 0 & \alpha_1 I_n & -(\delta_1 + \beta_1 + \beta_3)I_n \end{pmatrix}.$$

Let $\{\lambda_k\}_{k=1}^n (\lambda_1 \geq \cdots \geq \lambda_n)$ be n eigenvalues of the adjacency matrix A and the vector a_k be the eigenvector with respect to λ_k. The characteristic polynomial of matrix D is:

$$\chi_D(\lambda) = |\lambda I_{3n} - D|$$

$$= \begin{vmatrix} (\lambda + p_1 + q_1)I_n & -(\beta_2 - q_1)I_n & -(\beta_3 - q_1)I_n \\ 0 & -e^*\gamma A + (\lambda + \alpha_1 + \beta + \beta_2)I_n & -\delta_1 I_n \\ 0 & -\alpha_1 I_n & (\lambda + \delta_1 + \beta_1 + \beta_3)I_n \end{vmatrix}. \tag{6}$$

With Eq. (6) equal to 0, we have

$$\chi_D(\lambda) = (\lambda + p_1 + q_1)^n |\lambda I_{2n} - D'| = 0. \tag{7}$$

Obviously, $\lambda = -p_1 - q_1$ are its n eigenvalues which are less than 0. To guarantee the stability of the dying-out equilibrium, it is sufficient to request the largest eigenvalue of the following matrix, D', is less than 0 only:

$$D' = \begin{pmatrix} e^*\gamma A - (\alpha_1 + \beta + \beta_2)I_n & \delta_1 I_n \\ \alpha_1 I_n & -(\delta_1 + \beta_1 + \beta_3)I_n \end{pmatrix}.$$

Consider a specific eigenvalue λ and its corresponding eigenvector $b = (u^\top, v^\top)^\top$, with $u, v \in C^n$. This gives

$$\lambda \begin{pmatrix} u \\ v \end{pmatrix} = \begin{pmatrix} (e^*\gamma A - (\alpha_1 + \beta + \beta_2)I_n) \cdot u + \delta_1 I_n \cdot v \\ \alpha_1 I_n \cdot u - (\delta_1 + \beta_1 + \beta_3)I_n \cdot v \end{pmatrix}. \tag{8}$$

Immediately, we have $u = \dfrac{\lambda + \delta_1 + \beta_3 + \beta_1}{\alpha_1} v$. Substituting it into the first equation, we have

$$(e^*\gamma A - (\beta + \alpha_1 + \beta_2)I_n) \cdot u + \delta_1 I_n \cdot v = \lambda u$$

$$\Leftrightarrow (e^*\gamma A - (\beta + \alpha_1 + \beta_2)I_n) \cdot \frac{\lambda + \delta_1 + \beta_3 + \beta_1}{\alpha_1} v$$

$$+ \delta_1 I_n \cdot v = \frac{\lambda(\lambda + \delta_1 + \beta_3 + \beta_1)}{\alpha_1} v$$

$$\Leftrightarrow \frac{e^*\gamma(\lambda + \delta_1 + \beta_3 + \beta_1)}{\alpha_1} Av = \frac{(\lambda + \delta_1 + \beta_3 + \beta_1)(\lambda + \beta + \alpha_1 + \beta_2) - \delta_1\alpha_1}{\alpha_1} v. \tag{9}$$

Equation (9) implies that v is one of A's eigenvectors. Without loss of generality, letting $v = a_k$, we have

$$\frac{e^*\gamma(\lambda + \delta_1 + \beta_3 + \beta_1)}{\alpha_1} \lambda_k a_k = \frac{(\lambda + \delta_1 + \beta_3 + \beta_1)(\lambda + \beta + \alpha_1 + \beta_2) - \delta_1\alpha_1}{\alpha_1} a_k.$$

This implies a quadratic polynomial equation for a pair of eigenvalues of D':

$$\lambda^2 + (\delta_1 + \beta_3 + \beta_1 + \beta + \alpha_1 + \beta_2 - \gamma'\lambda_k)\lambda$$

$$+ (\delta_1 + \beta_3 + \beta_1)(\beta + \alpha_1 + \beta_2 - \gamma'\lambda_k) - \delta_1\alpha_1 = 0, \tag{10}$$

with $\gamma' = e^*\gamma$. It can be identified the bigger one is

$$\lambda = \frac{\sqrt{\Delta} - (\delta_1 + \beta_3 + \beta_1 + \beta + \alpha_1 + \beta_2 - \gamma'\lambda_k)}{2},$$

with

$$\Delta = (\gamma'\lambda_k + \delta_1 + \beta_3 + \beta_1 - \beta - \alpha_1 - \beta_2)^2 + 4\delta_1\alpha_1 \geq 0.$$

By the derivation of λ with respect to λ_k

$$\frac{\mathrm{d}\lambda}{\mathrm{d}\lambda_k} = \frac{\Delta^{-\frac{1}{2}} \cdot \frac{\mathrm{d}\Delta}{\mathrm{d}\lambda_k} + 2\gamma'}{4} = \frac{2\gamma'(\frac{\gamma'\lambda_k + \delta_1 + \beta_3 + \beta_1 - \beta - \alpha_1 - \beta_2}{\sqrt{\Delta}} + 1)}{4}$$

$$\geq \frac{2\gamma'(\frac{-|\sqrt{\Delta}|}{\sqrt{\Delta}} + 1)}{4} = 0, \tag{11}$$

it holds that λ is monotone increasing (with respect to λ_k). Therefore, the largest eigenvalue of D

$$\lambda_{\max} = \frac{\sqrt{\Delta} - (\delta_1 + \beta_3 + \beta_1 + \beta + \alpha_1 + \beta_2 - \gamma'\lambda_1)}{2} \tag{12}$$

by picking λ_1. It can be seen that $\lambda_{\max} < 0$ if and only if

$$\lambda_1 < \frac{\beta + \alpha_1 + \beta_2 - \frac{\delta_1\alpha_1}{\delta_1 + \beta_3 + \beta_1}}{\gamma \cdot \frac{p_1}{p_1 + q_1}}. \tag{13}$$

This completes the proof.

We provide a numerical example to show that our SEIC model is effective (see Figs. 2 and 3). We pick the "p2p-Gnutella05" network. Since it is a directed network, we add some edges to make the network undirected. We denote the modified network by "unGNU5". By calculation, the adjacency matrix of the graph of unGNU5 network has a largest eigenvalue $\lambda_1 \in (23.54, 23.55)$. Then we give two examples with two sets of parameters as follows:

$$p_1 = 0.1, q_1 = 0.9, \alpha_1 = 0.7, \delta_1 = 0.4, \beta = 0.5,$$
$$\beta_1 = 0.4, \beta_2 = 0.6, \beta_3 = 0.2, \gamma = 0.6, \tau = 25.33 > \lambda_1.$$

And

$$p_1 = 0.1, q_1 = 0.2, \alpha_1 = 0.4, \delta_1 = 0.4, \beta = 0.5,$$
$$\beta_1 = 0.4, \beta_2 = 0.4, \beta_3 = 0.2, \gamma = 0.5, \tau = 6.84 < \lambda_1.$$

We set four different initial states with $(0.1, 0.8, 0.1, 0)$, $(0.9, 0.05, 0.05, 0)$, $(0.3, 0.3, 0.4, 0)$, $(0.3, 0.15, 0.55, 0)$ and simulate the virus spread. As we can see from Fig. 2, the virus spreading dies out quickly regardless of the initial infection structure. And in Fig. 3, the virus doesn't die out and the system converges to an equilibrium near $(0.687, 0.270, 0.030, 0.013)$.

By setting some parameters to zeros, this SEIC model can be regarded as generalization of a few models. As shown by Fig. 4, for instance, if we set $\alpha_1, \delta_1, \beta_1, \beta_3 = 0$, the SEIC model can be seen as the SEI model and we have

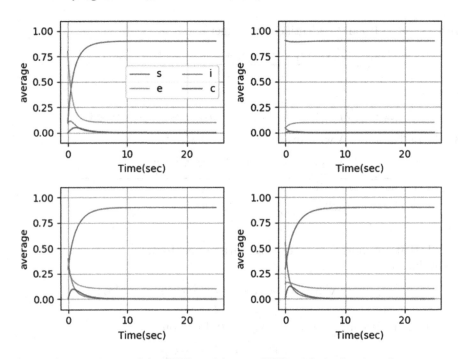

Fig. 2. The experiment of the SEIC model on unGNU5 with the first set of parameters.

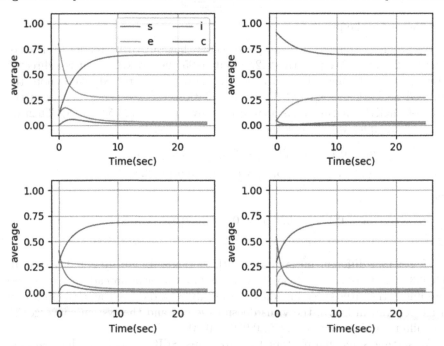

Fig. 3. The experiment of the SEIC model on unGNU5 with the second set of parameters.

Corollary 1. *The epidemic threshold of the SEI model is*

$$\tau_{SEI} = \frac{\beta + \beta_2}{\gamma \cdot \frac{p_1}{p_1 + q_1}}. \tag{14}$$

If we set $p_1, q_1, \beta_2, \beta_3 = 0$, the SEIC model can be seen as the EIC model, which is known as the SIR model. And we have

Corollary 2. *The epidemic threshold of the EIC model (known as the SIRS model) is*

$$\tau_{EIC} = \frac{\beta + \frac{\alpha_1 \beta_1}{\delta_1 + \beta_1}}{\gamma}. \tag{15}$$

If we set $p_1, q_1, \alpha_1, \delta_1, \beta_1, \beta_2, \beta_3 = 0$, the SEIC model can be seen as the EI model, which is the same as the SIS model. And we have

Corollary 3. *The epidemic threshold of the EI model (known as the SIS model) is*

$$\tau_{EI} = \frac{\beta}{\gamma}. \tag{16}$$

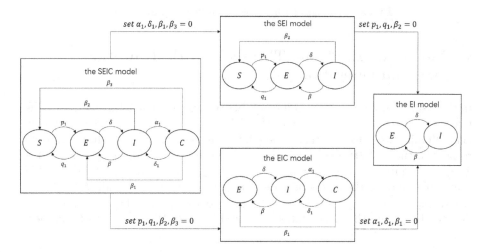

Fig. 4. State transition diagram of the EI, SEI, EIC and SEIC model.

The state transition diagrams of these four models are shown in Fig. 4.

From Fig. 5, we can see the monotone of the epidemic threshold τ of these four models with respect to different parameters. It is easy to see that

$$\tau_{SEIC} > \tau_{EIC} > \tau_{EI}$$
$$\tau_{SEIC} > \tau_{SEI} > \tau_{EI} \tag{17}$$

which means that the SEIC model has greater stability than the other three models.

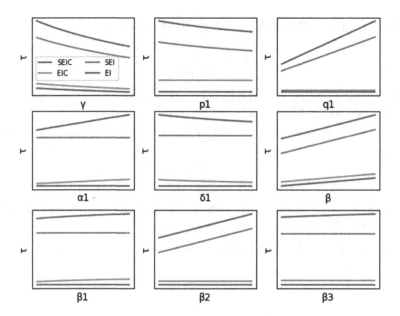

Fig. 5. τ changes with respect to different parameters.

4 Monotone Epidemic Threshold with Transition Diagram Operation

In the last section, the comparison result between the epidemic thresholds for different models (SEIC, EIC, SEI and EI) with the same network topology, namely, (17), illuminates us to investigate the relationship of the epidemic threshold with respect to the state transition diagram. For better exposition, let us consider a general formulation. Let $x_v = [x_{v,-p}, \cdots, x_{v,-1}, x_{v,1}, \cdots, x_{v,m-p}]^\top$ be variable vector to stand for the states of node v, $v \in V$. Then, we group all these states, the index $j = -p, \cdots, -1, 1, \cdots, m-p$, into two parts: the "Good states", denoted by $\mathcal{G}$, and the "Bad states", denoted by $\mathcal{B}$. In the term of mathematics,

Definition 2. *If the cybersecurity dynamical system of x_v, $v \in V$, which has p good states and $m-p$ bad states, possesses the dying-out equilibrium: $x_v^* = \{x_{v,-p}^*, \cdots, x_{v,-1}^*, x_{v,1}^*, \cdots, x_{v,m-p}^*\}$, $v \in V$, such that there exists disjoint index sets $\mathcal{G}$ and $\mathcal{B}$ satisfying (1). $\mathcal{G} = \{-1, \cdots, -p\}, \mathcal{B} = \{1, \cdots, m-p\}, 0 < p < m$; (2) $x_{v,j}^* = 0$ for all $j \in \mathcal{B}$ and $v \in V$ and $x_{v,k} > 0$ for all $k \in \mathcal{G}$ and $v \in V$ hold, then we call $\mathcal{G}$ is the "Good state" subset and $\mathcal{B}$ is the "Bad state" subset.*

Definition 3. *We group all state transition links into three parts:*

(i) *If the state transition link L is from $\mathcal{G}$ to $\mathcal{G}$ or from $\mathcal{B}$ to $\mathcal{B}$, then we call L the "Neighbour-link".*

(ii) If the state transition link L is from "Bad state" to "Good state", then we call L the "Cross-link".

(iii) Especially, we call the "−1 to 1" and "1 to −1" links the "Infect-links".

We conclude the evolution rules of this cybersecurity dynamical system:

1. There are only Neighbour-links within $\mathcal{G}$ and within $\mathcal{B}$ with parameters being constants;
2. There are no limits with Cross-links with parameters being constants;
3. The transition parameter of Infect-link from "good" to "bad" is formulated by (1) and from "bad" to "good" is constant. There are no other links except Neighbour-links, Cross-links and Infect-links;

The evolution rules of this cybersecurity dynamical system are shown by the state transition diagram (see Fig. 6), denoted by $\mathcal{E}_{p,m}$. Herein, we consider s specific operation on $\mathcal{E}_{p,m}$.

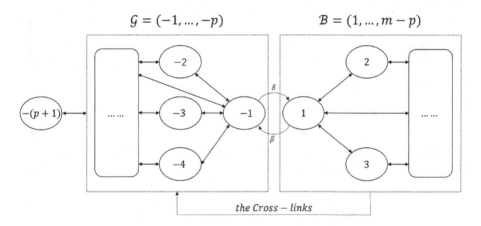

Fig. 6. The state transition diagram of $\mathcal{E}_{p,m}$ and the operation.

Theorem 2. *If a Good State "−(p + 1)" with its Neighbour-links to the "Good state" set on the left side of $\mathcal{E}_{p,m}$ (See Fig. 6), then the epidemic threshold of the new model $\mathcal{E}_{p+1,m+1}$ increases.*

Proof. Use the same approach used in Sect. 3, we just need to do some research about the linearization of the $\mathcal{E}_{p,m}$'s master equation where $x_{v,-1}$ is replaced by $1 - \sum_{\substack{k \in \mathcal{G} \cup \mathcal{B} \\ k \neq -1}} x_{v,k}$. Let us denote the coefficient matrix of the linearization equation by $D_{p,m}$. $D_{p,m}$ has the form as follows.

$$D_{p,m} = \left(\begin{array}{c|c} G_{(p-1)\times(p-1)} & F_{(p-1)\times(m-p)} \\ \hline O_{(m-p)\times(p-1)} & B_{(m-p)\times(m-p)} \end{array} \right)$$

(18)

Let us denote the parameter of the link from "a" to "b" by $p_{a,b}$. Since this operation can make $x^*_{v,-1}$ lower, we have

$$D_{p+1,m+1} = \begin{pmatrix} 0 & 0 & 0 \\ \hline 0 & G_{(p-1)\times(p-1)} & F \\ \hline 0 & O_{(m-p)\times(p-1)} & B_{(m-p)\times(m-p)} \end{pmatrix}$$

$$+ \begin{pmatrix} -\sum_{k=-1}^{-p} p_{-(p+1),k}I & p_{-p,-(p+1)}I \cdots p_{-2,-(p+1)}I & 0 \\ \hline p_{-(p+1),-p}I & -p_{-p,-(p+1)}I & \\ \vdots & & 0 \\ p_{-(p+1),-2}I & \ddots \quad -p_{-2,-(p+1)}I & \\ \hline 0 & 0 & \Delta B \end{pmatrix}$$

$$+ \begin{pmatrix} -p_{-1,-(p+1)}I & -p_{-1,-(p+1)}I \cdots -p_{-1,-(p+1)}I & -p_{-1,-(p+1)}I \cdots -p_{-1,-(p+1)}I \\ \hline -p_{-1,-p}I & & \\ \vdots & 0 & 0 \\ -p_{-1,-2}I & & \\ \hline 0 & 0 & 0 \end{pmatrix}$$

$$= \begin{pmatrix} G_{p\times p} & F' \\ \hline O_{(m-p)\times p} & B'_{(m-p)\times(m-p)} \end{pmatrix}$$

$$\tag{19}$$

Obviously, if the adjacency matrix A does not change, we have $B'_{(m-p)\times(m-p)} \leq B_{(m-p)\times m-p)}$. At the equilibrium $P^* = (x^*_{-(p+1)}, \cdots, x^*_{-2}, x^*_1, \cdots, x^*_{m-p})^\top$, we have

$$\frac{d}{dt}(P(t) - P^*) = D_{p+1,m+1}(P(t) - P^*). \tag{20}$$

Here, $P(t) = (x_{-(p+1)}(t), \cdots, x_{-2}(t), x_1(t), \cdots, x_{m-p}(t))^\top$. So that we just need to prove the stability of the zero point of system (20). Since our goal is to make sure that all nodes are not in Bad State, we only consider that whether $x^*_1, \cdots, x^*_{m-p}$ is stable at 0 point. And the problem is simplified to consider the following equation

$$\frac{d}{dt}Q(t) = B'_{(m-p)\times(m-p)}Q(t), \tag{21}$$

where $Q(t) = (x_1(t), \cdots, x_{m-p}(t))^\top$. In the model $\mathcal{E}_{p,m}$, we have

$$\frac{d}{dt}Q(t) = B_{(m-p)\times(m-p)}Q(t), \tag{22}$$

Let us denote the epidemic threshold of $\mathcal{E}_{p,m}$ and $\mathcal{E}_{p+1,m+1}$ by $\tau_{p,m}$ and $\tau_{p+1,m+1}$ respectively. Since $B'_{(m-p)\times(m-p)} \leq B_{(m-p)\times(m-p)}$, $Q(t) \geq 0$ and system (22) is local stable at zero point, the zero point of system (21) is also local stable which means

$$\lambda_1 < \tau_{p,m} \Rightarrow \lambda_1 < \tau_{p+1,m+1}. \tag{23}$$

So that we have

$$\tau_{p,m} < \tau_{p+1,m+1}. \tag{24}$$

This complete the proof.

5 Conclusions

For a large class of cybersecurity dynamical system models, the model is partially defined by the state transition diagram, the infection graph, and the parameter. How the dynamics of the model are influenced by the state transition diagram has lacked systematic research. In this paper, we presented a novel SEIC cybersecurity dynamical system model and derived its epidemic threshold, the critical values of parameters that insects the stability and instability of the dying-out equilibrium. This model is general and include a few existing models as its special cases. Also, we illustrated by this kind of models and proved that the epidemic threshold increase as adding new "Good state" with its "Neighbour-links" into the transition diagram in a specific way. However, the more profound and general results that how the threshold behaviour changes for the directed network topology and other diagram operation, for instance, adding "Bad states" or "Cross-links" between "Good states" and "Bad states" will be the orients of our future research.

References

1. Ball, F., Sirl, D., Trapman, P.: Threshold behaviour and final outcome of an epidemic on a random network with household structure. Adv. Appl. Probab. **41**(3), 765–796 (2009)
2. Chakrabarti, D., Wang, Y., Wang, C., Leskovec, J., Faloutsos, C.: Epidemic thresholds in real networks. ACM Trans. Inf. Syst. Secur. **10**(4), 1:1–1:26 (2008)
3. Cohen, F.: Computer viruses: theory and experiments. Comput. Secur. **6**(1), 22–35 (1987)
4. d'Onofrio, A.: A note on the global behaviour of the network-based SIS epidemic model. Nonlinear Anal.: Real World Appl. **9**(4), 1567–1572 (2008)
5. Ganesh, A., Massoulie, L., Towsley, D.: The effect of network topology on the spread of epidemics. In: Proceedings IEEE 24th Annual Joint Conference of the IEEE Computer and Communications Societies, vol. 2, pp. 1455–1466, March 2005
6. Hethcote, H.W.: The mathematics of infectious diseases. SIAM Rev. **42**(4), 599–653 (2000)
7. Kang, H., Fu, X.: Epidemic spreading and global stability of an SIS model with an infective vector on complex networks. Commun. Nonlinear Sci. Numer. Simul. **27**(1), 30–39 (2015)
8. Kephart, J.O., White, S.R.: Directed-graph epidemiological models of computer viruses. In: Proceedings of the 1991 IEEE Computer Society Symposium on Research in Security and Privacy, pp. 343–359, May 1991
9. Kephart, J.O., White, S.R., Chess, D.M.: Computers and epidemiology. IEEE Spectr. **30**(5), 20–26 (1993)

10. Kim, J., Radhakrishnan, S., Dhall, S.K.: Measurement and analysis of worm propagation on internet network topology. In: Proceedings of the 13th International Conference on Computer Communications and Networks (IEEE Cat. No. 04EX969), pp. 495–500, October 2004
11. Murray, W.H.: The application of epidemiology to computer viruses. Comput. Secur. **7**(2), 139–145 (1988)
12. Pastor-Satorras, R., Vespignani, A.: Epidemic spreading in scale-free networks. Phys. Rev. Lett. **86**, 3200–3203 (2001)
13. Shi, H., Duan, Z., Chen, G.: An SIS model with infective medium on complex networks. Phys. A: Stat. Mech. Appl. **387**(8), 2133–2144 (2008)
14. Wang, Y., Chakrabarti, D., Wang, C., Faloutsos, C.: Epidemic spreading in real networks: an eigenvalue viewpoint. In: Proceedings of the 22nd International Symposium on Reliable Distributed Systems, pp. 25–34, October 2003
15. Kermack, W.O., Mckendrick, A.G.: A contribution to the mathematical theory of epidemics. Proc. R. Soc. Lond. A: Math. Phys. Eng. Sci. **115**(772), 700–721 (1927)
16. Kermack, W.O., Mckendrick, A.G.: Contributions to the mathematical theory of epidemics. II.—the problem of endemicity. Proc. R. Soc. Lond. A: Math. Phys. Eng. Sci. **138**(834), 55–83 (1932)
17. Xu, S., Lu, W., Li, H.: A stochastic model of active cyber defense dynamics. Internet Math. **11**(1), 23–61 (2015)
18. Xu, S., Lu, W., Xu, L.: Push- and pull-based epidemic spreading in networks: thresholds and deeper insights. ACM Trans. Auton. Adapt. Syst. **7**(3), 32:1–32:26 (2012)
19. Xu, S., Lu, W., Xu, L., Zhan, Z.: Adaptive epidemic dynamics in networks: thresholds and control. ACM Trans. Auton. Adapt. Syst. **8**(4), 19:1–19:19 (2014)
20. Yang, M., Chen, G., Fu, X.: A modified SIS model with an infective medium on complex networks and its global stability. Phys. A: Stat. Mech. Appl. **390**(12), 2408–2413 (2011)

Characterizing the Optimal Attack Strategy Decision in Cyber Epidemic Attacks with Limited Resources

Dingyu Yan[1,2]([⊠]), Feng Liu[1,2], Yaqin Zhang[1,2], Kun Jia[1,2], and Yuantian Zhang[1,2]

[1] State Key Laboratory of Information Security, Institute of Information Engineering, Chinese Academy of Sciences, Beijing 100093, China
`yandingyu@iie.ac.cn`
[2] University of Chinese Academy of Sciences, Beijing 100049, China

Abstract. A cyber epidemic attack is considered as one effective cyber weapon in cyberspace. Generally speaking, due to the limited attack resource, the adversary needs to adjust their attack strategy timely to maximize the attack profits in the attack process. However, previous studies have not focused on the interaction between the cyber epidemic attack and the adversary's strategy from the perspective of the dynamics. This paper aims to investigate the relationship between the network security situation and the adversary's strategy decision with limited attack resources. We propose a new dynamical framework by coupling the adversary's strategy decision model to the cyber epidemic model. Through numerical results, we find the mutual effects between the network security situation and the adversary's strategy decision. Specifically, the selective attack strategy can help the adversary accumulate more attack resource compared to the random attack strategy.

Keywords: Cybersecurity dynamics · Cyber epidemic model
Attack strategy · Decision making model

1 Introduction

A cyber epidemic attack is considered to be one of the powerful cyber weapons in attacker's hands. In addition to being used to compromise the most machines on the Internet, e.g., Blaster worm and WannaCry ransomware [2], the cyber epidemic attack can be taken as an effective tool throughout the internal network, e.g., the stage of the lateral movement in one advanced persistent threat attack [11]. In this type of attack, attackers need to adjust their attack strategy, including selecting the optimal stepping stone to infect and exit the captured machines in order to be detected. Due to the finite human and material resource, the attacker must decide his optimal attack strategy to reduce the risk and maximize his attack profits. Thus, a study on the interaction between the cyber

© Springer Nature Switzerland AG 2018
F. Liu et al. (Eds.): SciSec 2018, LNCS 11287, pp. 65–80, 2018.
https://doi.org/10.1007/978-3-030-03026-1_5

epidemic attack and the attack strategy decision with limited attack resources will further enhance the understanding of this field in cybersecurity.

To date, a large number of works have investigated the cyber epidemic model theoretically [8,9], but these existing studies on cyber epidemic attacks fail the clarity regarding the attack strategy in the attack-defense process. The classic population model is based on the homogeneous assumption and the normal network models only consider the heterogeneous network topology. Lacking the heterogeneity of the attack strategy towards the users, these theoretical models assume the homogenous infection rate and recovery rate. Additionally, with no consideration of the attack cost in most of the theoretical models, the adversary has unlimited attack resource by default [14], which does not accord with the reality in cyberspace.

In this paper, we attempt to characterize the adversary's optimal attack strategy with finite resources and establish the relationship between the network security situation and the attack strategy decision. Our contribution consists mainly of two parts. First, we propose a new dynamical framework for characterizing the adversary's strategy decision in cyber epidemic attacks with limited resources. In the cyber epidemic model, we present an individual-based heterogeneous dynamical model, emphasizing more on the heterogeneous adversary's strategies towards each user. Considering all individual security states, we use a network-level dynamics to describe the evolution of the network security situation. Then, we analyze a sufficient condition that keeps the cyber system in a zero state depending on the above model. In the modeling the decision process of attack strategy, we adopt the Prospect Theory to calculate the adversary's expected utility and then obtain the adversary's optimal strategy decision by the solution of the 0-1 knapsack problem. Next, in order to explore the interaction between the optimal attack strategy and network security situation, we carry out a series of simulations. The numerical results show that: (1) There are some common patterns of relationship between the network security situation and adversary's strategy decision with respect to cyber epidemic attack scenarios. (2) Through the optimal combination of utility factors, the adversary can maximize their benefits with limited attack resources. (3) Compared to the random attack strategy, the selective attack strategy can help the adversary accumulate more attack resources and avoid being detected in some attack scenarios.

The remainder of our paper is organized as follows. We briefly introduce the related work in Sect. 2 and propose the dynamical framework in Sect. 3. The simulation results and analysis are presented in Sect. 4. We finally summarize the paper in Sect. 5.

2   Related Work

Due to a few papers focused on the relationship between the cyber epidemic attack and the attack strategy with limited resources, we list some existing study fields related to our research: cybersecurity dynamics and optimization in security strategy.

2.1 Cybersecurity Dynamics

Cybersecurity dynamics is a novel research field of cybersecurity, which describes the evolution of the security state of a cyber system [15]. As the basic theory of the cybersecurity dynamics, disease epidemics in Biology has studied for decades. The work of Kermack and McKendrick [8] starts the modern mathematical epidemic model. The theoretical epidemic model can be classified into two types: population model and network model [9]. The population model relies on the homogeneous approximation, which means that each individual is well-mixed or interacts with other individuals with the same probability. The network model considers the heterogeneous network and emphasizes the heterogeneity of the disease spreading. The cyber epidemic model often tends to the network model.

The early studies on cybersecurity dynamics focus on the network virus spreading. Kephart and White [5] establish the first homogenous virus model. Chakrabarti and Wang [1] present a heterogeneous epidemic model and find that the epidemic threshold is related to the largest eigenvalue of the adjacency matrix of network topology. By proposing an N-intertwined continuous model, Mieghem et al. [13] prove a new sufficient condition of epidemic threshold and give the bounds of the number of infected nodes. By establishing a push- and pull-based epidemic spreading model on the network, Xu et al. [16] give a more general epidemic threshold of the stability in the security state of the cyber system. Zheng et al. [18] prove the cybersecurity dynamic is always globally stable and analyze the meaning of these results for cybersecurity. Based on the heterogeneous network model, Li et al. [6] model an optimal defense approach to defend against the advanced persistent threat theoretically.

2.2 Optimization in Security Strategy

By adding economic factors, researchers focus on the optimal decision making in cybersecurity. Generally speaking, attackers hope to use less attack cost to cause the maximal sabotage or obtain the largest profits, while defenders aim to minimize their losses. The basic model is a two-player security model, which characterizes the interaction between one defender and one attacker by the game theory and optimization algorithm. For example, Pita et al. [10] design a deployed system to study the terrorist attack on the airport security. Yang et al. [17] bring the Prospect Theory and Quantal Response into the above model to increase the prediction accuracy. Moreover, some researchers attempt to model the security decision by dynamics. Lu et al. [7] study the interaction between strategic attackers and strategic defenders with the active cyber defense and then find the Nash equilibrium between strategic defenders and strategic attackers.

3 Theoretical Model

3.1 Model Assumption

Before modeling the cyber epidemic attack, we summarize some outstanding characters in the attack process and then provide some assumptions in this

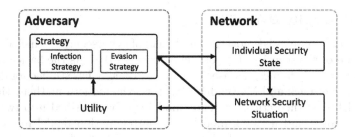

Fig. 1. Relationship between four elements in the model

model. In reality, each attacker cannot have the unlimited attack resources in the attack process. Thus, the adversary must make some decision and select the attack strategy reasonably to maximize the attack profits in the right moment, rather the static or random attack strategy. Thus, in this model, we assume that there is only one attacker, called adversary, launches a cyber epidemic attack on the network. He is responsible for deciding the attack strategy and manipulating the attack path. We divide the attack strategy into two classes: the infection strategy and the evasion strategy. The infection strategy represents that the adversary releases the malware, such as computer virus and worms, to compromise more nodes in the network. The evasion strategy means the adversary takes some evasion tool and techniques to avoid the defender's detection. In the cyber epidemic attack, the attacker not only ought to infect more nodes in the network but also guarantee the nodes he manipulates not to be detected or recovered by users. Under the assumption of limited attack resources, the adversary needs to select which nodes he wants to infect and which compromised nodes he wants to abandon.

Next, we list four main elements in our model: strategy, utility, individual security state and network security situation. Figure 1 shows the general relationship between these four elements. Generally speaking, in the view of the adversary, he must consider the current network security situation and his utility, and select the optimal attack strategy to maximize his profits. His attack strategy directly influences the individual security state of each node in the network. In the network-level security, all individual security states consist of the whole network security situation, which provides feedback to the adversary. Thus, we model a coupling dynamical framework to characterize the complex process mentioned above. This framework includes the dynamics for cyber epidemic attack and the model for attack strategy decision-making.

3.2   Dynamics for Cyber Epidemic Attacks

Given an arbitrary static undirected network $G = (Vt, Ed)$, Vt is the set of vertexes $Vt = \{vt_1, vt_2, \cdots, vt_n\}$ and Ed is denoted as the set of edges, $(vt_i, vt_i) \notin Ed$. The adjacency matrix of the network A is

Table 1. Main parameters in the dynamical model

G	The undirected network graph, $G = (Vt, Ed)$, with
A	The adjacency matrix of G
$x_i(t)$	The probability that node i is compromised by the attacker at time t
$\gamma(t)$	The infection probability that node is infected by one compromised neighbor node at time t
$\beta(t)$	The recovery probability that the compromised node becomes secure at time t
$X(t)$	The vector of the network secuirty situation at time t
$M(t)$	The system matrix at time t
$\pi_{ij}(t)$	The infection strategy towards secure node i by its compromised neighbor j at time t
$\sigma_i(t)$	The evasion strategy towards compromised node i at time t
$\Pi(\tau)$	The infection strategy matrix at time t
$diag(\sigma_i)$	The evasion strategy matrix at time t

$$A = (a_{ij})_{n \times n} = \begin{cases} 0 & (vt_i, vt_j) \notin Ed(t) \\ 1 & (vt_i, vt_j) \in Ed(t) \end{cases}.$$

In this model, each node has two security states: compromised state and secure state. We define $x_i(t)$ as the probability of being compromised state at time t, $x_i(t) \in [0, 1]$. The state transition parameters are: $\gamma(t)$ is the probability that the secure node is infected by one compromised neighbor node at time t; $\beta(t)$ is the probability that the compromised node becomes secure at time t. The main parameters in this dynamics are summarized in Table 1. The main equation of this dynamical model is

$$x_i(t+1) = \left(1 - \prod_{j=1}^{n}(1 - \gamma(t) a_{ij} \pi_{ij}(t) x_j(t))\right)(1 - x_i(t)) + (1 - \beta(t))\sigma_i(t) x_i(t), \quad (1)$$

where $\pi_{ij}(t)$ and $\sigma_i(t)$ refer to the infection strategy and evasion strategy separately. If the secure node i is regarded as the infection target at time t, the infection strategy $\pi_{ij}(t) = \pi_{ji}(t) = 1$. If the compromised node i is selected to use the evasion technique at time t, the evasion strategy $\sigma_i(t) = 1$. Converting these two strategy parameters into matrix form, we get the infection strategy matrix $\Pi(t) = (\pi_{ij}(t))_{n \times n}$ and the evasion strategy matrix $diag(\sigma_i)$. Thus, we can use these two matrices to represent the adversary's attack strategy in the dynamical model. Rewriting the Eq. (1) as

$$x_i(t+1) = (1 - \theta_i(t))(1 - x_i(t)) + z_i(t) x_i(t), \quad (2)$$

where $\theta_i(t) = 1 - \prod_{j=1}^{n}(1 - y_{ij}(t) x_j(t))$ and $y_{ij}(t) = \gamma(t) a_{ij} \pi_{ij}(t)$ and $z_i(t) = (1 - \beta(t))\sigma_i(t)$. $\theta_i(t)$ is the probability of the secure node become compromised.

$y_{ij}(t)$ is the relative infection probability that node i is infected by the compromised node j at time t with the infection strategy $\pi_{ij}(t)$ and $z_i(t)$ is the relative recovery probability of the compromised node i at time t with the evasion strategy $\sigma_i(t)$. Obviously, $\theta_i(t)$ and $z_i(t)$ is transition probability of the individual security state.

Through the linearization method mentioned in [13], we can rewrite Eq. (2), $x_i(t+1) \approx \sum_{i=1}^{n} y_{ij}(t) p_j(t) + z_i(t) p_i(t)$. Then, we write equation in matrix form for each node i, $i = 1, 2, \cdots, n$,

$$X(t+1) = (Y(t) + Z(t)) \cdot X(t) \tag{3}$$

where $Y(t) = \gamma(t) \cdot (A(t) \circ \Pi(t))$ and $Z(t) = (1 - \beta(t)) \cdot diag(\sigma_i)$.. Denote the system matrix by $M(t) = Y(t) + Z(t)$, then $X(t+1) = M(t) \cdot X(t) = \prod_{\tau=1}^{t+1} M(\tau) \cdot P(1)$. The vector $X(t)$ is considered to represent the current network situation, and the system matrix $M(t)$ is to characterize all the interactions between the attacker and the defender. If we consider this network as a cyber dynamical system, we use a triple $\langle A, M(t) \rangle$ to characterize this system.

3.3   Analysis on the Dynamical Model

For the adversary, if all compromised nodes is removed, it means this cyber epidemic attack fails. In our model, we call this security situation the zero state i.e. $\lim_{\tau \to \infty} x(\tau) = x_i^* = 0$, $i = 1, 2, \cdots, n$ or $X(t) = (0, 0, \cdots, 0)$. There exits two steady states: the zero state or trivial state and non-zero state when $t \to \infty$. In this subsection, we provide a sufficient condition to clear up all compromised nodes. In order to avoid this zero state, the adversary ought to adjust his attack strategy to avoid the following condition.

Theorem 1. *The cyber dynamical system would be in a zero state regardless of the initial configuration, if the attack strategies manipulated by the adversary at time τ, $\tau = 1, \cdots, t$, satisfies*

$$0 \leq \rho(A \circ \Pi(\tau)) < \frac{1 - (1 - \beta(\tau)) \max(\sigma_i)}{\gamma(\tau)} \tag{4}$$

where $\Pi(\tau)$ is the infection strategy matrix, σ_i is the evasion strategy for node i, $\gamma(\tau)$ is the infection probability that the node is infected by any compromised node, $\beta(\tau)$ is the recovery probability that the compromised node becomes secure. $\rho(\cdot)$ is the spectral radius of the matrix and $\circ$ is the Hadamard product.

Proof. For the discrete-time switched linear system of Eq. (3), if the system matrix has $\rho\left(\prod_{\tau=1}^{t+1} M(\tau)\right) < 1$, the network security situation $X(t) = (0, 0, \cdots, 0)$.

The system matrix $M(\tau)$, $\tau = 1, 2, \cdots, t$, is the real symmetric normal matrix, and its spectral radius $\rho(M(\tau)) = \sqrt{\lambda_1(M^2(\tau))} = \sqrt{\lambda_1(M^*(\tau)M(\tau))}$ $= \|S(\tau)\|_2 \cdot \prod_{\tau=1}^{t} \|M(\tau)\|_2 = \prod_{\tau=1}^{t} \rho(M(\tau))$. $\|\cdot\|_2$ is the 2-norm of matrix. By the theorem of 2-norm [3], $\left\|\prod_{\tau=1}^{t} M(\tau)\right\|_2 \leq \prod_{\tau=1}^{t} \|M(\tau)\|_2$ and $\rho\left(\prod_{\tau=1}^{t} M(k)\right) <$ $\left\|\prod_{\tau=1}^{t} M(\tau)\right\|_2$, we have the inequation $\rho\left(\prod_{\tau=1}^{t} M(\tau)\right) < \prod_{\tau=1}^{t} \rho(M(\tau))$.

If this cyber system satisfies $\rho(M(\tau)) < 1$, for each system matrix $\tau = 1, 2, \cdots, t$, we have $\rho\left(\prod_{\tau=1}^{t} M(\tau)\right) < 1$. Compute

$$\rho(M(\tau)) = \rho(Y(\tau) + Z(\tau)) \leq \gamma(\tau)\rho(A(\tau) \circ \Pi(\tau)) + (1 - \beta(\tau))\rho(diag(\sigma_i))$$
$$= \gamma(t)\rho(A(\tau) \circ \Pi(\tau)) + (1 - \beta(\tau))\max(\sigma_i),$$

we could obtain one sufficient condition of system stability,

$$\rho(M(\tau)) \leq \gamma(t)\rho(A(\tau) \circ \Pi(\tau)) + (1 - \beta(\tau))\max(\sigma_i) < 1.$$

Moreover, $A \circ \Pi(t)$ is the $n \times n$ non-negative symmetric matrix, $\rho(A \circ \Pi(\tau)) \geq 0$. Therefore, each node would be secure regardless of the initial condition if the cyber dynamical system satisfies at time $\tau = 1, \cdots, t$,

$$0 \leq \rho(A \circ \Pi(\tau)) < \frac{1 - (1 - \beta(\tau))\max(\sigma_i)}{\gamma(\tau)}. \qquad \square$$

If the adversary is unwilling to take the infection strategy to each node $i = 1, 2, \cdots, n$, i.e. $\Pi(\tau)$ is the zero matrix, $0 = \rho(A \circ \Pi(\tau)) < \frac{1 - (1 - \beta(\tau))\max(\sigma_i)}{\gamma(\tau)}$ always holds. Thus, abandoning the infection strategy would result in the disappearance of cyber epidemic attacks, which is in line with reality.

The spectral radius of the evasion strategy matrix $diag(\sigma_i)$ is $\max(\sigma_i) = \{0, 1\}$. $\max(\sigma_i) = 0$ means the adversary doesn't adopt the evasion strategy, and then the sufficient condition becomes $0 \leq \rho(A \circ \Pi(\tau)) < \frac{1}{\gamma(\tau)}$. When $\max(\sigma_i) = 1$, $0 \leq \rho(A \circ \Pi(\tau)) < \frac{\beta(\tau)}{\gamma(\tau)}$. We rewrite the inequation as $0 \leq \rho(A \circ \Pi(\tau)) \leq \rho(A \circ J) = \rho(A) < \frac{\beta(\tau)}{\gamma(\tau)}$, where J refers to the $n \times n$ all-ones matrix. Specially, if it is assumed that this cyber dynamical system is a linear time-invariant system, i.e. $\gamma(\tau) = \gamma$ and $\beta(\tau) = \beta$, $\tau = 1, \cdots, t$, the sufficient condition could be $\rho(A) < \frac{\beta}{\gamma}$, which is the main conclusion in the references [1].

3.4 Model for Attack Strategy Decision-Making

In this subsection, we attempt to characterize the primary process of strategy-making in the type of attack. We model the decision process with three steps: utility calculation, decision-making algorithm, and resources updating. First, the adversary should compute the expected utility of each attack strategy toward the node through subjective expectation. Second, due to limited attack resources, the attacker needs to choose nodes he takes the attack strategies towards selectively to maximize his attack resource. Third, the consequences of the attack strategy and cyber epidemic attack would affect the total resource.

The adversary's resource depends only on whether the two strategies are successful or not. We denote the new resource obtained from node i at time t by $U_i(t)$, and $U_i(t) \in \{R_i^{IS}(t), P_i^{IS}(t), R_i^{ES}(t), P_i^{ES}(t)\}$. $R_i^{IS}(t)$ refers to the reward if the infection strategy towards secure node i is successful; $P_i^{IS}(t)$ refers to the penalty if the infection strategy towards secure node i is failed; $R_i^{ES}(t)$ refers to the reward if the evasion strategy towards compromised node i is successful; $P_i^{ES}(t)$ refers to the penalty if the evasion strategy towards compromised node i is failed. We further model these four economic parameters: $R_i^{IS}(t) = G^{ES} - nghb_i(t) \cdot C^{IS}$, $P_i^{IS}(t) = -nghb_i(t) \cdot C^{IS}$, $R_i^{ES}(t) = G^{ES} - C^{ES}$ and $P_i^{ES}(t) = -C^{ES}$. $nghb_i(t)$ is defined as the number of compromised neighbors of node i and C^{IS} is the cost of one infection from one compromised node. Because the attacker can infect the targeted secure node i from its compromised neighbors, the total cost of infection strategy towards node i is $nghb_i(t) \cdot C^{IS}$. C^{ES} is the cost of evasion strategy towards each compromised node. Once infection strategy or evasion strategy is successful, the adversary would receive the gains G^{IS} and G^{ES} respectively.

We adopt the Prospect Theory [12] to calculate the expected utility of each attack strategy towards the node. The utility is

$$V_i(t) = \begin{cases} v\left(R_i^{IS}(t)\right) \cdot \omega\left(\theta_i(t)\right) + v\left(P_i^{IS}(t)\right) \cdot \omega\left(1 - \theta_i(t)\right) & \text{node } i \text{ is secure} \\ v\left(R_i^{ES}(t)\right) \cdot \omega\left(1 - \beta_i(t)\right) + v\left(P_i^{ES}(t)\right) \cdot \omega\left(\beta_i(t)\right) & \text{node } i \text{ is compromised} \end{cases}.$$

The value function $v(l)$, probability-weighting function $\omega(l)$ and parameters are proposed in [12].

After computing the utility value of each attack strategy to the node, the adversary needs to make decision about which nodes are selected as the strategy targets at time t. Due to limited attack resources, the attacker cannot afford taking attack strategies to all nodes. Thus, he should select a few nodes in order to maximize the total resource-. We adopt the 0-1 knapsack problem [4] to characterize this strategy decision process. $V_i(t)$ is the expected utility on node i at time t, $m_i(t)$ is the resource which the adversary spends on the strategy to node i, $r_i(t)$ is the adversary's decision-making for node i and $S(t)$ is adversary's total resource at time t. $r_i(t) = 1$ means the adversary will take the attack strategy towards node i at time t, and $r_i(t) = 0$ otherwise. The above problem is formulated as

$$\max \sum_{i=1}^{n} V_i(t) \cdot r_i(t)$$

$$s.t. \begin{cases} \sum_{i=1}^{n} m_i(t) \cdot r_i(t) \leq S(t) \\ r_i(t) \in \{0,1\}, 1 \leq i \leq n \end{cases}.$$

We define the resource $m_i(t)$ the adversary allocates on the node i as the cost of the attack strategy for this node

$$m_i(t) = \begin{cases} nghb_i(t) \cdot C^{IS} & \text{node } i \text{ is secure} \\ C^{ES} & \text{node } i \text{ is compromised} \end{cases}.$$

Obviously, adversary's total resource is updated timely. The new resource obtained from node i is one element of $\{R_i^{IS}(t), P_i^{IS}(t), R_i^{ES}(t), P_i^{ES}(t)\}$. Therefore, the total resource at time $t+1$ is $S(t+1) = S(t) + \sum_{i=0}^{n} U_i(t)$.

After modeling the attack strategy decision-making, we finally couple the attack strategy to the cyber epidemic model. The strategy decision $r_i(t)$ directly influence the infection strategy $\pi_{ij}(t)$ or anti-detection strategy $\sigma_i(t)$, and then further affect the dynamics for cyber epidemic attack of Eq. (3). When $r_i(t) = 1$, the infection strategy $\pi_{ij}(t) = \pi_{ji}(t) = 1$ if the node i is secure node, or evasion strategy $\sigma_i(t) = 1$ if the node i is compromised node; $\pi_{ij}(t) = \pi_{ji}(t) = 0$ or $\sigma_i(t) = 0$ when $r_i(t) = 0$.

4 Numerical Analysis

4.1 Simulation Setting

We develop a simulator to virtualize the interaction between the attack strategy decision and the cyber epidemic attack. First, we construct the network environment by Python. The three graphs are generated in these simulations: Regular network, Watts-Strogatz network and Barabasi-Albert network. The basic parameters of these networks are as follows.

Regular graph. This undirected regular network has 1000 nodes and 3000 edges. Each node degree is 6, i.e. the largest eigenvalue $\lambda_1^A = 6$.

Watts-Strogatz network. The synthetic Watts-Strogatz network has 1000 nodes and 3000 edges. The maximal node degree is 16; the average node degree is 6; the largest eigenvalue $\lambda_1^A = 7.2$.

Barabasi-Albert network. This synthetic graph has 1000 nodes and 4985 edges. The maximal node degree is 404; the average node degree is 9.97; the largest eigenvalue $\lambda_1^A = 34.22$.

Then, we build the attack scenario to simulate the process of cyber epidemic attacks. The cyber attack scenario is denoted by $\langle \gamma(t), \beta(t) \rangle$. In order to control the individual state transition and seek for the universal laws, the differences of each $\gamma(t)$ and $\beta(t)$ are weakened. Thus, $\gamma(t) \approx \gamma$ and $\beta(t) \approx \beta$. In Sect. 4.2, we investigate the interaction between the network security situation and the adversary's attack strategy with respect to 121 attack scenarios. Then we list the five typical attack scenarios to explore the impact of the utility on the network security situation in Sect. 4.3 and study the difference between the selective attack strategy and random attack strategy in Sect. 4.4.

Last, we construct the decision module to simulate the process of adversary's strategy decisions. The utility parameters are listed as follows. The initial utility of the adversary $S(0) = 1000$. The cost of one infection strategy $C^{IS} = 2$, the cost of evasion strategy on the compromised node $C^{ES} = 4$, the gain from the successful infection strategy $G^{IS} = 20$, and the gain from the successful evasion strategy $G^{ES} = 20$, by default. The total cost of infection strategy on node i is $2 \cdot nghb_i(t)$. The reward and penalty functions are $R_i^{IS}(t) = 20 - 2 \cdot nghb_i(t)$, $P_i^{IS}(t) = -2 \cdot nghb_i(t)$, $R_i^{ES}(t) = 16$ and $P_i^{ES}(t) = -4$.

In order to keep the validity of our simulations, the following results are the average value obtained after over 100 independent simulations, and each simulation is run for over 100 steps.

4.2 Effects of Cyber Epidemic Scenarios

This section mainly studies the variations of the network security situation and the adversary's strategy decision with respect to the cyber epidemic attack scenarios. We simulate 121 cyber epidemic scenarios $\langle \gamma(t), \beta(t) \rangle$, where the infection rate $\gamma(t)$ and the recovery rate $\beta(t)$ are the value of the set $\{0.0, 0.1, \cdots, 1.0\}$ respectively. Three security metrics are used to measure the network security situation and the adversary's strategy decision. The rate of compromised nodes refers to the percentage of compromised nodes in the network;

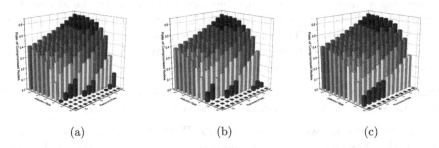

(a)   (b)   (c)

Fig. 2. Final compromised size with respect to cyber epiedmic scenarios. (a) Regular network. (b) Watts-Strogatz network. (c) Barabasi-Albert network.

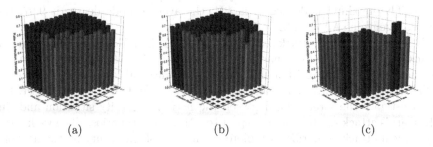

(a)   (b)   (c)

Fig. 3. Infection strategy with respect to cyber epiedmic scenarios. (a) Regular network. (b)Watts-Strogatz network. (c)Barabasi-Albert network.

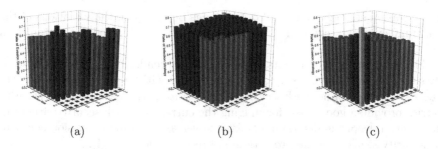

(a)   (b)   (c)

Fig. 4. Evasion strategy with respect to cyber epiedmic scenarios. (a) Regular network. (b) Watts-Strogatz network. (c)Barabasi-Albert network.

the rate of infection strategy and the rate of evasion strategy is the percentage of nodes taken by the infection strategy and the evasion strategy to secure nodes respectively.

For the rate of compromised nodes, although there are a few variations for three networks in Fig. 2, the common pattern of relationships between the network security situation and the attack scenario is that the rate of compromised nodes rises with the increase of the infection rate or the decrease of the recovery rate. When the adversary launches an invalid epidemic attack (i.e., $\gamma \approx 0$ and $\beta \neq 0$), all nodes are at secure state, and, both the rate of infection strategy and evasion strategy are 0. When the adversary starts a powerful epidemic attack (i.e., $\gamma \neq 0$ and $\beta \approx 0$), most nodes are compromised, but not all. Due to limited attack resources, the adversary cannot take the evasion measures to all compromised nodes. In our model, once one compromised node is not taken by the evasion strategy (i.e. $\sigma_i(t) = 0$), the transition probability $z_i(t) = (1 - \beta(t))\sigma_i(t) = 0$, and the individual security state of these nodes becomes secure at time t. Thus, in these attack scenarios, both the rate of compromised nodes and evasion strategy are not 100%.

Figures 3 and 4 show the rate of infection strategy and the rate of evasion strategy with respect to the interplay between the infection rate and the recovery rate. Generally, the rise in the infection rate γ leads to the increase in the adversary's infection strategy but has little influence on the evasion strategy decision. In contrast, the increasing of the recovery rate β improves the growth

Table 2. The factors and levels of the orthogonal array

Number	Factor	Level			
		1	2	3	4
A	G^{IS}	10	20	40	80
B	G^{ES}	10	20	40	80
C	C^{IS}	1	2	4	8
D	C^{ES}	1	2	4	8

in the evasion strategy. Thus, all other things being equal, the variations of the rate of infection strategy and evasion strategy size are subjected to the transition probability.

The above simulation results provide a general tendency of the network security situation and the adversary's strategy decision with respect to multiple cyber attack scenarios. For network security administrators, these variations of security metrics provide a good basis for judging the current network security situation. Moreover, a deeper understanding of the adversary's strategy decision can help the security staffs take the protection and recovery accordingly.

4.3   Effects of Utility Factors

To investigate the impacts of the adversary's utility on the network security situation, we further conduct simulations by orthogonal design with respect to the four primal utility parameters in this subsection. The four parameters at four levels are listed at Table 2. We select five typical cyber epidemic attack scenarios: $AS1 \langle \gamma = 0.2, \beta = 0.6 \rangle$, $AS2 \langle \gamma = 0.6, \beta = 0.2 \rangle$, $AS3 \langle \gamma = 0.2, \beta = 0.2 \rangle$, $AS4 \langle \gamma = 0.4, \beta = 0.4 \rangle$ and $AS5 \langle \gamma = 0.6, \beta = 0.6 \rangle$.

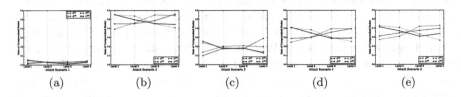

(a)   (b)   (c)   (d)   (e)

Fig. 5. Effects of 4 utility factors on the security situation of regular network. (a–e) attack scenario 1–5.

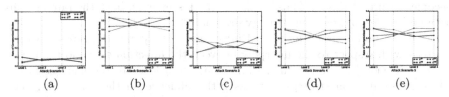

(a)   (b)   (c)   (d)   (e)

Fig. 6. Effects of 4 utility factors on the security situation of Watts-Strogatz network. (a–e) attack scenario 1–5.

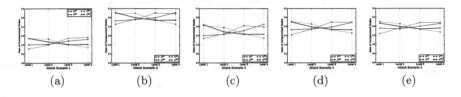

(a)   (b)   (c)   (d)   (e)

Fig. 7. Effects of 4 utility factors on the security situation of Barabasi-Albert network. (a–e) attack scenario 1–5.

In order to determine the impacts of these four factors on the network security situation, we firstly conduct the significance analysis in this section. We set the threshold value for the significance level p-value of our simulation, 0.05. If the p-value is less than 0.05, we consider this factor has a significant influence on the rate of compromised nodes. It is unexpected that there is no value less than the threshold value 0.05. This result indicates that these four utility factors have no significant effect on the network security situation. We think there are some reasons for this problem. First, the utility is just one factor in the adversary's strategy decision. Besides the utility factor, the network structure and the current network security situation, i.e., the adjacency matrix of the network topology A and transition probability, can affect decisions of the infection strategy and evasion strategy. Second, there is a complicated interaction between the network security situation and the adversary's strategy decision. It is impossible there is a linear relationship between the network security situation and the infection strategy or evasion strategy.

In addition to the significance analysis, the main effect of these four factors on the network security situation is studied in these simulations. The average values of the rate of compromised nodes with respect to the four factors are plotted in Figs. 5, 6 and 7. There are a few variations of these curves in these five attack scenarios, but the common trends indicate that increasing the gains and decreasing the cost of the infection and evasion strategy can improve the network security situation. We list optimal combinations with respect to the different attack scenarios and network environment in Table 3. Generally speaking, the higher attack gain or lower attack cost is benefits to the cyber epidemic attack. However, it is not a monotonous relationship between the rate of compromised nodes and utility factors. For example, compared to the other three values, when the gain of the successful infection strategy $G^s = 40$, the number of compromised nodes reaches the maximum in these simulations.

In our model, through the utility factor is not crucial to the network security situation, it influences the cyber epidemic attack to a certain extent. For adversaries, both the higher attack profits and the less attack cost can prompt them to take attack strategy to maximize the resource. Additionally, they need to decide the optimal combination of utility factors, instead of pursuing the higher profits or lower cost blindly. For normal users or network administrators, how to reduce attacker's benefits or increase the attack cost is always a challenge from the perspective of economy or management.

Table 3. The optimal combinations for utility factors

	AS1	AS2	AS3	AS4	AS5
Regular network	A4B3C1D1	A4B3C1D1	A3B4C1D1	A4B4C1D1	A4B3C1D1
WS network	A3B4C1D1	A3B4C1D1	A3B4C1D1	A4B4C1D1	A3B4C1D1
BA network	A4B4C1D1	A3B4C1D1	A3B4C1D1	A3B4C1D1	A4B4C1D1

4.4 Comparsion with Random Attack Strategy

This section is mainly to judge the effectiveness of the adversary's selective strategy decision with limited attack resources. We add a group of new simulation as the control group, in which the adversary decides the infection strategy and evasion strategy at random. First, the total amount of the strategy cost is no more than the total attack resources. Second, to make sure that the adversary does not exit all of the compromised nodes (i.e., the rate of evasion strategy is not zero), at least one compromised node is taken by the evasion strategy. Cyber attack scenarios are the same in Sect. 4.3. We denote the difference of the total resource between the selective attack strategy and the random attack strategy by $S(t) - S^R(t)$ to measure the effectiveness of the selective attack strategy, where $S^R(t)$ is the total resource of the random attack strategy decision.

Figure 8 presents the difference between the selective attack strategy and random attack strategy. It is obvious that the difference becomes larger and larger over time. It indicates that the selective attack strategy can help the adversary accumulate more resources than the random attack strategy. Specifically, in the attack scenarios of low infection rate and high recovery rate (e.g., $AS1$), the random attack strategy can make the rate of compromised nodes reaches to 0 when the time $t = 40$. This is because the random attack strategy does not emphasize the success rate of the attack strategy. In general, the selective attack strategy selects the relatively high-income and low protective nodes to infect and protects the crucial compromised nodes from the defender's detection.

Our simulation results indicate that the selective attack strategy is more effective than the random attack strategy. It cannot only help the adversary obtain more attack resources and higher profits but also can avoid being detected by the defender in some cyber epidemic attack scenarios.

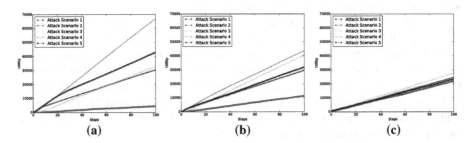

Fig. 8. Difference between the selective strategy and the random strategy. (a) Regular network. (b) Watts-Strogatz network. (c) Barabasi-Albert network.

5 Conclusion

This paper mainly studies the interaction between the network security situation and the adversary's attack strategy. We propose a new dynamical framework for characterizing the attack strategy decision in cyber epidemic attacks. In the modeling the cyber epidemic attack, an individual-based heterogeneous dynamics is established to emphasize the heterogeneity of the adversary's strategy. Then, we provide a sufficient condition that keeps the cyber dynamical system in a zero state. In modeling of adversary's strategy decision, we use the Prospect Theory to calculate the utility value of each strategy and then characterize the adversary's optimal strategy decision by the solution of the 0-1 knapsack problem. Through a serious of simulations on the cyber epidemic attack with selective attack strategy, we obtain some findings: (1) There are some common patterns of relationship between the network security situation and adversary's strategy decision with respect to cyber epidemic attack scenarios. (2) Through the optimal combination of utility factors, the adversary can maximize their benefits with limited attack resources. (3) Compared to the random attack strategy, the selective attack strategy can help the adversary accumulate more attack resources and avoid being detected in some attack scenarios.

Acknowledgment. The authors would like to thank the anonymous reviewers for their valuable comments and suggestions. This research was supported by the National Key Research & Development Program of China (Grant No.2016YFB0800102).

References

1. Chakrabarti, D., Wang, Y., Wang, C., Leskovec, J., Faloutsos, C.: Epidemic thresholds in real networks. ACM Trans. Inf. Syst. Secur. (TISSEC) **10**(4), 1 (2008)
2. Chen, Q., Bridges, R.A.: Automated behavioral analysis of malware: a case study of wannacry ransomware. In: IEEE International Conference on Machine Learning and Applications, pp. 454–460 (2017)
3. Horn, R.A., Johnson, C.R.: Matrix Analysis. Cambridge University Press, Cambridge (1990)
4. Jaszkiewicz, A.: On the performance of multiple-objective genetic local search on the 0/1 knapsack problem - a comparative experiment. IEEE Trans. Evol. Comput. **6**(4), 402–412 (2002)
5. Kephart, J.O., White, S.R.: Directed-graph epidemiological models of computer viruses. In: 1991 IEEE Computer Society Symposium on Research in Security and Privacy, Proceedings, pp. 343–359. IEEE (1991)
6. Li, P., Yang, X., Xiong, Q., Wen, J., Tang, Y.Y.: Defending against the advanced persistent threat: an optimal control approach. Secur. Commun. Netw. (2018)
7. Lu, W., Xu, S., Yi, X.: Optimizing active cyber defense. In: Das, S.K., Nita-Rotaru, C., Kantarcioglu, M. (eds.) GameSec 2013. LNCS, vol. 8252, pp. 206–225. Springer, Cham (2013). https://doi.org/10.1007/978-3-319-02786-9_13
8. Nowzari, C., Preciado, V.M., Pappas, G.J.: Analysis and control of epidemics: a survey of spreading processes on complex networks. IEEE Control. Syst. **36**(1), 26–46 (2016)
9. Pastor-Satorras, R., Castellano, C., Van Mieghem, P., Vespignani, A.: Epidemic processes in complex networks. Rev. Mod. Phys. **87**(3), 925 (2015)
10. Pita, J., John, R., Maheswaran, R., Tambe, M., Kraus, S.: A robust approach to addressing human adversaries in security games. In: Proceedings of the 20th European Conference on Artificial Intelligence, pp. 660–665. IOS Press (2012)
11. Sood, A.K., Enbody, R.J.: Targeted cyberattacks: a superset of advanced persistent threats. IEEE Secur. Priv. **11**(1), 54–61 (2013)

12. Tversky, A., Kahneman, D.: Advances in prospect theory: cumulative representation of uncertainty. J. Risk Uncertain. **5**(4), 297–323 (1992)
13. Van Mieghem, P., Omic, J., Kooij, R.: Virus spread in networks. IEEE/ACM Trans. Netw. (TON) **17**(1), 1–14 (2009)
14. Wang, W., Tang, M., Eugene, S.H., Braunstein, L.A.: Unification of theoretical approaches for epidemic spreading on complex networks. Rep. Prog. Phys. **80**(3), 036603 (2017)
15. Xu, S.: Cybersecurity dynamics. In: Proceedings of the 2014 Symposium and Bootcamp on the Science of Security, p. 14. ACM (2014)
16. Xu, S., Lu, W., Xu, L.: Push-and pull-based epidemic spreading in networks: thresholds and deeper insights. ACM Trans. Auton. Adapt. Syst. (TAAS) **7**(3), 32 (2012)
17. Yang, R., Kiekintveld, C., OrdóñEz, F., Tambe, M., John, R.: Improving resource allocation strategies against human adversaries in security games: an extended study. Artif. Intell. **195**, 440–469 (2013)
18. Zheng, R., Lu, W., Xu, S.: Preventive and reactive cyber defense dynamics is globally stable. IEEE Trans. Netw. Sci. Eng. **PP**(99), 1 (2016)

Computer Viruses Propagation Model on Dynamic Switching Networks

Chunming Zhang[✉]

School of Information Engineering, Guangdong Medical University,
Dongguan 523808, China
chunfei2002@163.com

Abstract. To explore the mechanism of computer viruses that spread on dynamic switching networks, a new differential equation model for computer viruses propagation is proposed in this paper. Then, to calculate the propagation threshold, two different methods are given. What's more, the stability of virus-free equilibrium in both linear and nonlinear model is proved. Eventually, some numerical simulations are given to illustrate the main results.

Keywords: Computer virus · Propagation model
Dynamic switching networks

1 Introduction

A time-varying network, also known as a temporal network, is a network whose links will change (dissipate and emerge). And the structure of it will be different in the distinct time [1, 2]. Therefore, this network can describe the real world more appropriately than static networks. For instance, people have different connections through the Internet during the day and the night [3].

The studies about time-varying network can be classified into two main types. Type 1 focuses on the influence of network's structure on computer viruses propagation; type 2 studies the effect of time interval on computer viruses spreading [2]. For example, in [4–6], authors proved that different structures of the network may derive different propagation thresholds. In [7, 8], authors presented that time interval is also a key factor in computer viruses propagation.

1.1 Related Work

Recently, Dynamic Switching Networks (*DSN*), a kind of time-varying networks, attracts lots of attention. *DSN* may include two or more sub-networks whose links would activate or dissipate at particular time. For example, in [9], authors firstly proposed a *SIS* propagation model on *DSN* which consists of two sub-networks. In [10, 11], the authors presented the different propagation thresholds of *SIS* propagation model on *DSN* in different ways.

On the other hand, the Susceptible-Latent-Breaking-Susceptible (*SLBS*) computer viruses propagation model has the following advantages compared with other models [12]. First, most of the previous model, like *SI*, *SIS*, *SIR*, and so on, ignore the notable

F. Liu et al. (Eds.): SciSec 2018, LNCS 11287, pp. 81–95, 2018.
https://doi.org/10.1007/978-3-030-03026-1_6

difference between latent and breaking-out computers [15, 17]. Second, some models, which contain E computers, neglect the fact that all infected computers possess infectivity [15, 16]. Therefore, *SLBS* model has become a hot research topic [12–18].

Hence, in this context, to better understand the impact of *DSN* topology on computer virus spreading. In this paper, we propose a novel *SLBS* computer virus propagation model based on *DSN*.

The subsequent materials of this paper are organized as follows. In Sect. 2, we present the *DSN* and computer viruses propagation model in detail; and then two kinds of methods to calculate thresholds and mathematical properties of the model are obtained in Sect. 3; in Sect. 4 some numerical simulation results are presented; eventually, in Sect. 5, we summarize this work.

2 Model Description

For the purpose of describing the model in detail, the following notations are proposed.

- $G = (V, E)$: the *DSN*, which consists of n time-varying sub-networks.
- $G_s = (V_s, E_s)$ $(s = 1, 2, \cdots, n)$: the sub-network of computer virus spread in the period form $t + (s-1)\Delta t$ to $t + s\Delta t$, and each sub-network Gs has N nodes.
- V_s: the set of nodes in G_s.
- E_s: the set of edges in G_s.
- $A_s = \left[a_{ij}^s\right]_{N \times N}$: the corresponding parameterized adjacency matrix of graph G_s.
- a_{ij}^s: the link from node i to node j in G_s, $a_{ij}^s \in \{0, 1\}$.

In addition, a *DSN* $G = (V, E)$ also must satisfy the following conditions.
(I) $V = V_1 = V_2 = \cdots V_n$;
(II) $E = \cup_{s=1}^{n} E_s$ and $E_{s_1} \cap E_{s_2} = \emptyset$ for all $s_1 \neq s_2$.
Condition (I) shows that nodes of all sub-networks are same. Condition (II) indicates that the edges of any two sub-networks are different (Fig. 1).

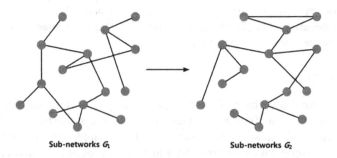

Sub-networks G_1 Sub-networks G_2

Fig. 1. The *DSN* with two sub-networks.

Under the traditional *SLBS* model, these nodes are classified into three groups: uninfected nodes (*S*-nodes), latent nodes (*L*-nodes), and breaking out nodes (*B*-nodes). Let $\xi_i(t) = 0$ (respectively, 1, 2) represent that node i is susceptible (respectively, latent, broken out) at time t. Then the state of the *DSN* at time t can be expressed as follows

$$\xi(t) = (\xi_1(t), \cdots, \xi_n(t)) \in \{0, 1, 2\}^n.$$

Let $s_i(t)$ (respectively, $l_i(t)$, $b_i(t)$) represent the probability that node i is susceptible (respectively, latent, broken out) at time t,

$$s_i(t) = \Pr(\xi_i(t) = 0),$$
$$l_i(t) = \Pr(\xi_i(t) = 1),$$
$$b_i(t) = \Pr(\xi_i(t) = 2).$$

Then, the following assumptions are given (see Fig. 2).

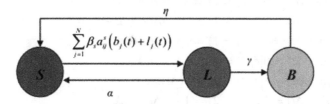

Fig. 2. State diagram of *SLBS* model on *DSN*.

(*H*1) In the sth sub-network G_s, the probability that a susceptible node i infected by a viral (include latent and breaking out) neighbor j is $\beta_s a_{ij}^s (b_j(t) + l_j(t))$, where β_s denotes the infection rate in the sth sub-network G_s. Then, a susceptible node i gets infected by all viral neighbors in the sth sub-network with probability per unit time
$$\sum_{j=1}^N \beta_s a_{ij}^s (b_j(t) + l_j(t)).$$

(*H*2) The probability a latent node becomes a broken out node is γ.
(*H*3) The probability a broken out node becomes a susceptible node is η.
(*H*4) The probability a latent node becomes a susceptible node is α.

First, we consider the spread of computer viruses in the first sub-network.

Let Δt denote a short time interval. Following formulas can be obtained from above assumptions:

$$s_i(t+\Delta t) = s_i(t)\,\Pr(\xi_i(t+\Delta t)=0|\xi_i(t)=0) + l_i(t)\,\Pr(\xi_i(t+\Delta t)=0|\xi_i(t)=1)$$
$$+ b_i(t)\,\Pr(\xi_i(t+\Delta t)=0|\xi_i(t)=2),$$
$$l_i(t+\Delta t) = s_i(t)\,\Pr(\xi_i(t+\Delta t)=1|\xi_i(t)=0) + l_i(t)\,\Pr(\xi_i(t+\Delta t)=1|\xi_i(t)=1)$$
$$+ b_i(t)\,\Pr(\xi_i(t+\Delta t)=1|\xi_i(t)=2),$$
$$b_i(t+\Delta t) = s_i(t)\,\Pr(\xi_i(t+\Delta t)=2|\xi_i(t)=0) + l_i(t)\,\Pr(\xi_i(t+\Delta t)=2|\xi_i(t)=1)$$
$$+ b_i(t)\,\Pr(\xi_i(t+\Delta t)=2|\xi_i(t)=2).$$

According to (*H1*)–(*H4*), we can derive the following equations:

$$\Pr(\xi_i(t+\Delta t)=0|\xi_i(t)=0) = 1 - \left(\sum_{j=1}^{N}\beta_1 a_{ij}^1(b_j(t)+l_j(t))\right)\Delta t + o(t),$$

$$\Pr(\xi_i(t+\Delta t)=1|\xi_i(t)=0) = \left(\sum_{j=1}^{N}\beta_1 a_{ij}^1(b_j(t)+l_j(t))\right)\Delta t + o(\Delta t),$$

$$\Pr(\xi_i(t+\Delta t)=2|\xi_i(t)=0) = o(\Delta t),$$
$$\Pr(\xi_i(t+\Delta t)=0|\xi_i(t)=1) = \alpha\Delta t + o(\Delta t),$$
$$\Pr(\xi_i(t+\Delta t)=1|\xi_i(t)=1) = 1 - \alpha\Delta t - \gamma\Delta t + o(\Delta t),$$
$$\Pr(\xi_i(t+\Delta t)=2|\xi_i(t)=1) = \gamma\Delta t + o(\Delta t),$$
$$\Pr(\xi_i(t+\Delta t)=0|\xi_i(t)=2) = \eta\Delta t + o(\Delta t),$$
$$\Pr(\xi_i(t+\Delta t)=1|\xi_i(t)=2) = o(\Delta t),$$
$$\Pr(\xi_i(t+\Delta t)=2|\xi_i(t)=2) = 1 - \eta\Delta t + o(\Delta t).$$

Substituting these equations into the above formulas and considering one order approximation, we get the following 3N-dimensional system:

$$s_i(t+\Delta t) = s_i(t)\left[1 - \left(\sum_{j=1}^{N}\beta_1 a_{ij}^1(b_j(t)+l_j(t))\right)\Delta t\right] + l_i(t)\alpha\Delta t + b_i(t)\eta\Delta t,$$

$$l_i(t+\Delta t) = s_i(t)\left(\sum_{j=1}^{N}\beta_1 a_{ij}^1(b_j(t)+l_j(t))\right)\Delta t + l_i(t)(1-\alpha\Delta t - \gamma\Delta t),\ 1\le i\le N. \tag{1}$$

$$b_i(t+\Delta t) = l_i(t)\gamma\Delta t + b_i(t)(1-\eta\Delta t),$$

Because $s_i(t)+l_i(t)+b_i(t)\equiv 1$, for all time, $s_i(t)$ can be expressed as $s_i(t)=1-l_i(t)-b_i(t)$. Then, the following 2N-dimensional subsystem can be derived:

$$l_i(t+\Delta t) = (1-b_i(t)-l_i(t))\left(\sum_{j=1}^{N}\beta_1 a_{ij}^1(b_j(t)+l_j(t))\right)\Delta t + l_i(t)(1-\alpha\Delta t - \gamma\Delta t),$$

$$\tag{2}$$

$$b_i(t+\Delta t) = l_i(t)\gamma\Delta t + b_i(t)(1 - \eta\Delta t),\ 1 \leq i \leq N.$$

Let $t_0 = t$, $t_1 = t+\Delta t,\ldots,t_n = t+n\Delta t, t_2 = t+2\Delta t$, system (2) can be expressed as:

$$l_i(t_1) = (1 - b_i(t_0) - l_i(t_0))\left(\sum_{j=1}^{N}\beta_1 a_{ij}^1(b_j(t_0) + l_j(t_0))\right)\Delta t + l_i(t_0)(1 - \alpha\Delta t - \gamma\Delta t),$$

$$b_i(t_1) = l_i(t_0)\gamma\Delta t + b_i(t_0)(1 - \eta\Delta t),\ 1 \leq i \leq N.$$

Similarly, according to the above method, we can obtain the system in one period at time t_0 to t_n which can be expressed as follows

$$l_i(t_s) = (1 - b_i(t_{s-1}) - l_i(t_{s-1}))\left(\sum_{j=1}^{N}\beta_s a_{ij}^s(b_j(t_{s-1}) + l_j(t_{s-1}))\right)\Delta t + l_i(t_{s-1})(1 - \alpha\Delta t - \gamma\Delta t),$$

$$b_i(t_s) = l_i(t_{s-1})\gamma\Delta t + b_i(t_{s-1})(1 - \eta\Delta t),\ 1 \leq s \leq n,\ 1 \leq i \leq N, \tag{3}$$

with initial conditions $0 \leq l_i(0)$, $b_i(0) \leq 1$.

As $p(t) << 1$, we consider one order approximation for the high dimensional model (3) as following linear form.

$$l_i(t_s) = \left(\sum_{j=1}^{N}\beta_s a_{ij}^s(b_j(t_{s-1}) + l_j(t_{s-1}))\right)\Delta t + l_i(t_{s-1})(1 - \alpha\Delta t - \gamma\Delta t), \tag{4}$$

$$b_i(t_s) = l_i(t_{s-1})\gamma\Delta t + b_i(t_{s-1})(1 - \eta\Delta t),\ 1 \leq s \leq n,\ 1 \leq i \leq N.$$

Let

$$p(t) = (l_1(t), \cdots, l_N(t), b_1(t), \cdots, b_N(t))^T,$$

I represents N-dimensional unit matrix, system (4) can be expressed as the following matrix notation.

$$p(t_s) = \begin{bmatrix} (1 - \alpha\Delta t - \gamma\Delta t)I + \beta_s A_s\Delta t & \beta_s A_s\Delta t \\ \gamma\Delta t I & (1 - \eta\Delta t)I \end{bmatrix}p(t_{s-1}),\ 1 \leq s \leq n. \tag{5}$$

And then, let

$$M_s = \begin{bmatrix} 1 - \alpha\Delta t - \gamma\Delta t + \beta_s A_s\Delta t & \beta_s A_s\Delta t \\ \gamma\Delta t & 1 - \eta\Delta t \end{bmatrix},\ 1 \leq s \leq n.$$

Then, we obtain

$$p(t_2) = M_2 M_1 p(t_0),$$

$$p(t_3) = M_3 M_2 M_1 p(t_0),$$

$$\cdots,$$

$$p(t_s) = M_s M_{s-1} \cdots M_2 M_1 p(t_0) = \prod_{j=1}^{s} M_j p(t_0),$$

$$\cdots,$$

$$p(t_n) = M_n M_{n-1} \cdots M_2 M_1 p(t_0) = \prod_{j=1}^{n} M_j p(t_0),$$

Let A represents the matrix $\prod_{j=1}^{n} M_j$. Let R_0 represent the largest eigenvalue of matrix $\prod_{j=1}^{n} M_j$.

Then, we can obtain the differential equation model in k period at time t_0 to kt_n which can be expressed as follows.

$$p(t_n) = A p(t_0),$$

$$p(2t_n) = A^2 p(t_0), \tag{6}$$

$$\cdots,$$

$$p(kt_n) = A^k p(t_0),$$

System (6) will be used as the differential equation model for *SLBS* computer virus propagation on *DSN*.

3 Theoretical Analysis

In this section, we focus on the propagation threshold of computer viruses, the stability of the virus-free equilibrium and the persistence of viral equilibrium.

Let R_0 represents the largest eigenvalue of matrix A.

Theorem 1. *Consider system* (6),

(a) The virus-free equilibrium $E_0 = (0, 0, \cdots, 0)_{2N \times 1}^{T}$ is exponentially stable if $R_0 < 1$.
(b) The virus-free equilibrium $E_0 = (0, 0, \cdots, 0)_{2N \times 1}^{T}$ is unstable if $R_0 > 1$.

Proof. Let $\lambda_{i,A}$ denote the i-th largest eigenvalue of A. Let $u_{i,A}$ denote eigenvector of A corresponding to $\lambda_{i,A}$.tr$A$ denotes the transpose of matrix A.

Then, by definition,

$$Au_{i,A} = \lambda_{i,A} u_{i,A}$$

Using the spectral decomposition, we get

$$A = \sum_{i=1}^{N} \lambda_{i,A} u_{i,A} \text{tr} u_{i,A},$$

and

$$A^k = \sum_{i=1}^{N} \lambda_{i,A}^k u_{i,A} \text{tr} u_{i,A}.$$

Considering (6), we get

$$p(kt_n) = \sum_{i=1}^{N} \lambda_{i,A}^k u_{i,A} \text{tr} u_{i,A} p(t_0).$$

As R_0 represents the largest eigenvalue of matrix A, without loss of generality, we obtain

$$R_0 \geq \lambda_{1,A} \geq \lambda_{2,A} \geq \lambda_{3,A} \cdots,$$

and for $\forall i$, $R_0^k \geq \lambda_{i,A}^k$.

System (6) can be represented as following format

$$
\begin{aligned}
p(kt_n) &= \sum_{i=1}^{N} \lambda_{i,A}^k u_{i,A} \text{tr} u_{i,A} p(t_0) \\
&= \lambda_{i,A}^k * C \\
&\leq R_0^k * C,
\end{aligned}
$$

where C is a constant vector. Since $R_0 < 1$, the values of $p(kt_n)$ are decreasing exponentially over time. $p(kt_n)$ is unstable, when $R_0 > 1$.

However, this condition is not simple. The relationship between the propagation threshold and the network structure can't be derived directly. In order to obtain the simple condition for computer viruses spreading, we should consider the continuous-time process of viruses spreading as an approximation to the discrete-time process. We examine the matrix $M_2 M_1$. Considering one order approximation, we get the following matrix.

$$
\begin{aligned}
M_2 M_1 &=
\begin{bmatrix}
(1 - \alpha\Delta t - \gamma\Delta t)I + \beta_2 A_2 \Delta t & \beta_2 A_2 \Delta t \\
\gamma\Delta t I & (1 - \eta\Delta t)I
\end{bmatrix}
\begin{bmatrix}
(1 - \alpha\Delta t - \gamma\Delta t)I + \beta_1 A_1 \Delta t & \beta_1 A_1 \Delta t \\
\gamma\Delta t I & (1 - \eta\Delta t)I
\end{bmatrix} \\
&=
\begin{bmatrix}
((1 - \alpha\Delta t - \gamma\Delta t)I + \beta_2 A_2 \Delta t)((1 - \alpha\Delta t - \gamma\Delta t)I + \beta_1 A_1 \Delta t) & ((1 - \alpha\Delta t - \gamma\Delta t)I + \beta_2 A_2 \Delta t)\beta_1 A_1 \Delta t \\
\quad + \beta_2 A_2 \gamma \Delta t^2 & \quad + \beta_2 A_2 \Delta t (1 - \eta\Delta t) \\
\gamma\Delta t((1 - \alpha\Delta t - \gamma\Delta t)I + \beta_1 A_1 \Delta t) + (1 - \eta\Delta t)\gamma\Delta t I & \gamma\beta_1 A_1 \Delta t^2 + (1 - \eta\Delta t)^2 I
\end{bmatrix} \\
&\geq
\begin{bmatrix}
(1 - 2(\alpha + \gamma)\Delta t)I + (\beta_1 A_1 + \beta_2 A_2)\Delta t & (\beta_1 A_1 + \beta_2 A_2)\Delta t \\
2\gamma\Delta t I & (1 - 2\eta\Delta t)I
\end{bmatrix}.
\end{aligned}
$$

Similarly,

$$
\prod_{j=1}^{n} M_j \geq
\begin{bmatrix}
(1 - n(\alpha + \gamma)\Delta t)I + \sum_{j=1}^{n} \beta_j A_j \Delta t & \sum_{j=1}^{n} \beta_j A_j \Delta t \\
n\gamma\Delta t I & (1 - n\eta\Delta t)I
\end{bmatrix}.
$$

Substituting the above matrix into (5), we get

$$
p(t_n) =
\begin{bmatrix}
(1 - n(\alpha + \gamma)\Delta t)I + \sum_{j=1}^{n} \beta_j A_j \Delta t & \sum_{j=1}^{n} \beta_j A_j \Delta t \\
n\gamma\Delta t I & (1 - n\eta\Delta t)I
\end{bmatrix} p(t).
\tag{7}
$$

Letting $\Delta t \to 0$, we get the following linear differential system:

$$
\begin{aligned}
\frac{dp(t)}{dt} &= \lim_{\Delta t \to 0} \frac{p(t_n) - p(t)}{n\Delta t} \\
&= \frac{
\begin{bmatrix}
(1 - n(\alpha + \gamma)\Delta t)I + \sum_{j=1}^{n} \beta_j A_j \Delta t & \sum_{j=1}^{n} \beta_j A_j \Delta t \\
n\gamma\Delta t I & (1 - n\eta\Delta t)I
\end{bmatrix} p(t) - p(t)
}{n\Delta t} \\
&=
\begin{bmatrix}
-(\alpha + \gamma)I + \frac{1}{n}\sum_{j=1}^{n} \beta_j A_j & \frac{1}{n}\sum_{j=1}^{n} \beta_j A_j \\
\gamma I & -\eta I
\end{bmatrix} p(t).
\end{aligned}
$$

Let

$$
H = \frac{1}{n}\sum_{j=1}^{n} \beta_j A_j,
$$

the above equation can be expressed as:

$$
\frac{dp(t)}{dt} =
\begin{bmatrix}
-(\alpha + \gamma)I + H & H \\
\gamma I & -\eta I
\end{bmatrix}_{2N \times 2N} p(t).
\tag{8}
$$

We assume $\lambda_{\max}$ represents the maximum eigenvalue of matrix H, W represents

$$\begin{bmatrix} -\alpha I - \gamma I + H & H \\ \gamma I & -\eta I \end{bmatrix}_{2N \times 2N}.$$

System (7) obviously has a unique virus-free equilibrium $E_0 = (0,0,\cdots,0)_{2N\times1}^T$. Let

$$R_1 = \frac{\eta+\gamma}{\eta(\alpha+\gamma)}\lambda_{max}. \tag{9}$$

Theorem 2. Consider linear system (8),

(a) The virus-free equilibrium $E_0 = (0,0,\cdots,0)_{2N\times1}^T$ is asymptotically stable if $R_1 < 1$.
(b) The virus-free equilibrium $E_0 = (0,0,\cdots,0)_{2N\times1}^T$ is unstable if $R_1 > 1$.

Proof. The characteristic equation of the Jacobian matrix of system (8) at E_0 is

$$\begin{aligned} \det(\lambda I - W) &= \det\begin{pmatrix} (\lambda+\alpha+\gamma)I - H & -H \\ -\gamma I & (\lambda+\eta)I \end{pmatrix}_{2N\times2N} \\ &= \det((\lambda+\alpha+\gamma)(\lambda+\eta)I - ((\lambda+\gamma+\eta)H) \\ &= 0. \end{aligned} \tag{10}$$

Equation (10) has two possible cases.

Case 1. $\alpha = \eta$. Then $R_1 = \lambda_{max}/\eta$, and Eq. (9) deduces into

$$(\lambda+\eta+\gamma)^N \det((\lambda+\eta)I - H) = 0.$$

This equation has a negative root $-\eta - \gamma$ with multiplicity N; and the remaining N roots of the equation are $\lambda_k - \eta$, $1 \leq k \leq N$. If $R_1 < 1$, then $\lambda_k - \eta \leq \lambda_{max} - \eta < 0$ for all k. Hence, all the roots of Eq. (10) are negative. So, the virus-free equilibrium of system (10) is asymptotically stable. On the contrary, if $R_1 > 1$, then $\lambda_{max} - \eta > 0$. So, Eq. (10) has a positive equilibrium. As a result, the virus-free equilibrium is unstable.

Case 2. $\alpha \neq \eta$. Then $-\eta - \gamma$ is not a root of Eq. (10). Thus,

$$\det\left(\frac{(\lambda+\alpha+\gamma)(\lambda+\eta)}{(\lambda+\gamma+\eta)}I - H\right) = 0.$$

This means that λ is a root of Eq. (10) if and only if λ is a root of equation

$$\lambda^2 + a_k\lambda + b_k = 0, \tag{11}$$

Where

$$a_k = \alpha + \gamma + \eta - \lambda_k,$$
$$b_k = (\alpha + \gamma)\eta - \lambda_k(\gamma + \eta).$$

If $R_1 < 1$, then $(\gamma + \eta)\lambda_k < (\gamma + \eta)\lambda_{max} < \eta(\alpha + \gamma)$, $\lambda_k < \lambda_{max} < \frac{\eta(\alpha+\gamma)}{\gamma+\eta} < \alpha + \gamma + \eta$ for all k, we have $a_k > 0$ and $b_k > 0$. According to the Hurwitz criterion, the two roots of Eq. (11) both have negative real parts. So, all roots of Eq. (10) have negative real parts. Hence, the virus-free equilibrium is asymptotically stable. Otherwise, if $R_1 > 1$, the equation $\lambda^2 + a_k\lambda + b_k = 0$ has a root with positive real part. As a result, Eq. (10) has a root with positive real part. Hence, the virus-free equilibrium is unstable.

The proof is complete.

4 Numerical Simulation

This section gives some numerical examples to illustrate the main results. Let $u\,(t)$ denote the percentage of infected nodes in all nodes at time t, $u(t) = \frac{1}{N}\sum_{i=1}^{N}(l_i(t) + b_i(t))$.

(1) Take a *DSN* with two Erdos–Renyi random sub-networks, each sub-network has 500 nodes. And the connection probability of the 1st and the 2nd sub-network is 0.8 and 0.6, respectively. The infection rate of the 1st and the 2nd sub-network is $\beta_1 = 0.0008$ and $\beta_2 = 0.0006$, respectively.

Case 1. System (6) with $\alpha = 0.4$, $\gamma = 0.5$, and $\eta = 0.4$ for different initial conditions, then $R_0 = 0.7174$, and $R_1 = 0.6247$. As $R_0 < 1$, and $R_1 < 1$, then computer virus would die out (see Fig. 3).

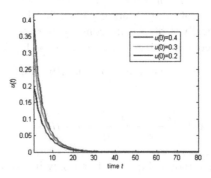

Fig. 3. Case 1.

Case 2. System (6) with $\alpha = 0.4$, $\gamma = 0.5$, and $\eta = 0.12$ for different initial conditions, then $R_0 = 1.1117$ and $R_1 = 1.4322$. As $R_0 > 1$, $R_1 > 1$, computer virus would persist (see Fig. 4).

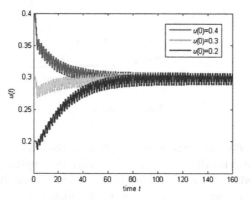

Fig. 4. Case 2.

(2) Take a *DSN* with two Barabási–Albert (BA) scale-free sub-networks on 500 nodes. The infected rate of the 1st and the 2nd sub-network is $\beta_1 = 0.002$ and $\beta_2 = 0.003$, respectively.

Case 3. System (6) with $\alpha = 0.8$, $\gamma = 0.7$, and $\eta = 0.6$ for different initial conditions. As $R_0 = 0.2692 < 1$, and $R_1 = 0.2223 < 1$, computer virus would die out (see Fig. 5).

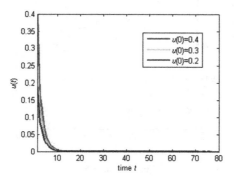

Fig. 5. Case 3.

Case 4. System (6) with $\alpha = 0.1$, $\gamma = 0.5$, and $\eta = 0.1$ for different initial conditions. As $R_0 = 1.1093 > 1$, $R_1 = 1.5425 > 1$, computer virus would persist (see Fig. 6).

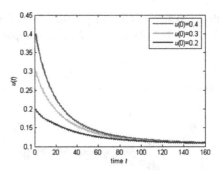

Fig. 6. Case 4.

(3) Considering a *DSN* consists of three sub-networks, each sub-network has 500 nodes. The sub-network of the 1st, 2nd, and 3rd is complete connected network, random network and scale-free network, respectively. And the connection probability of the random sub-networks is 0.7. Besides, the infected rate of the 1st, 2nd, and 3rd sub-network is $\beta_1 = 0.0005$, $\beta_2 = 0.0005$, and $\beta_3 = 0.003$, respectively.

Case 5. System (6) with $\alpha = 0.8$, $\gamma = 0.7$, and $\eta = 0.4$ for different initial conditions. As $R_0 = 0.3784 < 1$ and $R_1 = 0.3386 < 1$, then computer virus would die out (see Fig. 7).

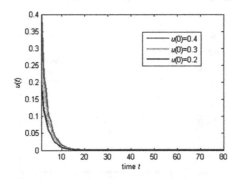

Fig. 7. Case 5.

Case 6. System (6) with $\alpha = 0.1$, $\gamma = 0.6$, and $\eta = 0.1$ for different initial conditions. As $R_0 = 1.2674 > 1$ and $R_1 = 1.8401 > 1$, then computer virus would persist (see Fig. 8).

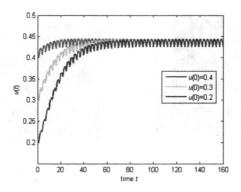

Fig. 8. Case 6.

(4) Considering a *DSN* consists of three sub-networks, each sub-network has 100 nodes. The sub-network of the 1st, 2nd, and 3rd is complete connected network, random network and scale-free network, respectively. And the connection probability of the random sub-networks is 0.7. Besides, the infection rate of the 1st, 2nd, and 3rd sub-network is $\beta_1 = 0.002$, $\beta_2 = 0.002$, $\beta_3 = 0.004$, respectively.

Case 7. Considering above network, values of R_0 as a function of varying η and γ with fixed the parameter $\alpha = 0.1$ is shown in Fig. 9.

Case 8. Considering above network, values of R_1 as a function of varying η and γ with fixed the parameter $\alpha = 0.1$ is shown in Fig. 10.

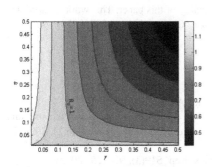

Fig. 9. Case 7.

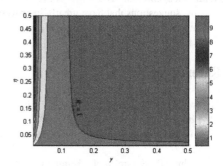

Fig. 10. Case 8.

From Figs. 9 and 10, we can find out the curve of $R_0 = 1$ and the curve of $R_1 = 1$ are very similar.

Case 9. Considering above network, values of R_0 as a function of varying η and α with fixed the parameter $\gamma = 0.2$ is shown in Fig. 11.

Case 10. Considering above network, values of R_1 as a function of varying η and α with fixed the parameter $\gamma = 0.2$ is shown in Fig. 12.

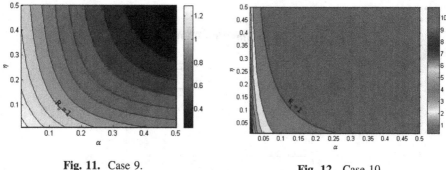

Fig. 11. Case 9.   **Fig. 12.** Case 10.

By comparing Fig. 11 with Fig. 12, we can discover that the curve of $R_0 = 1$ is similar to the curve of $R_I = 1$

5   Conclusion

To explore the propagation mechanism of computer viruses on *DSN*, a novel computer virus propagation model has been proposed. Two ways of calculating the propagation threshold R_0, R_1 are given, respectively. Then, the stability of virus-free equilibrium in both linear and nonlinear model has been proved. Finally, some numerical simulations have also been given.

Acknowledgements. The author is indebted to the anonymous reviewers and the editor for their valuable suggestions that have greatly improved the quality of this paper. This work is supported by Natural Science Foundation of Guangdong Province, China (#2014A030310239).

References

1. Wikipedia Homepage. https://en.wikipedia.org/wiki. Accessed 19 Jan 2017
2. Lou, F., Zhou, Y., Zhang, X., Zhang, X.: Review on the research progress of the structure and dynamics of temporal networks. J. Univ. Electron. Sci. Technol. China **46**(1), 109–125 (2017)
3. Holme, P., Saramäki, J.: Temporal networks. Phys. Rep. **519**(3), 97–125 (2013)
4. Perra, N., Gonçalves, B., Pastorsatorras, R., Vespignani, A.: Activity driven modeling of time varying networks. Sci. Rep. **2**(6), 469 (2012)
5. Han, Y., Lu W., Xu, S.: Characterizing the power of moving target defense via cyber epidemic dynamics. In: 2014 Symposium and Bootcamp on the Science of Security (HotSoS 2014) (2014)
6. Guo, D., Trajanovsk, S., Van, B.R., Wang, H., Van, M.P.: Epidemic threshold and topological structure of susceptible-infectious-susceptible epidemics in adaptive networks. Phys. Rev. E Stat. Nonlinear Soft Matter Phys. **88**(1), 042802 (2013)
7. Wang, X., Liu, S., Song, X.: A within-host virus model with multiple infected stages under time-varying environments. Appl. Math. Comput. **66**, 119–134 (2015)

8. Rocha, L.E., Liljeros, F., Holme, P.: Simulated epidemics in an empirical spatiotemporal network of 50,185 sexual contacts. PLOS Comput. Biol. **7**(3), e1001109 (2011)
9. Peng, C., Xu, M., Xu, S., Hu, T.: Modeling multivariate cybersecurity risks. J. Appl. Stat. (2018, accepted)
10. Sanatkar, M.R., White, W.N., Natarajan, B., Scoglio, C.M., Garrett, K.A.: Epidemic threshold of an SIS model in dynamic switching networks. IEEE Trans. Syst. Man Cybern. Syst. **46**(3), 345–355 (2016)
11. Wu, Q., Zhang, H., Small, M., Fu, X.: Threshold analysis of the susceptible-infected-susceptible model on overlay networks. Commun. Nonlinear Sci. Numer. Simul. **19**(7), 2435–2443 (2014)
12. Yang, L.X., Yang, X.: A new epidemic model of computer viruses. Commun. Nonlinear Sci. Numer. Simul. **19**(6), 1935–1944 (2014)
13. Yang, L.X., Yang, X., Wu, Y.: The impact of patch forwarding on the prevalence of computer virus: a theoretical assessment approach. Appl. Math. Model. **43**, 110–125 (2017)
14. Yang, L.X., Yang, X., Liu, J., Zhu, Q., Gan, C.: Epidemics of computer viruses: a complex-network approach. Appl. Math. Comput. **219**(16), 8705–8717 (2013)
15. Yang, L.X., Yang, X., Tang, Y.Y.: A bi-virus competing spreading model with generic infection rates. IEEE Netw. Sci. Eng. **5**(1), 2–13 (2018)
16. Yang, L.X., Yang, X., Zhu, Q., Wen, L.: A computer virus model with graded cure rates. Nonlinear Anal. Real World Appl. **14**(1), 414–422 (2013)
17. Chen, H., Cho, J., Xu, S.: Poster: quantifying the security effectiveness of network diversity. In: 2018 Symposium and Bootcamp on the Science of Security (HotSoS 2018) (2018)
18. Zhang, C., Huang, H.: Optimal control strategy for a novel computer virus propagation model on scale-free networks. Phys. A **451**, 251–265 (2016)

Advanced Persistent Distributed Denial of Service Attack Model on Scale-Free Networks

Chunming Zhang[✉], Junbiao Peng, and Jingwei Xiao

School of Information Engineering, Guangdong Medical University,
Dongguan 523808, China
chunfei2002@163.com

Abstract. Advanced persistent distributed denial of service attack (APDDoS), a common means for network attack, is a huge threat to network security. Based on the degree-based mean-field approach (*DBMF*), this paper first proposes a novel APDDoS attack model on scale-free networks to better understand the mechanism of it on scale-free networks. And then, this paper also discusses some mathematical properties of this model, including its threshold, equilibriums, their stabilities and systemic persistence. Finally, some effective suggestions are given to suppress or reduce the loss of APDDoS attack according to numerical simulation.

Keywords: Advanced persistent distributed denial of service attacks ·
Attacked threshold · Defensive strategies · Stability

1 Introduction

With the rapid development of modern technologies, the Internet has integrated into every corner of our life, which is a great help for us. However, as the saying goes: "every coin has two points". The Internet can also cause great damage to us through the cyber-attacks which include SQL injection attacks, hijacking attacks, DoS attacks and so on [1]. Because there are so many kinds of attacks on the Internet, it is more and more difficult for us to prevent them. What is worse, the damage caused by cyber-attacks is increasing at an accelerating rate.

DoS attack (denial of service attack) is a cyber-attack in which the perpetrator seeks to make a machine or network resource unavailable to its intended users by temporarily or indefinitely disrupting services of a host connected to the Internet. Denial of service is typically accomplished by flooding the targeted machine or resource with superfluous requests in an attempt to overload systems and prevent some or all legitimate requests from being fulfilled [2]. What is more, distributed denial-of-service attack (DDoS attack) is the incoming traffic flooding the victim originates from many different sources. This effectively makes it impossible to stop the attack simply by blocking a single source.

In addition, advanced persistent threat (APT) means that hackers have rich resources and use advanced attack methods to continuously attack the target. It is an

© Springer Nature Switzerland AG 2018
F. Liu et al. (Eds.): SciSec 2018, LNCS 11287, pp. 96–112, 2018.
https://doi.org/10.1007/978-3-030-03026-1_7

important threat to cyber security, also does great harm to us [3]. Combining DDoS and APT, hackers create a new attack way, APDDoS attack. With characteristics of clear aim, well resource and exceptional skills, APDDoS attack would put a bigger threat to cyber-security. For example, in 2017, Ukrainian postal system suffered an APDDoS attack lasting for two days, which caused countless losses [4]. Another famous APDDoS attack has been reported in [5] that five Russian banks suffered the most serious cyber-attack in January, 2016, which lasted for nearly 12 h.

The procedure of APDDoS attack is as follows (Fig. 1).

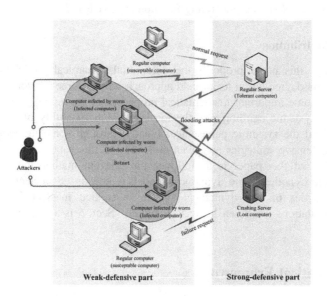

Fig. 1. Schematic diagram of APDDoS attack.

(1) Spreading worms. Worms usually hide in phishing websites (malicious websites) or phishing files (malicious information). Once visitors click the infected websites or files, the worm will be activated. Then the spreading process will trigger off, such as self-replicating, transplanting and making the host download malware autonomously. Besides, it allows victim to spread the worms by interacting or communicating. In this way, these infected computers are controlled by the attackers as special machines, and the infected network is so-called "botnets".

(2) Lunching flooding attack. When there are enough infected computers in the botnet, the hacker can manipulate them through remote control and send instructions to guide their behaviors. In the course of APDDOS attack, hackers often initiate flooding attacks so as to cause a particular server cannot response to normal access. Due to its low cost, it has been favored by hackers.

1.1 Related Work

It is known that the topology of network is vital to determine the effectiveness of cyber-attacks [6–12]. In reality, the actual network structure can be better described by the scale-free network than the fully-connected network or the random network [13]. The degree distribution $P(k)$ of nodes in a scale-free network obeys the power-law distribution, i.e. $P(k) \sim k^{-\tau}$, where k is the degree of the computer and $2 < \tau < 3$ [14–16].

In addition, there are a lot of methods to study the dynamics of propagation on networks, including individual-based mean-field theory (*IBMF*), degree-based mean-field approach (*DBMF*), and generating function approach [17–19].

1.2 Our Contribution

In this context, this paper proposes the differential dynamical model of APDDoS attacks based on degree-based mean-field approach on scale-free networks. This paper also discusses some important mathematical properties of the model, such as attacked threshold, the systemic equilibriums, the local and global stability of the attack-free equilibrium, and the systemic persistence. Finally, through some numerical simulations, some defensive strategies are given at the end of this paper.

The outline of this paper is as follows: the relevant mathematical framework, including basic hypothesis and dynamical model, is introduced in Sect. 2; the mathematical properties of this dynamical system is studied in Sect. 3; while some numerical simulations are given in Sect. 4. Finally, Sect. 5 is a summary of the full paper.

2 Mathematical Framework

According to their capabilities of defending cyber-attacks, computers on the networks can be divided into two parts: the weak-defensive part and the strong-defensive part (Fig. 1).

Computers in the weak-defensive part are vulnerable to malicious software attacks. Once a computer is infected by worms, it will soon download other malwares to assist attackers. Inspired by epidemic model, this part also can be divided into two groups: susceptible computer (Susceptible) which has not been infected yet and infected computer (Infected) that has been infected by malicious software. To simplify the notation, susceptible computer and infected computer can be denoted by S node and I node, respectively.

In another part of the network (strong-defensive part), the computer usually equips with firewall, which means the attack from general malicious software such as worms cannot affect it easily. So, flooding attack is the only way to attack it. This part can also be divided into two groups: tolerant computer (Tolerant) and lost computer (Lost). Tolerant computers stand for those normal computers, which are able to temporarily withstand the APDDoS attack. On the contrary, lost computers are the computers which are broken down after APDDoS attack and unable to response to requests. At the same way, tolerant computer and lost computer can be represented by T node and L node, respectively.

Based on the above assumptions, the following variables are given:

- Λ: The maximum degree of the node, i.e. $k \in [1, \Lambda]$.
- S_k: S nodes with degree k.
- I_k: I nodes with degree of k.
- T_k: T nodes with degree k.
- L_k: L nodes with degree k.
- $S_k(t)$: The probability of S_k at time t.
- $I_k(t)$: The probability of I_k at the time t.
- $T_k(t)$: The probability of T_k at time t.
- $L_k(t)$: The probability of L_k at time t.

There are several reasonable hypotheses about the system as follows:

(H1) System is closed, which means no computer can move in or out. Therefore, at any time t, the following relationship, $S_k(t) + I_k(t) + T_k(t) + L_k(t) \equiv 1$, applies to all k.

(H2) An S_k node is converted to an I_k node with the probability of β due to unsafe operations of an S_k node.

(H3) An I_k node recovers to an S_k node with the probability of γ due to the reinstallation of the system or the other operations that remove the malwares.

(H4) A T_k node turns into an L_k node with the probability of α due to APDDoS attacks overwhelm the T_k node's resistance.

(H5) An L_k node converts to a T_k node with the probability of η by restarting the server or replacing the system hardware.

(H6) The density of the weak-defensive part in whole is ϕ, the entire strong-defensive part is $1 - \phi$, at any time t, there are $I_k(t) + S_k(t) = \phi$, and $T_k(t) + L_k(t) = 1 - \phi$.

(H7) An S_k node fully connects to all I nodes from I_1 to I_Λ at time t with the average probability $\Theta(t)$. Let $<k>$ stand for the average node degree $\langle k \rangle = \sum_k kP(k)$.

The following relationship can be given:

$$\Theta(t) = \frac{1}{\langle k \rangle} \sum_k kP(k)I_k(t).$$

Based on the above hypotheses, the dynamical model of the system can be expressed as follows:

$$\begin{cases} \frac{dS_k(t)}{dt} = -\beta k S_k(t)\Theta(t) + \gamma I_k(t), \\ \frac{dI_k(t)}{dt} = \beta k S_k(t)\Theta(t) - \gamma I_k(t), \ k \in [1, \Lambda]. \\ \frac{dT_k(t)}{dt} = -\alpha k T_k(t)\Theta(t) + \eta L_k(t), \\ \frac{dL_k(t)}{dt} = \alpha k T_k(t)\Theta(t) - \eta L_k(t), \end{cases} \quad (1)$$

The initial conditions of the system are $0 \leq I_k(t)$, $S_k(t) \leq \phi$, $0 \leq L_k$ (t), $T_k(t) \leq 1 - \phi$, where $k \in [1, \Lambda]$.

Furthermore, the state transition diagram of system can be described as follows (Fig. 2):

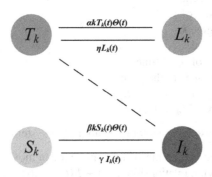

Fig. 2. State transition diagram of system (the dashed line on the graph means the attack from I node to T node).

3 Theoretical Analysis

This section deals with the mathematical properties of the system (1), such as attacked threshold, the equilibrium, the stability of the attack-free equilibrium, and the persistence of the system.

In (H6) we know that $S_k(t) = \phi - I_k(t)$, $T_k(t) = 1 - \phi - L_k(t)$, so system (1) can be simplified as the following 2Λ dimensional differential system:

$$\begin{cases} \frac{dI_k(t)}{dt} = \beta k(\phi - I_k(t))\Theta(t) - \gamma I_k(t), \\ \frac{dL_k(t)}{dt} = \alpha k(1 - \phi - L_k(t))\Theta(t) - \eta L_k(t), \end{cases} \quad k \in [1, \Lambda] \quad (2)$$

At the same time, the initial conditions of the system are $0 \leq I_k(t) \leq \phi$, $0 \leq L_k(t) \leq 1 - \phi$, where $k \in [1, \Lambda]$.

In the following, system (2), which is equivalent to system (1), will be deeply researched.

3.1 Attacked Threshold

As an important indicator to judge whether the system will suffer APDDoS attack, threshold plays an important role in predicting system behaviors.

First, the definition of E_Λ and $O_{i \times j}$ is given here, respectively. E_Λ is a $\Lambda \times \Lambda$ identity matrix, and $O_{i \times j}$ is an $i \times j$ zero matrix.

Referring to the method of calculating attacked threshold discussed in [18].

Let

$$R_0 = \rho\left(FV^{-1}\right).$$

Here $\rho(\mathbf{A})$ represents the eigenvalue of the matrix $\mathbf{A}$ [18].

According to the above method, in system (2), let $x = (I_1(t), I_2(t), \ldots, I_\Lambda(t),$ $L_1(t), L_2(t), \ldots, L_\Lambda(t))$, therefore,

$$
f = \begin{pmatrix} f_1 \\ f_2 \\ \vdots \\ f_\Lambda \\ f_{1+\Lambda} \\ f_{2+\Lambda} \\ \vdots \\ f_{2\Lambda} \end{pmatrix} = \begin{pmatrix} \beta(\phi - I_1(t))\Theta(t) \\ 2\beta(\phi - I_2(t))\Theta(t) \\ \vdots \\ \Lambda\beta(\phi - I_\Lambda(t))\Theta(t) \\ \alpha(1 - \phi - L_2(t))\Theta(t) \\ 2\alpha(1 - \phi - L_2(t))\Theta(t) \\ \vdots \\ \Lambda\alpha(1 - \phi - L_\Lambda(t))\Theta(t) \end{pmatrix}, \quad V = \begin{pmatrix} V_1 \\ V_2 \\ \vdots \\ V_\Lambda \\ V_{1+\Lambda} \\ V_{2+\Lambda} \\ \vdots \\ V_{2\Lambda} \end{pmatrix} = \begin{pmatrix} \gamma I_1(t) \\ \gamma I_2(t) \\ \vdots \\ \gamma I_\Lambda(t) \\ \eta L_1(t) \\ \eta L_2(t) \\ \vdots \\ \eta L_\Lambda(t) \end{pmatrix}.
$$

Let $F = \begin{pmatrix} M_1 & M_2 \\ M_3 & M_4 \end{pmatrix}$ where M_1, M_2, M_3, and M_4 are all $\Lambda \times \Lambda$ matrix. So we have the following relationships

$$
M_1 = \begin{bmatrix} \frac{\partial f_1(x_0)}{\partial I_1(t)} & \frac{\partial f_1(x_0)}{\partial I_2(t)} & \cdots & \frac{\partial f_1(x_0)}{\partial I_\Lambda(t)} \\ \frac{\partial f_2(x_0)}{\partial I_1(t)} & \frac{\partial f_2(x_0)}{\partial I_2(t)} & \cdots & \frac{\partial f_2(x_0)}{\partial I_\Lambda(t)} \\ \vdots & \vdots & \ddots & \vdots \\ \frac{\partial f_\Lambda(x_0)}{\partial I_1(t)} & \frac{\partial f_\Lambda(x_0)}{\partial I_2(t)} & \cdots & \frac{\partial f_\Lambda(x_0)}{\partial I_\Lambda(t)} \end{bmatrix}, \quad M_2 = \begin{bmatrix} \frac{\partial f_1(x_0)}{\partial L_1(t)} & \frac{\partial f_1(x_0)}{\partial L_2(t)} & \cdots & \frac{\partial f_1(x_0)}{\partial L_\Lambda(t)} \\ \frac{\partial f_2(x_0)}{\partial L_1(t)} & \frac{\partial f_2(x_0)}{\partial L_2(t)} & \cdots & \frac{\partial f_2(x_0)}{\partial L_\Lambda(t)} \\ \vdots & \vdots & \ddots & \vdots \\ \frac{\partial f_\Lambda(x_0)}{\partial L_1(t)} & \frac{\partial f_\Lambda(x_0)}{\partial L_2(t)} & \cdots & \frac{\partial f_\Lambda(x_0)}{\partial L_\Lambda(t)} \end{bmatrix},
$$

$$
M_3 = \begin{bmatrix} \frac{\partial f_{1+\Lambda}(x_0)}{\partial I_1(t)} & \frac{\partial f_{1+\Lambda}(x_0)}{\partial I_2(t)} & \cdots & \frac{\partial f_{1+\Lambda}(x_0)}{\partial I_\Lambda(t)} \\ \frac{\partial f_{2+\Lambda}(x_0)}{\partial I_1(t)} & \frac{\partial f_{2+\Lambda}(x_0)}{\partial I_2(t)} & \cdots & \frac{\partial f_{2+\Lambda}(x_0)}{\partial I_\Lambda(t)} \\ \vdots & \vdots & \ddots & \vdots \\ \frac{\partial f_{2\Lambda}(x_0)}{\partial I_1(t)} & \frac{\partial f_{2\Lambda}(x_0)}{\partial I_2(t)} & \cdots & \frac{\partial f_{2\Lambda}(x_0)}{\partial I_\Lambda(t)} \end{bmatrix}, \quad M_4 = \begin{bmatrix} \frac{\partial f_{1+\Lambda}(x_0)}{\partial L_1(t)} & \frac{\partial f_{1+\Lambda}(x_0)}{\partial L_2(t)} & \cdots & \frac{\partial f_{1+\Lambda}(x_0)}{\partial L_\Lambda(t)} \\ \frac{\partial f_{2+\Lambda}(x_0)}{\partial L_1(t)} & \frac{\partial f_{2+\Lambda}(x_0)}{\partial L_2(t)} & \cdots & \frac{\partial f_{2+\Lambda}(x_0)}{\partial L_\Lambda(t)} \\ \vdots & \vdots & \ddots & \vdots \\ \frac{\partial f_{2\Lambda}(x_0)}{\partial L_1(t)} & \frac{\partial f_{2\Lambda}(x_0)}{\partial L_2(t)} & \cdots & \frac{\partial f_{2\Lambda}(x_0)}{\partial L_\Lambda(t)} \end{bmatrix}.
$$

There are also the following relationships:

$$\frac{\partial \Theta(t)}{\partial I_t} = \frac{tP_t}{\langle k \rangle}, \quad \frac{\partial I_i(t)}{\partial I_j(t)} = 0, (i \neq j). \tag{3}$$

As

$$\frac{\partial f_j(x_0)}{\partial I_t} = \frac{\partial \frac{\beta(\phi - l_j)}{\langle k \rangle} j \sum_k k P_k I_k}{\partial I_t} = \frac{j\beta}{\langle k \rangle}\left(\phi t P_t - t P I_j\right)\Big|_{x=x_0} = \frac{j\beta\phi}{\langle k \rangle} t P_t,$$

then

$$M_1 = \frac{\beta\phi}{\langle k \rangle} \begin{bmatrix} P_1 & 2P_2 & \cdots & \Lambda P_\Lambda \\ 2P_1 & 4P_2 & \cdots & 2\Lambda P_\Lambda \\ \vdots & \vdots & \ddots & \vdots \\ \Lambda P_1 & 2\Lambda P_2 & \cdots & \Lambda^2 P_\Lambda \end{bmatrix}.$$

Also

$$\frac{\partial f_{j+\Lambda}(x_0)}{\partial I_t} = \frac{\partial \alpha(1-\phi-L_j)j\sum_k kP_k I_k}{\partial I_t} = j\alpha\left(\frac{(1-\phi)}{\langle k \rangle}tP_t - L_j\frac{\partial\Theta(t)}{\partial I_t}\right)\Big|_{x=x_0}$$

$$= j\alpha\frac{(1-\phi)}{\langle k \rangle}tP_t.$$

so that

$$M_3 = \frac{\alpha(1-\phi)}{\langle k \rangle} \begin{bmatrix} P_1 & 2P_2 & \cdots & \Lambda P_\Lambda \\ 2P_1 & 4P_2 & \cdots & 2\Lambda P_\Lambda \\ \vdots & \vdots & \ddots & \vdots \\ \Lambda P_1 & 2\Lambda P_2 & \cdots & \Lambda^2 P_\Lambda \end{bmatrix}.$$

And as

$$\Theta(t)|_{x=x_0} = 0,$$

$$\frac{\partial f_{j+\Lambda}(x_0)}{\partial L_t} = \frac{\partial \alpha j(1-\phi-L_j)\Theta(t)}{\partial L_t}\Big|_{x=x_0} = 0,$$

hence there is $M_4 = O_{\Lambda\times\Lambda}$. Finally, **F** and **V** can be transformed into following expressions:

$$F = \begin{pmatrix} \frac{\beta\phi\langle k^2 \rangle}{\langle k \rangle}\cdot E_\Lambda & O_{\Lambda\times\Lambda} \\ \frac{\alpha(1-\phi)\langle k^2 \rangle}{\langle k \rangle}\cdot E_\Lambda & O_{\Lambda\times\Lambda} \end{pmatrix}, V = \begin{pmatrix} \gamma\cdot E_\Lambda & O_{\Lambda\times\Lambda} \\ O_{\Lambda\times\Lambda} & \eta\cdot E_\Lambda \end{pmatrix}.$$

From the above deduction,

$$R_0 = \rho\left(FV^{-1}\right) = \rho\left(\frac{M_1}{\gamma}\right) = \frac{\beta\phi\langle k^2 \rangle}{\gamma\langle k \rangle}.$$

Here R_0 is the attacked threshold of system (2).

The above results are consistent with the Hurwitz criterion [18]. All the roots of the characteristic equations have real parts, and system (2) exists E_0 as its equilibrium.

Example 1: In system (2), fixing $\beta = 0.01$, $\phi = 0.5$, and $\gamma = 0.6$, while varying the values of τ and Λ, the heat map is used to observe the change of R_0 which is negatively correlated with τ and Λ (see Fig. 3a). Similarly, fixing $\Lambda = 200$, $\tau = 2$, $\gamma = 0.85$, changing the value of β and ϕ, the following drawing show the change of R_0, which is positively associated with β and ϕ (see Fig. 3b).

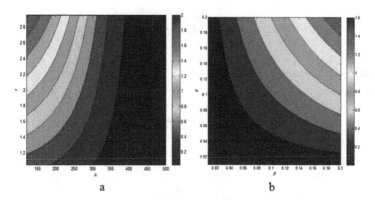

a   b

Fig. 3. Heat map of the change of R_0 in different situations.

3.2   Equilibrium

Theorem 1. If $R_0 < 1$, $E_0 = (0, \cdots, 0)_{2\Lambda}$ is a unique attack-free equilibrium of system (2), and there is $I_k(t) = L_k(t) = 0$ for all k.

Proof. Let

$$\frac{dI_k(t)}{dt} = \frac{dL_k(t)}{dt} = 0,$$
$$\Theta(t) = 0 \text{ for } I_k(t) = L_k(t) = 0.$$

Hence, it's not hard to find that this vector E_0 is a unique attack-free equilibrium of system (2).

Theorem 2. System (2) has a unique attacked equilibrium E^* if $R_0 > 1$.

Proof. Let

$$\frac{dI_k(t)}{dt} = \frac{dL_k(t)}{dt} = 0,$$

there exists

$$I_k^*(t) = \frac{\beta \phi k \Theta^*(t)}{\beta \phi k \Theta^*(t) + \gamma}, \quad L_k^*(t) = \frac{\alpha(1 - \phi)k\Theta^*(t)}{\alpha k \Theta^*(t) + \eta},$$

where

$$\Theta^*(t) = \frac{1}{\langle k \rangle} \sum_k k P_k I_k^*(t).$$

Substituting $I_k^*(t)$ into the above equation of $\Theta^*(t)$, and then

$$\Theta^*(t) = \frac{1}{\langle k \rangle} \sum_k \left(k P_k \frac{\beta \phi k \Theta^*(t)}{\beta \phi k \Theta^*(t) + \gamma} \right).$$

Construct the function $f(x)$ as follows:

$$f(x) = 1 - \frac{\beta \phi}{\langle k \rangle} \sum_k \frac{k^2 P_k}{\beta k x + \gamma}.$$

It is easy to get that $f'(x) > 0$, and

$$f(0) = 1 - \frac{\beta \phi}{\langle k \rangle} \sum_k \frac{k^2 P_k}{\gamma} = 1 - R_0.$$

When $R_0 < 1$, $f(x) > f(0) > 0$, and further, $\Theta^*(t) = 0$ which indicates $I_k = L_k = 0$. The conclusion follows Theorem 1. When $R_0 > 1$, $f(0) < 0$, and thus,

$$f(\xi) = 1 - \frac{\beta \phi}{\langle k \rangle} \sum_k \frac{k^2 P_k}{\beta k \xi + \gamma} > 1 - \frac{\beta \phi}{\langle k \rangle} \sum_k \frac{k^2 P_k}{\beta k \xi} = 0.$$

So, there is a unique root between 0 and ξ. When $\Theta(t) = \Theta*(t)$, equilibrium $E^* = (I_1^*(t), \ldots, I_A^*(t), L_1^*(t), \ldots, L_A^*(t))$.

3.3   The Global Stability of Attack-Free Equilibrium E_0

This section will discuss the global stability of attack-free equilibrium E_0.

At first, a simply connected compact set of system (2) can be described as

$$\Omega = \{x = (I_1, I_2, \ldots, I_A, L_1, L_2, \ldots, L_A) | 0 \leq I_i \leq \phi, 0 \leq L_i \leq 1 - \phi, \ i \in [1, A]\}.$$

Lemma 3 [19]. For any compact set C is invariant for $\frac{dx}{dt} = f(x)$ which is defined in the system. If each point y in ∂C (the boundary of C), the vector f (y) is tangent or pointing into the set.

Lemma 4. In system (2), compact set Ω is positive and invariant. Because $x(0) \in \Omega$, so $x(t) \in \Omega$ for all $t > 0$.

Proof. Let us define 4 sets containing Λ element in $\partial\Omega$, that is,

$$S_i = \{x \in \Omega | x_i = 0, \, i = 1, \ldots, \Lambda\}, \quad T_i = \{x \in \Omega | x_i = 0, \, i = \Lambda + 1, \ldots, 2\Lambda\},$$
$$U_i = \{x \in \Omega | x_i = \phi, \, i = 1, \ldots, \Lambda\} \quad R_i = \{x \in \Omega | x_i = 1 - \phi, \, i = \Lambda + 1, \ldots, 2\Lambda\}.$$

And

$$\xi_i = \left(0, \, \ldots, \, 0, \, \overset{i}{-1}, \, 0, \, \ldots, \, 0\right), \, \eta_i = \left(0, \, \ldots, \, 0, \, \overset{i+\Lambda}{-1}, \, 0, \, \ldots, \, 0\right)$$
$$\zeta_i = \left(0, \, \ldots, \, 0, \, \overset{i}{1}, \, 0, \, \ldots, \, 0\right), \, v_i = \left(0, \, \ldots, \, 0, \, \overset{i+\Lambda}{1}, \, 0, \, \ldots, \, 0\right),$$

as their respectively outer vector. So when $1 \leq i \leq \Lambda$, there are

$$\left(\frac{dx}{dt}\bigg| x \in Si, \, \xi i\right) = -i\beta\phi \frac{1}{\langle k \rangle} \sum_{k \neq i} kP_k x_k \leq 0, \, \left(\frac{dx}{dt}\bigg| x \in Ti, \, \eta i\right) = -i\frac{\alpha(1 - \phi)}{\langle k \rangle} \sum_{k \neq i} kP_k x_k \leq 0,$$
$$\left(\frac{dx}{dt}\bigg| x \in Ui, \, \zeta i\right) = -\gamma\phi \leq 0, \, \left(\frac{dx}{dt}\bigg| x \in Ri, \, vi\right) = -\eta(1 - \phi) \leq 0,$$

which is accordingly with the result of Lemma 3.

Lemma 5 [20]. System (2) can be rewritten in a compact vector form as

$$\frac{dx(t)}{dt} = \mathbf{A}x(t) + \mathbf{H}(x(t)), \, x \in D,$$

where $\mathbf{A}$ is an $2\Lambda \times 2\Lambda$ matrix and $\mathbf{H}(x(t))$ is continuously differentiable in a region $\mathbf{D}$ which includes the origin. Then

$$\mathbf{A} = \begin{pmatrix} M1 & O_{\Lambda \times \Lambda} \\ M_3 & \eta \cdot E_\Lambda \end{pmatrix}.$$

Besides, $\mathbf{H}(x(t)) = \Theta(t)(g_1, \, \ldots, \, g_\Lambda, \, g_1{}^*, \ldots, \, g_\Lambda{}^*)$, where $g_j = -j\beta I_j(t), \, g_j{}^* = -j\alpha L_j(t)$. Also as $\mathbf{H}(x) \in C^1(D)$, $\lim_{x \to 0} ||\mathbf{H}(x)|| / ||x|| = 0$. Assuming that system (2) exists a compact set $C \subset D$ is positive invariant containing the origin, a positive number r, and a positive eigenvalue of $\mathbf{A}^T$. Therefore, the following relationship can be given:

(C1) $(x, \, \omega) \geq r||x||$ if $x \in C$.
(C2) For all $x \in C$, $(\mathbf{H}(x), \, \omega) \leq 0$.
(C3) The origin that $x = 0$ is the largest positively invariant set contained in $N = \{x \in C \, |(\mathbf{H}(x)\cdot\omega) = 0\}$.

Defining the eigenvector $\omega = (\omega_1, \omega_2, \ldots, \omega_{2\Lambda})$ of $\mathbf{A}^{\mathrm{T}}$ and its corresponding eigenvalue is $s(\mathbf{A}^{\mathrm{T}})$, then the following assumptions can be drawn:

(1) The origin that $x = 0$ is global asymptotical stable when $s(\mathbf{A}^{\mathrm{T}}) < 0$.
(2) If $s(\mathbf{A}^{\mathrm{T}}) > 0$, there is a $m > 0$, such as $x(0) \in C-\{0\}$, will satisfy $\liminf_{t\to\infty}\|x(t)\| \geq m$.

The proof for E_0 as a global asymptotic stability is as follows.

Theorem 6. In system (2), if $R_0 < 1$, E_0 is global asymptotic stable in Ω.

Proof. Let $C = \Omega$, and focus on the real part of $\frac{\mathrm{d}x(t)}{\mathrm{d}t} = \mathbf{A}x(t) + \mathbf{H}(x(t))$.

Because $\mathbf{A}^{\mathrm{T}}$ is irreducible and a_{ij} in $\mathbf{A}$ is nonnegative whenever $i \neq j$, then let $\omega = (\omega_1, \ldots, \omega_{2\Lambda}) > 0$ and $\omega_0 = \min_{1 \leq i \leq 2\Lambda}\omega_i$. For all $x = \Omega$,

$$(x, \omega) \geq \omega_0 \left(\sum_{i=0}^{2\Lambda} x_i^2 \right)^{\frac{1}{2}} = \omega_0\|x\|, \quad (\mathbf{H}(x), \omega) = -\Theta(x)\sum_{i=1}^{\Lambda} i\omega_i(x_i + x_{i+\Lambda}) \leq 0.$$

Additionally, $(\mathbf{H}(x), \omega) = 0$ means $x = 0$. Finally, this condition coincided with the first assumption in Lemma 5.

Example 2. In system (2), fixing $\beta = 0.04$, $\phi = 0.5$, $\gamma = 0.72$, $\alpha = 0.02$, $\eta = 0.36$, $\Lambda = 200$ and $\tau = 2$, then $R_0 = 0.9451 < 1$, which means there is no attacked equilibrium (see Fig. 4).

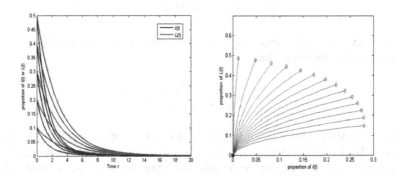

Fig. 4. If $R_0 < 1$, system (2) doesn't have attacked equilibrium.

3.4   Persistence of System

When the first assumption in Lemma 5 and Theorem 6 is satisfied, so that $\exists k_0, 1 \leq k_0 \leq \Lambda$.

$$\lim_{t\to\infty} \inf\{I_{k_0}(t), L_{k_0}(t)\} > 0,$$

also

$$\lim_{t\to\infty} \inf \Theta(t) = \lim_{t\to\infty} \inf \frac{1}{\langle k \rangle} \sum_k kP_k I_k(t) \geq \frac{1}{\langle k \rangle} k_0 P_{k_0} I_{k_0}(t) > 0.$$

Further, as

$$\frac{\mathrm{d}(I_k(t))}{\mathrm{d}t} = \beta(\phi - I_k(t))k\Theta(t) - \gamma I_k(t) = \beta\phi k\Theta(t) - (\beta k\Theta(t) + \gamma)I_k(t)$$
$$\geq \beta\phi k\Theta(t) - (\beta k\Theta(t) + \gamma)\lim_{t\to\infty} \inf\{I_k(t)\},$$

so that

$$\lim_{t\to\infty} \inf\{I_k(t)\} \geq \frac{\beta\phi k\Theta(t)}{\beta k\Theta(t) + \gamma} > 0.$$

Also there is

$$\frac{\mathrm{d}(L_k(t))}{\mathrm{d}t} = \alpha(1 - \phi - L_k(t))k\Theta(t) - \eta L_k(t) = \alpha(1 - \phi)k\Theta(t) - (\alpha k\Theta(t) + \eta)L_k(t)$$
$$\geq \alpha(1 - \phi)k\Theta(t) - (\alpha k\Theta(t) + \eta)\lim_{t\to\infty} \inf\{L_k(t)\},$$

which manifests

$$\lim_{t\to\infty} \inf\{L_k(t)\} \geq \frac{\alpha(1 - \phi)k\Theta(t)}{\alpha k\Theta(t) + \eta} > 0.$$

The proof is completed.

Example 3. In system (2), fixing $\beta = 0.34$, $\phi = 0.5$, $\gamma = 0.23$, $\alpha = 0.76$, $\eta = 0.24$, $\Lambda = 200$ and $\tau = 2$, then $R_0 = 25.1489 > 1$, which indicates system is persistent (see Fig. 5).

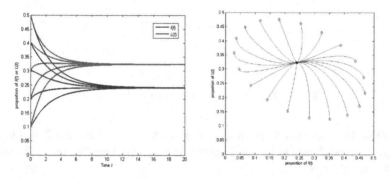

Fig. 5. System is persistent when $R_0 > 1$.

4 Numerical Simulations

This section mainly concentrates on the change of system (4) under different parameters.

$$
\begin{cases}
\dfrac{dI_k(t)}{dt} = \beta k(\phi - I_k(t))\Theta(t) - \gamma I_k(t), \\[2mm]
\dfrac{dL_k(t)}{dt} = \alpha k(1 - \phi - L_k(t))\Theta(t) - \eta L_k(t).
\end{cases}
\tag{4}
$$

In order to detailed discuss, the tokens $I(t)$ and $L(t)$ are defined here,

$$
I(t) = \sum_k I_k(t)P(k),
$$

$$
L(t) = \sum_k L_k(t)P(k).
$$

In system (4), $I_k(t)$ can be affected by the parameters β, ϕ, γ, Λ and τ, yet any parameter can influence $L_k(t)$.

Example 4. In system (4), fixing $\phi = 0.72$, $\gamma = 0.3$, $\Lambda = 200$ and $\tau = 2$, and varying β, the graph of the change of $I(t)$ can be given (see Fig. 6a). Also, the ratio of $I(t)$ and β are positive.

Example 5. In system (4), fixing $\phi = 0.38$, $\gamma = 0.26$, $\alpha = 0.35$, $\eta = 0.18$, $\Lambda = 200$ and $\tau = 2$, and varying β, the graph of the change of $L(t)$ can be given (see Fig. 6b). The ratio of $L(t)$ and β is positive.

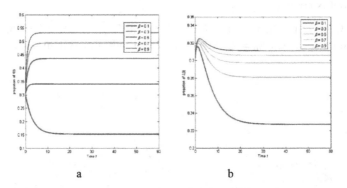

a   b

Fig. 6. The change of $I(t)$ and $L(t)$ in different β.

Example 6. In system (4), fixing $\beta = 0.68$, $\phi = 0.6$, $\Lambda = 200$ and $\tau = 2$, and varying γ, the graph of the change of $I(t)$ can be given (see Fig. 7a). From the graph, the ratio of $I(t)$ and γ are negative.

Example 7. In system (4), fixing $\beta = 0.75$, $\phi = 0.2$, $\alpha = 0.6$, $\eta = 0.13$, $\Lambda = 200$ and $\tau = 2$, and varying γ, the graph of the change of $L(t)$ can be obtained (see Fig. 7b). The ratio of $L(t)$ and β are negative, too.

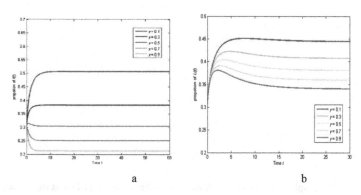

a   b

Fig. 7. The graphs that $I(t)$ and $L(t)$ respectively changes with different γ.

Example 8. In system (4), fixing $\beta = 0.76$, $\gamma = 0.42$, $\Lambda = 200$ and $\tau = 2$, and varying ϕ, the graph of the change of $I(t)$ can be given (see Fig. 8a). The ratio of $I(t)$ and γ are positive.

Example 9. In system (4), fixing $\beta = 0.53$, $\gamma = 0.17$, $\alpha = 0.38$, $\eta = 0.02$, $\Lambda = 200$ and $\tau = 2$, and varying ϕ, the graph of the change of $L(t)$ can be obtained (see Fig. 9b). From the graph, when enlarging ϕ, $L(t)$ will increase at first, and then descend.

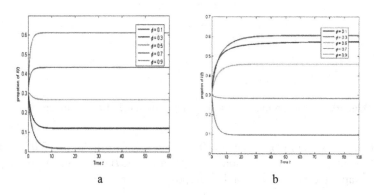

a   b

Fig. 8. The graphs that $I(t)$ and $L(t)$ respectively changes with different ϕ.

Example 10. In system (4), fixing $\beta = 0.46$, $\phi = 0.5$, $\gamma = 0.18$, and $\tau = 2$, and varying Λ, the graph of the change of $I(t)$ can be given (see Fig. 9a). From the graph, the ratio of $I(t)$ and Λ are positive.

Example 11. In system (4), fixing $\beta = 0.67$, $\phi = 0.4$, $\alpha = 0.41$, $\eta = 0.24$, $\gamma = 0.22$, and $\tau = 2$, and varying Λ, the graph of the change of $L(t)$ can be obtained (see Fig. 9b). The ratio of $L(t)$ and Λ are positive as well.

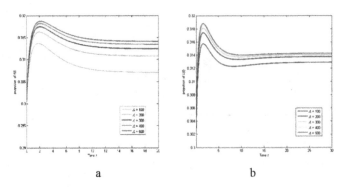

a   b

Fig. 9. The graphs that show the changes of value of $I(t)$ and $L(t)$ at different Λ.

Example 12. In system (4), fixing $\beta = 0.2$, $\phi = 0.6$, $\gamma = 0.33$, $\alpha = 0.63$, $\Lambda = 200$, and $\tau = 2$, while varying η, the graph of the change of $L(t)$ can be given (see Fig. 10). From the graph, the ratio of $L(t)$ and η are negative.

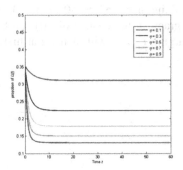

Fig. 10. The graph that shows the changes of value of $L(t)$ at different η.

Example 13. In system (4), fixing $\beta = 0.72$, $\phi = 0.42$, $\gamma = 0.48$, $\eta = 0.05$, $\Lambda = 200$, and $\tau = 2$, while varying α, the graph of the change of $L(t)$ can be given (see Fig. 11). From the graph, the ratio of $L(t)$ and α are positive.

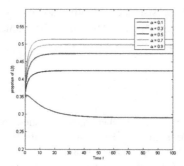

Fig. 11. The graph that shows the changes of value of $L(t)$ at different α.

Based on the above simulation results, this paper presents some of the following effective recommendations:

(1) Recognizing and detecting the computer malware, such as regularly executing anti-viruses or reinstalling computers, the value of γ will rise, and the density of I node and L node can be controlled.
(2) Enhancing the filtering capability of firewall of the tough-resist part, and then α will reduce, which is possible to inhibit the proportion of L node from incensement.
(3) Through rebooting the tough-resist part computer or replacing their hardware or other similar measures, the density of L node will reduce as the increase of η.
(4) Artificially controlling the scale of the network, that also means changing the parameter Λ, are almost infeasible. However, if the network limits Λ by controlling the number of connected node in the network, the probability of L node and the number of L node will descend.
(5) Changing Λ by adjusting the network structure is hard to achieve. But such as controlling of the gap between the biggest and the smallest degree in the network and other measures provide a special way to change Λ, then it will shrink the proportion of I node and L node.
(6) Also, according to some particular measures, adjusting the ratio of the tough-resist part and the feeble-resist part of the network by controlling the connections of the tough-resist part's computer in the network or similar actions will change the parameter ϕ. Sifting out some nodes in the feeble-resist part, which means increasing ϕ, can decrease the density of I node. But, L node's density can reach its goal only if taking the appropriate value of ϕ.

5   Conclusion

To better understand the mechanism of APDDoS attack, this paper proposes an APDDoS attack model based on degree-based mean-field on a scale-free network. This paper discusses some mathematical properties of the model, such as its thresholds, equilibrium stability, and persistence. Finally, some proposals for reducing or exhibiting APDDoS attack are given after doing the numerical simulations of the model.

References

1. http://www.hackmageddon.com/2016-cyber-attacks-statistics/. Accessed 19 Jan 2018
2. Official website of the Department of Homeland Security Homepage.https://www.us-cert.gov/ncas/tips/ST04-015. Accessed 28 June 2018
3. https://www.academia.edu/6309905/Advanced_Persistent_Threat_-_APT. Accessed July 2018
4. http://www.bbc.com/news/technology-40886418. Accessed 19 Mar 2018
5. http://www.bbc.com/news/technology-37941216. Accessed 13 June 2018
6. Xu, S., Li, W.L.H.: A stochastic model of active cyber defense dynamics. Internet Math. **11**(1), 23–61 (2015)
7. Xu, M., Schweitzer, K., Bateman, R., Xu, S.: Modeling and predicting cyber hacking breaches. IEEE Trans. Inf. Forensics Secur. **13**(11), 2856–2871 (2018)
8. Yang, L.X., Draief, M., Yang, X.: The optimal dynamic immunization under a controlled heterogeneous node-based SIRS model. Phys. A **450**, 403–415 (2016)
9. Gan, C., Yang, X., Liu, W., Zhu, Q., Jin, J., He, L.: Propagation of computer virus both across the internet and external computers: a complex-network approach. Commun. Nonlinear Sci. Numer. Simul. **19**(8), 2785–2792 (2014)
10. Du, P., Sun, Z., Chen, H., Cho, J., Xu, S.: Statistical estimation of malware detection metrics in the absence of ground truth. IEEE Trans. Inf. Forensics Secur. **13**(12), 2965–2980 (2018)
11. Zhang, C., Huang, H.: Optimal control strategy for a novel computer virus propagation model on scale-free networks. Phys. A **451**, 251–265 (2016)
12. Yang, L.X., Yang, X., Wu, Y.: The impact of patch forwarding on the prevalence of computer virus: a theoretical assessment approach. Appl. Math. Model. **43**, 110–125 (2017)
13. Barabási, A., Albert, R.: Emergence of scaling in random networks. Science **286**(5439), 509 (1999)
14. Albert, R., Barabási, A.: Statistical mechanics of complex networks. Rev. Mod. Phys. **74**(1) (2001)
15. Chen, H., Cho, J., Xu, S.: Quantifying the security effectiveness of firewalls and DMZs. In: 2018 Symposium and Bootcamp on the Science of Security (HotSoS 2018) (2018)
16. Yang, L.X., Yang, X., Liu, J., Zhu, Q., Gan, C.: Epidemics of computer viruses: a complex-network approach. Appl. Math. Comput. **219**(16), 8705–8717 (2013)
17. Pastor-Satorras, R., Castellano, C., Mieghem, P.V., Vespignani, A.: Epidemic processes in complex networks. Rev. Mod. Phys. **87**(3), 925 (2015)
18. Fu, X., Small, M., Chen, G.: Propagation Dynamics on Complex Networks: Models, Methods and Stability Analysis, 1st edn. Higer Education Press, China (2013)
19. Yorke, J.A.: Invariance for ordinary differential equations. Math. Syst. Theory **1**(4), 353–372 (1967)
20. Lajmanovich, A., Yorke, J.A.: A deterministic model for gonorrhea in a nonhomogeneous population. Math. Biosci. **28**(3), 221–236 (1976)

Attacks and Defenses

Security and Protection in Optical Networks

Qingshan Kong[(⊠)] and Bo Liu

Institute of Information Engineering, Chinese Academy of Science (CAS),
Beijing, China
kongqingshan@iie.ac.cn

Abstract. We address emerging threats to the security of optical networks, mainly loss of the confidentiality of user data transmitted through optical fibers and disturbances of network control, both of which could seriously damage the entire network. Distributed acoustic sensors can be used to detect these threats to the fiber-optic infrastructure before they cause damage to the infrastructure and proactively re-route the traffic towards links were no threat is detected. In this talk we will review our recent progress on distributed acoustic sensing and will provide some key considerations for the deployment of these systems in connection with their use in the protection of optical networks.

Keywords: Optical network · Security · Fiber optics sensors
Phase-sensitive optical time-domain reflectometry · Scattering Rayleigh

1 Introduction

Transport layer security (or secure sockets layer) can tunnel an entire network's traffic, working at the boundary between layers 4 (transport layer) and 5 (session layer). Layer 2, the virtual private network, uses a combination of Ethernet and generalized multi-protocol label switching (GMPLS).

In contrast to security technologies for layer 2 and the aforementioned layers, security protection in layer 1 has not been attracting much attention. The importance of layer 1 security should be stressed because once a security breakdown occurs, a quick stopgap measure will not be easily implemented, but it takes a painfully long time to remedy a physically damaged photonic layer. There have been studies on photonic network security. Medard et al. raised early on that security issues of the physical layer, suggesting possible attacks such as crosstalk attacks at optical nodes and fiber tapping [1]. This was followed by studies on monitoring and localization techniques of crosstalk attacks [2, 3], quality of service (QoS) degrading/disruptive attacks, such as optical amplifier gain competition attacks [4], and low-power QoS attacks [5]. Attack-aware routing and wavelength assignment of optical path networks have recently gained attention [6–8].

One may simply assume that network facilities and outside plants can be physically isolated from adversaries. However, optical fiber cables are exposed to physical attacks in customer premises owing to the wide use of fiber-to-the-home systems, and tapping of the optical signal from a fiber could be easily done by using inexpensive equipment [9]. Recently, risk of information leakage occurring in a fiber cable has been pointed

F. Liu et al. (Eds.): SciSec 2018, LNCS 11287, pp. 115–125, 2018.
https://doi.org/10.1007/978-3-030-03026-1_8

out [10]. A small fraction of optical signals, even in a coated fiber, often leaks into adjacent fibers in a cable at the bending points. The amount of light leakage is small but detectable with a photon counting detector.

New threats are also emerging as the photonic network becomes multidomain, being opened to the upper layers, other operators, and end users. Figure 1 depicts the typical architecture of a photonic network, including the IP over wavelength division multiplexing (WDM) network, consisting of the optical path network, IP network, and the control plane. The IP and optical path networks are tightly integrated with the WDM interfaces of the optical cross connects (OXCs), which are directly connected to IP routers to set up a desired optical path by wavelength switching. Routing, signaling, and link management are supported by GMPLS in the control plane. Today, confidential control signals are carried through out-of-band channels in optical fibers, or sometimes over a dedicated control network. Hackers may have the opportunity to easily access them and maliciously control the network with the control information, which could seriously damage the entire photonic network.

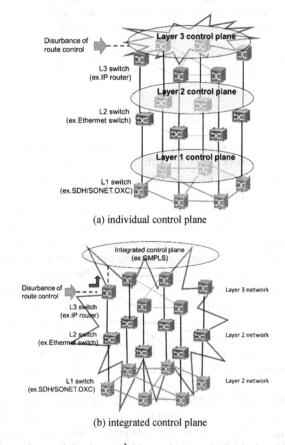

(a) individual control plane

(b) integrated control plane

Fig. 1. Comparison of potentially threatened layers between individual and integrated types of network control technologies

This paper is organized as follows. Potential threats to security in IP over optical path networks are discussed in Sect. 2, followed by a discussion on the principle of distributed optical sensing in Sect. 3. In Sect. 4, application of distributed acoustic sensor is presented, followed by concluding remarks in Sect. 5.

2   Threats to Security in Photonic Networks

Threats to security in photonic networks will be of a huge variety and extension in the near future. Cyber attacks are not be within the scope of this paper. Our concern is new threats, those that have recently occurred or will likely take place in the near future. From a management perspective, security failures and attacks on AONs can be broadly classified into two main types: direct and indirect. The former are more related to physical network components and can be directly implemented on different AON components such as taps and optical fibers. In contrast, the latter are unlikely to be performed directly. In this case, an attacker attempts to use indirect means, taking advantage of possible vulnerabilities of AON components and other transmission effects (e.g., crosstalk effects) to gain access to the network. In comparison to direct attacks, indirect attacks require expert diagnostic techniques and more sophisticated management mechanisms to ensure the secure and proper function of the network. However, either type of attack may be targeted at three major AON components: optical fiber cables, optical amplifiers, and switching nodes.

2.1   Control Plane

Automatic switched optical network/GMPLS control plane technology for automated path control of a photonic network was developed in the past decade. In the past few years, it has been deployed in service provider commercial networks. This control plane technology provides network operators with advanced network functions such as multilayer network operation and user control. The control plane technology can change the traditional closed network operation to an open-controlled network. This change is beneficial for saving both operation expenditure (OPEX) and capital expenditure (CAPEX) of networks as well as for creating new services.

This technology also introduces new threats to the security of photonic network operation [11]. In the IP layer, multiprotocol label switching (MPLS) is used as a control plane in various network service provider networks. The MPLS packets use interfaces identified by their IP addresses, and the MPLS control packets use the same interfaces and addresses. Some malicious users may access the devices and channels in these lower layers and may pretend to be a network operator and flow incorrect network information to confuse the IP network through the MPLS control plane. However, in the traditional control plane configuration, photonic networks cannot be disturbed by a malicious user from the IP layer because it is controlled by the isolated control plane from the IP layer's control plane, as shown in Fig. 1(a).

The introduction of the GMPLS control plane exposes devices in a photonic network to a malicious user in the IP layer because the GMPLS control plane can be configured as an integrated control plane from layers 1 to 3, which is shown in Fig. 1

(b). A potential serious problem in this architecture is that a malicious user can change and confuse a carrier's database of the network configuration through the IP layer. Hacking and a photonic network in this way would be a likely threat. This can be partially prevented by IPsec; however, the protocols used are always threatened by advances in mathematics and computer technologies, or may have already been cracked. Hence, it is not a perfect solution.

2.2 Optical Path Network

Possible targets of attacks on an optical path network include devices such as optical fibers, OXC, and reconfigurable optical add–drop multiplexers (ROADMs). Access networks will be an easy target for attacks since the optical signals are at a relatively low bit rate and most of the facilities, such as optical fiber cables, are installed in the open outside plant. Moreover, passive optical network (PON) systems, in which an optical fiber is shared by typically up to 32 users, have been widely deployed in access networks, as shown in Fig. 2(a). This point-to-multipoint network topology is inherently prone to security threats, for example, tapping by detecting the leakage of light signal at the bent portion and spoofing by connecting an unauthorized optical network unit (ONU). To prevent such attacks, encryption, such as AES for payload data and authentication for individual ID of the ONU, is generally used for communication between the optical line terminal (OLT) and each ONU. Thus, PON systems provide reasonable security using currently available techniques. However, it seems worth pursuing newly emerging PL1sec technologies in the long run. Jamming by injecting high-power light from the optical fiber is another possible attack, which would paralyze the PON with the breakdown of the receiver, leading to service denial, as shown in Fig. 2(a). This can be prevented by isolating the drop fiber from the optical splitter. For example, jamming light can be shut out by attaching an optical gate, controlled by a photovoltaic module to the fiber [12].

High cross-talk in wavelength selective switches can be exploited by an attacker to perform in band jamming by injecting a very high power attack signal. In-band jamming attack is difficult to localize, and causes service disruption without breaking or disrupting the fiber by jamming the data signal in legitimate light path. Therefore, it is necessary to minimize the crosstalk of a switch as far as possible. Switch crosstalk depends on coherence time, polarization, phase mismatch and input power of the switch, where first three factors are design dependent. The crosstalk can be severe if the power of the attack signal is very high and it can lead to denial of service by jamming the switch.

Another target of attack may be network nodes. As Medard et al. suggested [2], crosstalk attack is possible, which occurs in the optical switch at the node, as illustrated in Fig. 2(b). When an attacker injects high-power light on the same wavelength as the signal from an input port of the switch, its leaked light energy can significantly affect the normal connections passing through the same switch and can propagate to the next node.

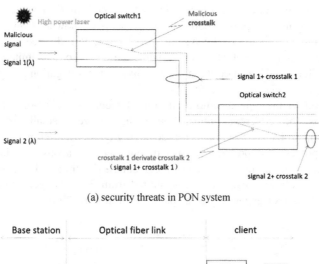

(a) security threats in PON system

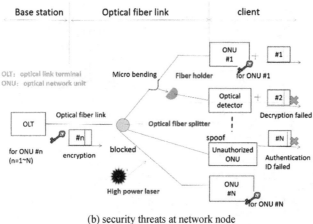

(b) security threats at network node

Fig. 2. Security threats (a) in PON system (b) at network node

3 Principle of Distributed Optical Sensing

Distributed optical sensing based of φOTDR is gaining a great deal of interest in a wide number of distinct areas, e.g., for structure health monitoring, aerospace or material processing [13–17]. φOTDR-based sensors are routinely employed for the monitoring of vibrations and displacements over large perimeters. This fact, together with their potential for higher spatial resolution and bandwidth than other available distributed sensors make φOTDR an interesting technology solution for a wide number of applications [16].

φOTDR-based sensing schemes operate similarly to OTDR technology, but using a highly coherent optical pulse instead of an incoherent one. The received power trace is then produced by coherent interference of the light reflected via Rayleigh scattering in the inhomogeneities of the fiber. In φOTDR operation, dynamic range, resolution, and signal-to-noise ratio (SNR) are closely related parameters. Thus, the probe pulse should have high energy for long-range capabilities with enough SNR. This can be achieved by either increasing the pulse width or the pulse peak power. However, the first solution leads to a reduction of the system spatial resolution (defined as the minimum spatial separation of two resolvable events) while the second one is limited by the onset of nonlinear effects, such as modulation instability, in its propagation along the sensing fiber [16, 17].

Figure 3 shows the typical setup used to implement a φOTDR-based sensor. This laser used as the coherent optical source has a very small frequency drift (<1 MHz/min), which is important for achieving good interference stability. The modulation process is preferably carried out by an acoustic-optic modulator (AOM) with a maximum insertion loss of 6 dB and the rise time of 10 ns, the repetition rate and pulse width are designed and generated from the pulse generator, which are 8 kHz and 200 ns (corresponding to a spatial resolution of 20 m).

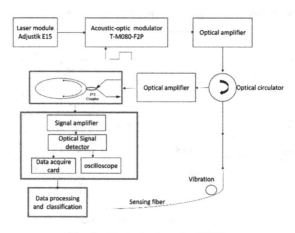

Fig. 3. Typical setup of φOTDR

The pulsed light is amplified by an Erbium doped fiber amplifier (EDFA), and then filtered by a dense wavelength division multiplexing (DWDM) in order to eliminate the amplified spontaneous emission (ASE) noise of the EDFA. The adjusted lights are launched into the fiber via a circulator, then propagating along the fiber and generate the coherent back Rayleigh scattered (RS) light. The RS light is amplified and then detected by a high sensitivity balanced photo detector (PD) with 10 MHz bandwidth. The original RS curves are sampled by an oscilloscope with a data acquisition (DAQ) board of 200 MS/s sampling rate in each trigger period. The external vibration signal working as the phase perturbation could be introduced upon the fiber at certain distance from the beginning of the fiber line. Finally, the signals are processed and analyzed by the computing module of the oscilloscope in real time.

The power evolution as a function of time for each point along the FUT was obtained by monitoring equivalent points in consecutive traces. The FFT of this power evolution will therefore present the frequencies measured for each point.

The resulting traces show a static, noise-like interference pattern, which is only altered by variations in the state of the fiber, such as vibrations or strain changes. Time and frequency of vibration signal are shown in Fig. 4. Hence, those variations can be continuously detected from the analysis of the backscattered trace.

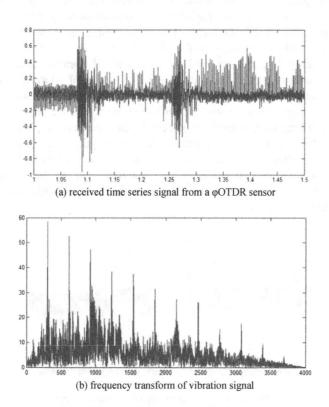

(a) received time series signal from a φOTDR sensor

(b) frequency transform of vibration signal

Fig. 4. Time and frequency of vibration signal

4 Distributed Acoustic Sensors in Optical Network

In this Section, we review our recent progress in DAS-based systems for prevention of integrity threats along optical fibers. The Section is divided into two main blocks, each of them describing a key development in φOTDR-based DAS that has been carried out in our group, greatly contributing to the current state of maturity of this technology. The first block present innovative advances related to the fundamentals of the technology, while other block are focused on applications that could inspire novel procedures or readily be employed for the prevention of failures in telecommunication networks.

4.1   Long Range φOTDR Systems Using Distributed Raman Amplification

As introduced in Sect. 3, for a given resolution of the φOTDR system the increase of the input pump peak power will increase the dynamic range and SNR, this approach being limited by the onset of nonlinear effects. Several solutions have been proposed to improve the performance of φOTDR such as the use of signal post-processing algorithms. Still, a significant increase of the sensing range can only be achieved using optical amplification. In particular, we have demonstrated vibration detection of up to 380 Hz over a distance of 125 km with a spatial resolution of 10 m using distributed Raman amplification along the FUT. Two kinds of vibration signal are shown in Fig. 5. The achievable range is then comparable with the typical distance between nodes of a fiber link ($\sim$ 100 km). Raman amplification can be engineered to keep the power of the optical pulse almost constant along the whole fiber length, generating a trace with sufficiently high visibility at all locations. The main concern of using Raman amplification is the relative intensity noise (RIN) transferred from the Raman pump to the signal. This problem can be easily solved by using balanced photodetection, which can completely eliminate the RIN.

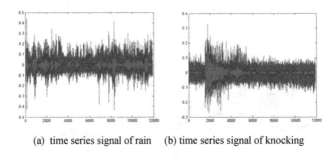

(a) time series signal of rain   (b) time series signal of knocking

Fig. 5. Two kinds of vibration signal (a) rain (b) knocking

The bandwidth of the acquired acoustic signals covers frequencies up to 380 Hz, but experiments were carried out by analyzing frequencies up to 100 Hz, since frequencies above 100 Hz do not convey meaningful information. The low limit of the spectral range was set to 1 Hz, since the window size in the ST-FFT expands 1 s. The relevant parameters related to the energy-in-bands computation in the feature extraction are: the acoustic frame size (which in the system is set to 1 s), the acoustic frame shift (set to 5 ms), the number of FFT points (set to 8192) for the ST-FFT, and the number of frequency bands that defines the number of components in the feature vectors (set to $P = 100$). These values were chosen based on their best performance in preliminary experiments.

4.2   Applications of φOTDR for Early Detection of Threats

φOTDR based sensors have already been proposed and tested for critical safety applications in areas as energy source transmission via pipelines. A system for detection and classification of threats in the vicinity of a long gas pipeline has been proposed and successfully demonstrated based on φOTDR technology. The system relies on the deployment of a standard telecommunication optical fiber in parallel with the pipeline. This vibration-based sensor monitors potentially dangerous activities near the pipeline in a remote, cost-effective and highly reliable fashion. Moreover, the classification of a complete set of relevant activities based on the sensed vibration have been performed by means of pattern recognition strategies.

A single GMM component per class has been used for model training in the pattern classification stage, as a baseline setup to allow for robust training and easier generalization. To increase the statistical significance of the system performance estimation, the experiments are carried out using a leave-one-out cross-validation (CV) strategy, on a location basis. Since data were recorded in six different locations, the CV comprises six folds, where the data recorded in all the locations except one were used for training, and the evaluation was done on data of the unused location (thus ensuring full independence between the training and testing subsets).

Classification is conducted on a frame-by-frame basis. Therefore, a feature vector is calculated for each 1 s frame within every 12 s length recorded file. All the vectors are used in the pattern classification stage, either as training or testing data. Therefore, given the feature extraction parameters, there are 415 feature vectors for each recorded file.

An initial analysis was carried out aiming at checking whether meaningful and discriminative patterns for each machine activity pair exist. To do so, spectrograms were computed from randomly selected acoustic files. These acoustic files are those corresponding to a highest energy meter for a given machine activity pair in a certain location according to the 12 s length duration of each acoustic file in the database. To provide a general idea on the signal characteristics, some examples of these spectrograms are shown in Fig. 6, where it can be seen that the signals have a high level of noise and that, in general, each machine activity pair exhibits a reasonably consistent spectral behavior, hence allowing for the use of pattern classification strategies.

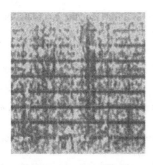 

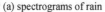

(a) spectrograms of rain   (b) spectrograms of knocking

Fig. 6. Classification by spectrograms (a) rain (b) knocking

This approach can further increase the cost-effectiveness of the system as the number of false alarms can be significantly reduced.

This proposed operation procedure could inspire a similar strategy for detecting integrity threats in communication networks due to construction works analogous to those affecting pipelines. In this case, the optical fiber used for sensing could be the same fiber transporting the data traffic or even a dark fiber of the network.

5   Conclusion

We have addressed emerging threats to the security of photonic networks, reviewed of our recent progress on DAS based on φOTDR, paying special attention to those properties that could be of high interest for the prevention of threats in optical fiber links. Some of the more significant developments achieved by our group are briefly described; namely, the use of distributed Raman amplification to increase the range of operation of φOTDR sensors in at least one order of magnitude.

Distributed acoustic sensing is a continuously growing technology with strong potential to become a critical tool in future network survivability strategies.

Additionally, a practical, cost-effective approach proposed for integrity threat detection of pipelines is described, which is based on φOTDR together with pattern recognition strategies. This approach has a strong potential for serving as baseline in future survivable optical telecommunication networks. Finally, The combination of φOTDR technology for fiber link failure prevention and current strategies for node congestion control and traffic re-routing could rise as a promising arrangement to significantly reduce the network disruption rate and associated data loss.

Acknowledgment.   The authors are grateful to:

Special thanks to Weiqing Huang at electronics and communication Lab, Institute of information engineering, CAS, for his patience and support throughout this project.

Yanyun Xu at electronics and communication Lab, Institute of information engineering, CAS for help with this project.

The research was supported by the National Natural Science Foundation of China (No. 61601460).

References

1. Medard, M., Marquis, D., Barry, R.A., Finn, S.G.: Security issues of all-optical networks. IEEE Netw. **11**(3), 42–48 (1997)
2. Wu, T., Somani, A.K.: Cross-talk attack monitoring and localization in all-optical networks. IEEE/ACM Trans. Netw. **13**(6), 1390–1401 (2005)
3. Rejeb, R., Leeson, M.S., Green, R.J.: Fault and attack management in all-optical networks. IEEE Commun. Mag. **44**(11), 79–86 (2006)
4. Deng, T., Subramaniam, S.: Analysis of optical amplifier gain competition attack in a point-to-point WDM link. In: International Society for Optical Engineering, vol. 4874, pp. 249–261, July 2002

5. Deng, T., Subramaniam, S.: Covert low-power QoS attack in all optical wavelength routed networks. In: Proceedings of Global Telecommunication Conference, vol. 3, pp. 1948–1952 (2004)
6. Liu, G., Ji, C.: Resilience of all-optical network architectures under in-band crosstalk attacks: a probabilistic graphical model approach. IEEE J. Sel. Areas Commun. **25**(3), 2–17 (2007)
7. Skorin-Kapov, N., Chen, J., Wosinska, L.: A new approach to optical networks security: attack aware routing and wavelength assignment. IEEE/ACM Trans. Netw. **18**(3), 750–760 (2010)
8. Machuca, C.M., Tomkos, I., Tonguz, O.: Failure location algorithm for transparent optical networks. IEEE J. Sel. Areas Commun. **23**(8), 1508–1519 (2005)
9. The Wolf Report (in German). http://www.youtube.com/watch?v=2DvaubDDbss
10. Fujiwara, M., Miki, S., Yamashita, T., Wang, Z., Sasaki, M.: Photon level crosstalk between parallel fibers installed in urban area (2010). arXiv:quant-ph/1008.0893. http://xxx.lanl.gov/abs/1008.0893
11. Farrel, A.: Control plane resilience and security in GMPLS networks: Fact and fiction. Presented at the Adrian Farrel Old Dog Consulting, UK (2008). http://pil.yamanaka.ics.keio.ac.jp/2008/info/pdf/iPOP2008_1-1.pdf
12. Ramanitra, H., Chanclou, P., Belfqih, Z., Moignard, M., Le Bras, H., Schumacher, D.: Scalable and multi-service passive optical access infrastructure using variable optical splitters. Presented at the Optical Fiber Communications, Anaheim, CA (2006)
13. Zhou, D., Subramaniam, S.: Survivability in optical networks. IEEE Netw. **14**(6), 16–23 (2000)
14. Cisco Press Book: Quality of service design overview. In: Enterprise QoS Solution Network Design Guide. Cisco Systems, San Jose (2005). ISBN: 1587051761
15. Mallika, Mohan, M.: Multiple link failure in optical network. IJRET **2**(2), 4378–4381 (2013)
16. Barrias, A., et al.: A review of distributed optical fiber sensors for civil engineering applications. Sensors **16**(5), 748–782 (2016)
17. Martins, H.F., et al.: Distributed vibration sensing over 125 km with enhanced SNR using phi-OTDR over a URFL cavity. J. Lightwave Technol. **33**(12), 2628–2632 (2015)

H-Verifier: Verifying Confidential System State with Delegated Sandboxes

Anyi Liu[✉] and Guangzhi Qu

Department of Computer Science and Engineering, Oakland University,
Rochester, MI 48309, USA
{anyiliu,gqu}@oakland.edu

Abstract. As a viable technology that supports ubiquitous, versatile, and cost-efficient IT solution for various applications, the wide adoption of the cloud computing is still hindered by the lack of online anomaly detection and poor accountability. Although cloud providers facilitate trusted computing with the support of hardware and software, to construct a trusted computing base (TCB) in a hostile environment with a minimal size is still non-trivial. It is desired to have a general solution that supports trusted computing regardless of the underlying hardware and software. In this paper, we present a system, namely *H-Verifier*, which verifies the states of the confidential system with cryptographic support. To ensure data confidentiality, H-Verifier leverages homomorphic encryption (HE), partitions the model of the monitored system, and stores the partitions distributively. To track the system states, the partitions are updated against the ciphertext via the standard HE operations. Since both the model and audit events are encrypted, H-Verifier does not require a TCB to be constructed on the computational nodes. H-Verifier overcomes the performance curse of HE and makes sure that only a limited number of HE operations are required online. H-Verifier is capable of performing trusted computing without relying on special hardware and thus can be widely deployed in various sandboxes and/or enclave. The experimental results demonstrate that H-Verifier can achieve reasonable performance for model initialization, updating, and verification for an online system in the cloud.

Keywords: Homomorphic encryption · Finite-state automaton
Sandbox

1 Introduction

As a ubiquitous, versatile, and cost-efficient IT solution, cloud computing has been widely adopted as a feasible technology to facilitate various services and applications. While the cloud computing offers the appealing features, such as elasticity and low cost, it has also been abused by the adversaries. Extensive research has shown that adversaries took advantage of the appealing features of the cloud and have exaggerated the loss caused by the cloud-based

© Springer Nature Switzerland AG 2018
F. Liu et al. (Eds.): SciSec 2018, LNCS 11287, pp. 126–140, 2018.
https://doi.org/10.1007/978-3-030-03026-1_9

intrusions [1], malicious services [2–4], and underground ecosystems [5,6]. The recently announced the Security, Trust & Assurance Registry (STAR) [7] by the Cloud Security Alliance explicitly defines three levels of audit certification: self-auditing, third-party auditing, and continuous, near real-time verification of security compliance, which articulates the importance of real-time verification and auditing. To counter the capability of the adversary and grantee the timely detection of any violation of security properties, the runtime auditing, system verification, and intrusion detection become urgent to cloud providers to ensure the security status in the cloud and to be responsive to the cybercrime and intrusions.

However, several challenges to the area hinder the real-time verification and auditing. First, it is difficult to standardize the techniques of secure audit log generation and real-time tenant's system status verification. To increase the cloud tenants' trust in the designated infrastructure and platform, cloud providers must ensure the security compliance with the support of trusted computing. To construct a trusted execution environment (TEE), hardware and software are used to construct a trusted computing base (TCB) in a hostile environment with a minimal size. Existing systems primarily focus on constructing the root of trust (RoT) with the trusted hardware or hypervisor [8–12]. Commodity technologies, such as Intel System Management Mode (SMM) [13], Trusted Execution Technology (TXT) [14], and Intel Software Guard Extensions (SGX) [15] are proprietary products and lack of the cross-platform guarantee. Second, although the technology, such as virtual machine introspection (VMI) [16–18], allows the virtual artifacts to be identified and collected from the self-provisioned VMs, the correctness of the technology largely relies on the trustworthiness of the hypervisor or the privileged VM. Moreover, to reconstruct the virtual artifact and verify the security properties of the monitor system from the low-level observations requires to bridge the semantic gap [19], which is non-trivial. Thus, a general solution is desired regardless of the underlying infrastructure and the supporting technologies to construct the TEE.

In this paper, we present an online system, namely *H-Verifier*, which is capable of identifying the status of a system through the confidential audit log with the aid of collaborative sandboxes[1]. To ensure the confidentiality of the audit log, H-Verifier partitions the model of the monitored system and encrypts the model by leveraging the homomorphic encryption (HE) [20]. The partitions are securely updated on different computational nodes. The major innovative contribution H-Verifier is that it overcomes the performance curse of HE by only introducing a limited number of HE operations when updating the partitions. Since the computational nodes only keep the ciphertext of the model and data, no additional TCB is needed on the computational nodes, which allows it to perform trusted computing without relying on special hardware and can be widely deployed in various sandboxes, including virtual machine, container, and enclave. The experimental results demonstrate that H-Verifier is capable of identifying

---

[1] We use *sandbox* and *enclave* interchangeably throughout this paper.

the status of the monitor system and achieving a reasonable overhead for model initialization, updating, and verification for an online system in the cloud.

The rest of the paper is organized as follows. First, we review the related work Sect. 2. Then, we describe the threat model in Sect. 3. After that, we present the system design and elaborate the methodology in Sect. 4 and the evaluation results in Sect. 5. We also discuss the limitation of our current design and proposed the future work in Sect. 6. Finally, we conclude the paper in Sect. 7 .

2   Related Work

As a cryptosystem that allows the untrusted party to perform computing on the encrypted data, while still preserves ciphertext secret, the Homomorphic Encryption (HE) has been widely adopted in various applications [21–23]. Li et al. [22] presented a distributed incremental data aggregation scheme, in which data collected from smart meters can be aggregated along the route from the source meter to the collector unit. Homomorphic encryption is used to protect user's private data en route. As a result, the involved meters cannot see any intermediate or final result. Hong et al. [23] proposed a collaborative search log sanitization scheme, which allows multiple parties to collaboratively generate search logs with boosted utility while satisfying differential privacy. To this end, a protocol, namely *CELS*, is proposed to meet the privacy-preserving objectives. Comparing with the above applications of HE, the unique feature of our approach is that it encrypts the model and apply HE re-encryption to record the model's status change. Our approach facilitates online model checking and verification, without revealing its secret. Furthermore, the encrypted model can be deployed on a platform whose TCB has not been authenticated. Although HE shows the benefits of privacy and secrecy guarantees, researchers also show that both HE schemes are prohibitively slow and has only supported limited crypto operations [24].

3   The Threat Model

To specify the threat model without loss of generality, we assume that the sandbox of the state verifier, which generates and maintains the secret keys (including HE's and OPE's) is secure. Given that the secret inside a sandbox could be leaked either from the VM [25,26] or enclave [27–29] through the side-channel attacks, we also assume that the system is unbreachable during the process of the secret keys generation. In addition, the integrity of the pseudo-random number generator (PRNG) has been attested. Furthermore, we assume that once the mutual trust is established, the secret keys used for encryption are *ephemeral* and thus cannot be stolen by the inside attacker through the race condition [30] and the side-channel attack [31]. Finally, we assume that the information of e-Relations, which predominates the update of the secure model, should also be secured.

H-Verifier assumes that the cloud provider is *honest but curious* and does not impose any assumption on the trustworthiness of the state updater. Thus, it is resilient against the exploits that breach the stand-alone sandbox of state updaters. For each sandbox, the adversary owns the capabilities of (1) stealing the ciphertext of the model; (2) running the brute force attack to break the ciphertext, and (3) eavesdropping the communication between the sandboxes. Our current design might still be vulnerable to the advanced collusion attack, in which the collusive adversary records the memory locations of the HE operations in all sandboxes and infers the rules of the transition function. In such a manner, the adversary can replace the ciphertext of the secure model with any arbitrary value, and thus break our system. The countermeasure of how to mitigate the collusion attack is discussed in Sect. 6.

4 System Design

In this section, we first present the system architecture of H-Verifier. Then, we describe the design of the encrypted model readily to be verified. After that, we detail the procedure and algorithms that initialize, update, and verify the encrypted model.

4.1 The System Architecture

H-Verifier is designed to identify the state of the monitored system/program against the specified formal model and encrypted system log. The primary challenge that H-Verifier intends to overcome is to facilitate trusted computing without solely relying on the guarantee of the TCB. It also prevents the plaintext of the system log from being recorded by the honest but curious cloud provider. To this end, H-Verifier is designed to fulfill three objectives: (1) it ensures the *confidentiality* of the formal model that specifies the intended behavior of the monitored system/program. The secrecy of the model does not only depends on the hardness of the sandbox or enclave, but also the cryptographic scheme used to generate the model; (2) it ensures that the state of system/program is verifiable during the runtime, without leaking the secret that how the model is verified; (3) it is resilient against the replay attack [32] and the side channel attacks [25,27], even when the infrastructure is compromised. The bottom line is that H-verifier keeps the secrecy of both the system log and the formal model.

To achieve these objectives, we design H-Verifier as illustrated in Fig. 1, which consists of three major components: *Event Generator*, *State Verifier*[2], and *State Updater*. To separate the functionalities, the components can be placed inside either the *heavy-weight* sandboxes such as the virtual machines (VMs), or the *light-weight* ones such as the containers and enclaves. H-Verifier works in two phases: the *auditing* and the *verification* phase. During the auditing phase, H-Verifier updates the system model upon the observed system events. Specifically, the event generator generates the raw system log e and timestamp t in plaintext

---

[2] In the real application, the *Event Generator* and *State Verifier* can be deployed in the same sandbox.

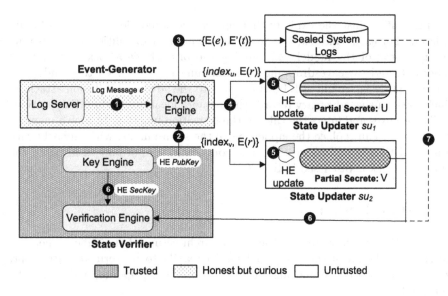

Fig. 1. The system architecture of *H-Verifier*.

(step 1), encrypts them with the HE public key, *PubKey*, which is generated by the state verifier (step 2), and seals them into the system log repository for the future verification purpose (step 3). Rather than sending the data in plaintext across the boundary of the sandbox, the plaintext data are encrypted by the HE and Order-Preserving Encryption (OPE) cipher (E and E') [33] respectively, which produce a ciphertext pair $\{E(e), E'(t)\}$ (step 3). This process ensures that neither the key-related information nor the plaintext log will leave the sandbox unencrypted. Then, the tuples $\{index_u, E(r)\}$ and $\{index_v, E(r)\}$ are sent to two state updaters (su_1 and su_2), respectively (step 4). $E(r)$ is the HE ciphertext of a pseudo-random number r. The detail description of $index_u$, $index_v$, and $E(r)$ will be presented in Sect. 4.3. When the tuple reaches to each state updaters, it will be recomputed with the security model, which is also in the form of HE ciphertext but has been partitioned into two parts, namely U and V (step 5). The details of how to partition and update the model are also described in Sect. 4.3. During the verification phase, H-Verifier identifies the current state of the system being monitored. Specifically, the state verifier first retrieves the HE secret key *SecKey* from the local key repository. Then, it acquires the ciphertext of U and V from the state updaters (step 6). Since both U and V are encrypted by HE cipher, they are only decipherable inside the state verifier. Optionally, the sealed log might be fed into the state verifier for the offline verification (step 7).

H-Verifier is designed to demonstrate at least four advantages. First, it prevents the single-point failure caused by the compromised node. Since the jobs of the event generation, system auditing, and state verification are separated, the security of H-Verifier primarily relies on the trustworthiness of state verifier, which keeps the secret keys confidentially. Second, the model never saves as plaintext in sandboxes, which preserves the secret of the model from being stolen by the malicious insider or the honest but curious privileged user. The sandboxes of state updater do not store any secret key, which also prevents the leakage of the secret key caused by the side-channel attacks [25,27]. Third, although the encrypted model is updated by recomputing with the ciphertext of the event log, the rules used to verify the system state is decoupled from the model, and thus do not depend upon the updated model. In the worst case, even the ciphertext of the model can be breached by the adversary, she still cannot figure out the state of the model because both the initial values of the elements in the model and the updating ciphertext are randomly chosen. Last but not least, instead of keeping the model as a monolithic piece, the model is partitioned into n pieces ($n \geq 2$), which are updated in an individual sandbox without any dependency. The HE re-computing against the partitioned model mitigates the runtime overhead caused by solving the large polynomial of HE. To increase the degree of obfuscation, we discuss the measure of how to partition the formal model into n ($n >= 2$) parts in Sect. 6.

4.2 Constructing Secure Model

To identify the state of the monitored system/program with both the encrypted formal model and the encrypted system log, at least two challenges are needed to be overcome. First, we need to formalize the model in a way that it is expressive enough to represent the general system state based on observations. Second, the model should be encrypted in a way that it will be difficult for the adversary to learn any criteria how the state of the monitored system is determined. To overcome these challenges, we first formalize the model as the finite state machine (FSM), which has been extensively applied as an efficient model to verify the system state. It has been adopted in various fields, such as modeling verification [34] and intrusion detection [35].

Definition 1 (The Security Model $\mathcal{M}$). The model used to identify the verifiable state of a cloud service can be defined as a deterministic finite state machine (FSM) $\mathcal{M}$, which is a quintuple $\mathcal{M} = (\Sigma, S, s_0, \Delta, F)$:

- Σ is an *event alphabet* with a finite number of symbols. In our system, each symbol e is an observable audit event generated by a cloud service.
- S is a finite set of the states.
- s_0 is the initial state, where $s_0 \in S$.
- Δ is a state-transition function: $\Delta : S \times \Sigma \rightarrow S$.
- F is the set of final states. In accordance with the general definition of FSM, we include an additional state $s_e \in F$, which is used to indicate an erroneous final state that leads the FSM to halt with errors.

As an important design objective, once the model is generated, it should be encrypted in a way that it is difficult for the adversary to learn how the state of the monitored system is determined. Our methodology is based on the key observation: if we can successfully conceal (1) the information of the alphabet Σ in the transition function and (2) the correlation between current state S_c and the next state S_n in one transition, we will prevent the adversary from inferring the state of a system from the encrypted model. In order to conceal the information of the transition function, we decouple the actions of FSM update and verification. In particular, the FSM update refers to the actions that apply the HE re-encryption against the partitioned model upon new observations; whereas the FSM verification refers to the actions that apply the HE re-encryption and decryption to cancel out the intermediate states recorded by the partition and therefore determine the final state of the FSM.

To generate an encrypted model that can be easily updated and verified, we further refine the problem by answering three questions: (1) *how to partition and encrypt the model in a way that the partial model alone cannot be used to infer the entire model?* (2) *how to protect the secret of the transition function, even when the content of the partial model is disclosed to the adversary?* and (3) *how to bound the overall computational overhead of model update and verification, with respect to the HE operations imposed to the model?* To answer the first question, we define a data structure for an FSM $\mathcal{M}$, namely *dual-vector* $DV(\mathcal{M})^3$, which is used to keep the state information of an FSM. The definition of $DV(\mathcal{M})$ is listed below:

Definition 2 (The Dual-Vector $DV(\mathcal{M})$). A $DV(\mathcal{M})$ comprises two vectors of finite sizes, namely $U[sizeof(U)]$ and $V[sizeof(V)]$, where the functions $sizeof(U)$ and $sizeof(V)$ return the sizes of vectors U and V respectively. The initial values of the element are first randomly chosen and then encrypted with the HE public key.

To answer the second question, we define two types of relations, namely *e-Relations* and *i-Relations*, which can be used as the alternatives to the original transition function of an FSM for the state update and verification purposes. Instead of keeping the transition function confidential, we use the information kept in the *e-Relations* to update the FSM based on the observable events, while we use the information kept in the *i-Relations* to verify the state of the FSM. The definitions of *e-Relations* and *i-Relations* are listed below:

Definition 3 (*e-Relations* and *i-Relations*). Given an FSM $\mathcal{M}$ and its transition function $\mathcal{M}.\Delta$, for each transition $\delta_i \in \mathcal{M}.\Delta$, we define a mapping relationship $\mathbb{M} : \delta_i \rightarrow \{index_u^i, index_v^i\}$, in which $index_\alpha^i$ ($\alpha = u$ or v) refers to the index corresponding to the vectors U and V, respectively.

- The *explicit relations* (*e-Relations*) is an ordered pair $E(i) = \{index_u^i, index_v^i\}$, where the states S_i and S_{i+1} satisfy the transition function δ_i: $S_i \times e_i \rightarrow S_{i+1}$.

---

[3] Our approach allows more than two vectors to be used, though the current design only uses two vectors.

– The *implicit relations* (*i-Relations*) is an ordered pair $I(i) = \{index_v^i, index_u^{i+1}\}$, where the transition $\delta_i: S_i \times e_i \rightarrow S_{i+1}$ is corresponding to the e-Relation $\{index_u^i, index_v^i\}$ and the transition $\delta_{i+1}: S_{i+1} \times e_j \rightarrow S_{i+2}$ is corresponding to the e-Relation $\{index_u^{i+1}, index_v^{i+1}\}$.

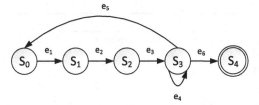

Trans.	U	V
δ_0	1	4
δ_1	7	13
δ_2	5	6
δ_3	10	15
δ_4	14	8
δ_5	16	17

(a) The sample finite state machine $\mathcal{M}_s$.

(b) The transition function $\mathcal{M}_s.\Delta$ and its corresponding e-Relations.

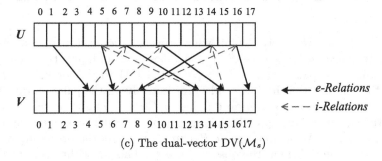

(c) The dual-vector DV($\mathcal{M}_s$)

Fig. 2. An example FSM and its corresponding dual vector.

To explain the concepts of *e-Relations* and *i-Relations*, we use the sample FSM illustrated in Fig. 2.

Example 1. As illustrated in Fig. 2a, the sample FSM $\mathcal{M}_s$ comprises an event alphabet $\Sigma = \{e_i\}$ ($0 \leq i \leq 5$), the set of states $S = S_i$ ($0 \leq i \leq 4$), the initial state S_0, and the final state set $F = \{S_4\}$. In Fig. 2b, each row in the table represents an e-Relation. Accordingly, the solid arrows point from the elements of vector U to those of V are the e-Relations, while the dotted arrows point from the elements of vector V to those of U are the i-Relation. In this example, the transitions $\delta_1 : S_0 \times e_0 \rightarrow S_1$ (shown in row 2) is mapped to the index pair $\{1, 4\}$, whose corresponding e-Relation (shown as the solid arrow) points from $U[1]$ to $V[4]$. Similarly, the transition $\delta_2 : S_1 \times e_1 \rightarrow S_2$ (the row 3) is mapped to the e-Relation points from $U[7]$ to $V[13]$. Thus, the i-Relation that corresponds to δ_1 and δ_2 is $\{4, 7\}$, which is the dotted arrow points from $V[4]$ to $U[7]$.

4.3 Updating Secure Model

A major objective of partitioning the model is to ensure that each partition is updated independently, and thus mitigates the chance of correlation. To achieve this objective, the vectors U and V are deployed in different sandboxes and updated independently upon the observed events. However, to update the partitions in the sandboxes of the state updaters is non-trivial because U and V only keep the HE ciphertext as their elements, they only accept the HE ciphertext, in order to update the model in the state updaters.

Algorithm. *Update_Partitions.*

Input: The pair $P_i = \{index_\alpha, E(r)\}$ ($\alpha = u$ or v) and the current vectors U and V.
Output: The updated vectors U' and V'.
1: **if** the state updater contains U **then**
2:     $Sub(U[index_u], E(r))$;
3: **else**
4:     $Add(V[index_v], E(r))$;
   End of Algorithm

To do this, we apply the following conversion for each plaintext event e_i: for the transition $\delta_i: S_i \times e_i \rightarrow S_{i+1}$ that takes e_i as an input, the event generator produces two pairs, namely $P_i = \{index_\alpha, E(r)\}$ ($\alpha = u$ or v), and send them to the sandbox that hosts U and V respectively. In the pairs, $index_\alpha$ ($\alpha = u$ or v) refers to the indexes in an e-Relation $E(i) = \{index_u^i, index_v^i\}$, while $E(r)$ is the ciphertext of a pseudorandom number r that is encrypted by HE public key $PubKey$. Algorithm *Update_Partitions* presents the procedure of updating vectors U and V upon the observed events. This algorithm uses two standard HE functions: namely Add for HE addition and Sub for HE subtraction. The algorithm is executed each time when a data pair is received by the state updater. For the sandbox that contains U, the element $U[index_u]$ will be *homomorphically* subtracted by $E(r)$. Otherwise, the element $V[index_v]$ will be *homomorphically* added by $E(r)$. Of course, the values of index $index_\alpha$ must also be encrypted to keep its confidentiality. Since Algorithm *Update_Partitions* ensures that each transition of $\mathcal{M}_s$ can be translated into an HE operations (either addition or subtraction) and imposed to each vector, we answer the third question mentioned in Sect. 4.3 that the time complexity of algorithm *Update_Partitions* is $O(1)$.

Whenever there is a need of checking the current state of the monitored program with respect to its corresponding FSM, the algorithm *Verification_State* is executed, which takes current values of U and V, as the input. The values of U and V might have been updated before verification. It outputs the ID of the state as defined by the FSM if success, or -1 if fail. To understand the algorithm, two standard HE functions are needed for HE encryption and HE decryption, namely En for De. Two additional functions *Lookup_expl* and *Lookup_impl* are needed to retrieve the indexes of the explicit and the implicit relations, respectively. For the verification purpose, the original copies of U and V, namely V_{part}^{org} and U_{part}^{org}, are also needed. The algorithm contains two parts. The lines 1 - 8 cancel out the states, which have been involved in the state transition during in run-time, but are included in the set of final states. The line 10 - 15 traverse the transition function and determine which state is the final state.

Algorithm. *Verification_State.*

Input: The updated vectors U'_{part} and V'_{part}, the original copy of partitions U^{org}_{part} and V^{org}_{part}, and the pseudorandom number r.

Output: The ID of the current state of the monitored system S_m if success, or -1 if fail. LineComment *Cancel out the non-final states.*

1: **for each** $\delta_i \in \Delta$
2:     $(index_v, index_u) \leftarrow Lookup\_imp~(i)$;
3:     $temp \leftarrow Add(EV[index_v], EV[index_u])$;
4:     **if** $De(temp) == V[index_v] + U[index_u]$ **then**
5:         $diff = De(EV[index_v]) - V[index_v]$;
6:         $temp\_V[index_v] \leftarrow Sub(EV[index_v], En(diff))$;
7:         $temp\_U[index_u] \leftarrow Add(EU[index_u], En(diff))$;
8: ▷ *Now, start to traverse the transition function and determine the final state*
9: **for each** $\delta_i \in \Delta$
10:     $(index_u, index_v) \leftarrow Lookup\_exp~(i)$;
11:     **if** $(De(temp\_U[index_u]) == U^{org}_{part}[index_u])$ **and** $(De(temp\_V[index_v]) == V^{org}_{part}[index_v] + r)$ **then**
12:         return i;
13: **if** $De(temp) == V[index_v] + U[index_u]$ **then**
14:     return -1;
    End of Algorithm

---

5   Implementation and Evaluation

We implemented the prototype of H-Verifier with nearly 500 lines of `C++` code. We used `HElib` [36] as the library to facilitate the generic HE operations. The evaluation results were collected from the physical machine which is equipped with Intel i7-6600U CPU 2.60 GHz, 4-core processor, 20 GB of RAM. In the following, we first analyze the computational overhead and then present the scalability of our model.

5.1   Computational Overhead

The first set of experiments measures the time elapsed for bootstrapping, updating, and verifying the model for different sizes of the vector, which is illustrated in Fig. 3 and Table 1. From the experiments, we have made the following observation: First, regardless of bootstrapping and verification, the average time spent for manipulating one element in a vector is nearly constant ($\sim$33 ms for bootstrapping and $\sim$14 ms for verification). Therefore, the accumulative time that bootstraps and verifies the vectors are linear to the size of a vector. Second, since the e-Relations is a pair of two indexes in U and V respectively, only one element in each vector is updated for an observable event during the runtime. As shown in Table 1, the average time spent in each sandbox is nearly constant (∼2.6 ms) regardless of the size of a vector. This property gives us the lower bound of the applications that can adapt our approach without losing the accountability. Third, the increasing size of the model, in particular, the increasing size of its transition function, requires the larger vectors to hold the HE ciphertext. However, the increasing size of its transition function is not necessarily linear to the size of vectors. Some dummy data are kept in the vectors for the purpose of obfuscation because only the elements at the indexes of the e-Relations and i-Relations contribute to the FSM updated and verified respectively. Similar results can be found in Fig. 3b for the state verification.

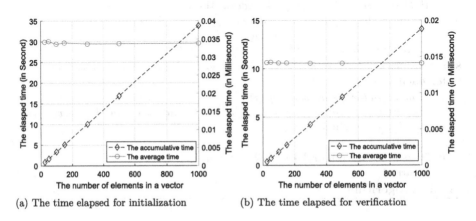

(a) The time elapsed for initialization   (b) The time elapsed for verification

Fig. 3. The time elapsed for the incurred HE operations.

Table 1. The time elapsed for secure model update (in Millisecond).

	U	V
Mean	2.669	2.698
Std. Deviation	0.578	0.618

6   Discussion

In this section, we discuss some limitation of the proposed scheme, propose some possible solutions, and describe some directions for our future study.

First, although homomorphic encryption offers the good characteristics to compute over the ciphertext, its low efficiency prevents it from being applied to the high-performance applications [37], which seems to defeat the purpose of online state verification. We made the similar observation through our experiment. However, we found that the online component (the state updator) of

H-Verifier only incurs one HE re-computation (either addition or subtraction) for one element in a vector, and its computational overhead is nearly constant. Meanwhile, the steps that consume more time, such as bootstrapping and verification, are performed offline. Therefore, our approach still holds the great promise to be adopted for various online auditing applications without losing the soundness. In our future study, we will test more real-world applications and study the performance gaps.

Second, our current scheme does not resilient against the collusion attack, in which the adversary controls all the state updater and records all the HE operations. In particular, the adversary records the HE addition and subtraction in each sandbox, identifies the updated elements in each vector, and infers the e-Relations. She can thus infer an i-Relations by correlating two adjacent e-Relations. To counter this attack, we can use the following scheme to increase the degree of randomness: First, instead of saving partitions in two vectors, we may use multiple vectors, say m ($m > 2$) vectors. To update a vector, a one-dimensional matrix of indexes (with an average dimension of n) will be sent to a state updater so that multiple elements, instead of one element in the vector, will be updated. However, during the verification process, only one pair of the index will be selected out of $m \times n$ possibilities. This approach will introduce the degree of randomness and mitigate the collusion attack. The only sacrifice is that it requires more sandboxes and will incur higher online overhead in each sandbox.

Third, in this paper, we primarily focus on retaining the secrecy of the model and without having to construct the TCB. Our current implementation requires the model to be generated as the results of the static analysis from the source code. The model that we have studied is deterministic, instead of probabilistic. As a future direction, we will apply the learning algorithms, such as Hidden Markov Model (HMM), to generate the non-deterministic model and consider the probabilistic model as well. Moreover, we will consider the side channel attack and the forensic analysis, which observe the CPU usage of H-Verifier and infer the execution path of the monitored system.

7   Conclusions

Despite its appealing features, such as ubiquity, elasticity, and low-cost, the cloud computing is still hindered by the limitation of real-time verification, detection, and accountability. Cloud providers intended to facilitate trusted computing with the supporting hardware and software, which lacks interoperability and the cross-platform security guarantee. In this paper, we present an online system, namely *H-Verifier*, which verifies the status of the confidential system with collaborative sandboxes. To ensure data confidentiality, H-Verifier leverages homomorphic encryption (HE), partitions the model of the monitored system, and stores the partition model distributively. To track the system status, the partitioned model is updated against the ciphertext through the general HE operations. To keep both the model and events encrypted, H-Verifier does not require any TCB to be constructed on the computational nodes. Only a limited number of HE operations are needed to track the status of an online system. H-Verifier does not rely on any special hardware and thus can be widely deployed in a variety of environment. The evaluation demonstrates that H-Verifier can achieve reasonable performance overhead for model initialization, updating, and verification for an online system in the cloud.

Acknowledgment. This work is partially supported by the National Science Foundation under awards Grants No. DGE-1723707 and the Michigan Space Grant Consortium. Any opinions, findings, and conclusions or recommendations expressed in this material are those of the authors and do not necessarily reflect the views of the funding agencies. We also thank Aditi Patil for the preliminary implementation.

References

1. Darwish, M., Ouda, A., Capretz, L.: Cloud-based DDoS attacks and defenses. In: Proceedings of 2013 International Conference on Information Society, pp. 67–71 (2013)
2. Ciancaglini, V., Balduzzi, M., McArdle, R., Rösler, M.: Below the surface: exploring the deep web (2015). https://www.trendmicro.com/cloud-content/us/pdfs/security-intelligence/white-papers/wp_below_the_surface.pdf
3. Symantec: Avoiding the hidden costs of the cloud. https://www.symantec.com/content/en/us/about/media/pdfs/b-state-of-cloud-global-results-2013.en-us.pdf
4. Samani, R., Paget, F.: Cybercrime exposed: cybercrime-as-a-servic (2013). http://www.mcafee.com/jp/resources/white-papers/wp-cybercrime-exposed.pdf
5. Goodin, D.: Zeusbot found using Amazon's EC2 as C&C server. http://www.theregister.co.uk/2009/12/09/amazon_ec2_bot_control_channel/
6. Ryan, M.D.: Cloud computing security: the scientific challenge, and a survey of solutions. J. Syst. Softw. **86**(9), 2263–2268 (2013)
7. Alliance, C.S.: CSA security, trust & assurance registry (STAR). https://cloudsecurityalliance.org/star/#_overview
8. Santos, N., Rodrigues, R., Gummadi, K.P., Saroiu, S.: Policy-sealed data: a new abstraction for building trusted cloud services. In: Proceedings of 21st USENIX Security Symposium, pp. 175–188 (2012)
9. Sirer, E.G., et al.: Logical attestation: an authorization architecture for trustworthy computing. In: Proceedings of 23rd ACM Symposium on Operating Systems Principles, pp. 249–264 (2011)
10. Butt, S., Lagar-Cavilla, H.A., Srivastava, A., Ganapathy, V.: Self-service cloud computing. In: Proceedings of 2012 ACM Conference on Computer and Communications Security, pp. 253–264 (2012)
11. Zhang, F., Chen, J., Chen, H., Zang, B.: Cloudvisor: retrofitting protection of virtual machines in multi-tenant cloud with nested virtualization. In: Proceedings of 23rd ACM Symposium on Operating Systems Principles, pp. 203–216 (2011)
12. Ko, R.K., et al.: TrustCloud: a framework for accountability and trust in cloud computing. In: Proceedings of 2011 IEEE World Congress on Services, pp. 584–588 (2011)
13. Intel: Intel. 64 and IA-32 architectures software developer's manual. Technical report. http://www.intel.com/content/www/us/en/processors/architectures-software-developer-manuals.html

14. Intel Corporation: Intel trusted execution technology: software development guide. Technical report. http://download.intel.com/technology/security/downloads/3151 68.pdf
15. McKeen, F., et al.: Intel software guard extensions support for dynamic memory management inside an enclave. In: Proceedings of Hardware and Architectural Support for Security and Privacy, pp. 101–109 (2016)
16. Hay, B., Nance, K.: Forensics examination of volatile system data using virtual introspection. ACM SIGOPS Oper. Syst. Rev. **42**(3), 74–82 (2008)
17. Fu, Y., Lin, Z.: Space traveling across VM: automatically bridging the semantic gap in virtual machine introspection via online kernel data redirection. In: 2012 IEEE Symposium on Security and Privacy, pp. 586–600, May 2012
18. Garfinkel, T., Rosenblum, M.: A virtual machine introspection based architecture for intrusion detection. In: Proceedings of Network and Distributed Systems Security Symposium, pp. 191–206 (2003)
19. Fu, Y., Lin, Z.: Bridging the semantic gap in virtual machine introspection via online kernel data redirection. ACM Trans. Inf. Syst. Secur. **16**(2), 7:1–7:29 (2013). https://doi.org/10.1145/2505124
20. Gentry, C.: Fully homomorphic encryption using ideal lattices. In: Proceedings of the Forty-first Annual ACM Symposium on Theory of Computing, STOC 2009, pp. 169–178. ACM, New York (2009). https://doi.org/10.1145/1536414.1536440
21. Hirt, M., Sako, K.: Efficient receipt-free voting based on homomorphic encryption. In: Preneel, B. (ed.) EUROCRYPT 2000. LNCS, vol. 1807, pp. 539–556. Springer, Heidelberg (2000). https://doi.org/10.1007/3-540-45539-6_38
22. Li, F., Luo, B., Liu, P.: Secure information aggregation for smart grids using homomorphic encryption. In: 2010 First IEEE International Conference on Smart Grid Communications, pp. 327–332 (2010)
23. Hong, Y., Vaidya, J., Lu, H., Karras, P., Goel, S.: Collaborative search log sanitization: toward differential privacy and boosted utility. IEEE Trans. Dependable Secur. Comput. **12**(5), 504–518 (2015). https://doi.org/10.1109/TDSC.2014. 2369034
24. Brakerski, Z., Vaikuntanathan, V.: Efficient fully homomorphic encryption from (standard) LWE. In: Proceedings of the 2011 IEEE 52nd Annual Symposium on Foundations of Computer Science, FOCS 2011, Washington, DC, USA, pp. 97–106. IEEE Computer Society (2011). https://doi.org/10.1109/FOCS.2011.12
25. Zhang, Y., Juels, A., Reiter, M.K., Ristenpart, T.: Cross-VM side channels and their use to extract private keys. In: Proceedings of 2012 ACM conference on Computer and communications security, pp. 305–316. ACM, New York (2012)
26. Yarom, Y., Falkner, K.: Flush+reload: a high resolution, low noise, L3 cache side-channel attack. In: 23rd USENIX Security Symposium (USENIX Security 14), San Diego, CA, pp. 719–732. USENIX Association (2014). https://www.usenix. org/conference/usenixsecurity14/technical-sessions/presentation/yarom
27. Lee, S., Shih, M.-W., Gera, P., Kim, T., Kim, H., Peinado, M.: Inferring fine-grained control flow inside SGX enclaves with branch shadowing. In: 26th USENIX Security Symposium (USENIX Security 17), Vancouver, BC, pp. 557–574. USENIX Association (2017). https://www.usenix.org/conference/ usenixsecurity17/technical-sessions/presentation/lee-sangho
28. Brasser, F., Müller, U., Dmitrienko, A., Kostiainen, K., Capkun, S., Sadeghi, A.-R.: Software grand exposure: SGX cache attacks are practical. In: 11th USENIX Workshop on Offensive Technologies (WOOT 17), Vancouver, BC. USENIX Association (2017). https://www.usenix.org/conference/woot17/workshop-program/ presentation/brasser

29. Guanciale, R., Nemati, H., Baumann, C., Dam, M.: Cache storage channels: Alias-driven attacks and verified countermeasures. In: 2016 IEEE Symposium on Security and Privacy (SP), pp. 38–55, May 2016. https://doi.org/10.1109/SP.2016.11
30. Dean, D., Hu, A.J.: Fixing races for fun and profit: how to use access(2). In: Proceedings of 13th USENIX Security Symposium, p. 14 (2004)
31. Schwarz, M., Weiser, S., Gruss, D., Maurice, C., Mangard, S.: Malware guard extension: using SGX to conceal cache attacks. CoRR, vol. abs/1702.08719 (2017)
32. Dua, G., Gautam, N., Sharma, D., Arora, A.: Replay attack prevention in Kerberos authentication protocol using triple password. CoRR, vol. abs/1304.3550 (2013)
33. Boldyreva, A., Chenette, N., Lee, Y., O'Neill, A.: Order-preserving symmetric encryption. In: Joux, A. (ed.) EUROCRYPT 2009. LNCS, vol. 5479, pp. 224–241. Springer, Heidelberg (2009). https://doi.org/10.1007/978-3-642-01001-9_13
34. Lee, D., Yannakakis, M.: Principles and methods of testing finite state machines-a survey. Proc. IEEE **84**(8), 1090–1123 (1996)
35. Bhatkar, S., Chaturvedi, A., Sekar, R.: Dataflow anomaly detection. In: 2006 IEEE Symposium on Security and Privacy (S&P 2006), 21–24 May 2006, Berkeley, California, USA, pp. 48–62 (2006). https://doi.org/10.1109/SP.2006.12
36. HElib: the library that implements homomorphic encryption (HE). https://github.com/shaih/HElib
37. Gentry, C.: A fully homomorphic encryption scheme. Ph.D. dissertation, Stanford, CA, USA, AAI3382729 (2009)

Multi-party Quantum Key Agreement Against Collective Noise

Xiang-Qian Liang, Sha-Sha Wang, Yong-Hua Zhang, and Guang-Bao Xu[✉]

Shandong University of Science and Technology, Qingdao, Shandong 266590, China
{xiangqian.liang,xu_guangbao}@163.com

Abstract. In this paper, two multi-party quantum key agreement protocols are proposed with logical W states which can resist the collective-dephasing noise and the collective-rotation noise. By using the decoy logical photons method and the delayed measurement, the security and fairness of the protocols are guaranteed. By using the dense coding method and block transmission technique, the efficiency of the two protocols can be improved. The efficiency analysis indicates that the proposed two quantum key agreement (QKA) protocols are efficient by comparing with other multi-party QKA protocols.

Keywords: Quantum key agreement · Logical W state
Collective-dephasing noise · Collective-rotation noise

1 Introduction

In view of fundamental principles of quantum mechanics, the security of quantum cryptography is guaranteed. Since the first quantum key distribution (QKD) protocol was put forward by Bennett and Brassard in 1984 [1], quantum cryptography has got swift and violent development. In 2000, Shor et al. [2] proved the security of BB84. Then, different types of quantum cryptographic protocols have been put forward, including quantum key distribution [3–6], quantum secure direct communication [7–9], quantum signature [10–13], quantum key agreement [14–28] and so on.

Quantum key agreement (QKA) permits two or more participants to generate the final shared key, and no one can decide the final generated key alone. In 2004, based on quantum teleportation, the first QKA protocol was put forward by Zhou et al. [14]. However, Tsai et al. [15] pointed out that Zhou et al.'s protocol could not resist the dishonest participant attack. Later, Hsueh et al. [16] designed a QKA protocol which was not safe in resisting a controlled-Not attack. Based on BB84, Chong and Hwang [17] put forward a QKA protocol that permitted two parties to consult the final shared key. The protocol was fair by analyzing. Based on maximally entangled states and Bell states, Chong et al. [18]

Supported by the National Natural Science Foundation of China (61402265) and the Fund for Postdoctoral Application Research Project of Qingdao (01020120607).

F. Liu et al. (Eds.): SciSec 2018, LNCS 11287, pp. 141–155, 2018.
https://doi.org/10.1007/978-3-030-03026-1_10

designed a QKA protocol. But these QKA protocols [14–18] only involved two participants. Next, let's pay attention to multi-party QKA (MQKA) protocols. In 2013, based on entanglement swapping, Shi and Zhong [19] proposed the first MQKA protocol. Afterwards, many MQKA protocols [24–27] were put forward and the their security were proved. The MQKA protocols [24–27] are mainly based upon Bell states or single particles. Recently, some MQKA protocols were put forward based on GHZ-states and four-qubit cluster states, including Xu et al.'s protocol [25] and Sun et al.'s protocol [28]. Obviously, the above MQKA protocols were proposed based on an environment without noise. However, because of the defect of channel, channel noise inevitably is produced when the particles are transferred. In order to avoid being detected, an eavesdropper may try to camouflage his attacks with noise in a quantum noise channel. So it is important to reduce the effect of noise when designing a QKA protocol. Later, the methods of resisting collective noise were proposed: quantum error-correcting codes [29], quantum error rejection [30–32], decoherence-free space [33], entanglement purification [34] and so on. In 2003, the decoherence-free subspace (DFS) [33] was proposed which could resist the collective noise because the qubits of the DFS were changeless toward the collective noise. In 2014, Huang et al. [23] first introduced two corresponding variables on the collective-noise channels. At the same time, Huang et al. [35] put forward a QKA protocol which was immune to collective decoherence by utilizing decoherence-free states. On account of the fact that a few the QKA protocols against collective noise were proposed, we consider designing new multi-party QKA protocols against the collective noise.

In this paper, we propose two multi-party quantum key agreement protocols against collective noise. The final common key is generated by all participants which obtain the final shared key simultaneously. The outsider eavesdropper and dishonest participants cannot obtain the shared key without introducing any error.

The rest of the paper is organized as follows. In Sect. 2, we introduce the preliminaries: quantum states, unitary operations, entangled states, the collective noises and the logical W states. In Sect. 3, we give the QKA protocols against collective noise. In Sect. 4, the security analysis is given. In Sect. 5, efficiency analysis is discussed. Section 6, a short conclusion is given.

2   Preliminaries

2.1   Quantum States, Unitary Operations and Entangled States

First, we present the four quantum states: $|0\rangle$, $|1\rangle$, $|+\rangle$, $|-\rangle$. Where $|+\rangle = \frac{1}{\sqrt{2}}(|0\rangle + |1\rangle)$, $|-\rangle = \frac{1}{\sqrt{2}}(|0\rangle - |1\rangle)$. We can describe the four quantum states in the form of vectors:

$$|0\rangle = \begin{pmatrix} 1 \\ 0 \end{pmatrix}, |1\rangle = \begin{pmatrix} 0 \\ 1 \end{pmatrix}, |+\rangle = \frac{1}{\sqrt{2}}\begin{pmatrix} 1 \\ 1 \end{pmatrix}, |-\rangle = \frac{1}{\sqrt{2}}\begin{pmatrix} 1 \\ -1 \end{pmatrix}.$$

Second, we introduce the four unitary operations:

$$\sigma^0 = I = |0\rangle\langle 0| + |1\rangle\langle 1|,$$
$$\sigma^1 = X = |0\rangle\langle 1| + |1\rangle\langle 0|,$$
$$\sigma^2 = Z = |0\rangle\langle 0| - |1\rangle\langle 1|,$$
$$\sigma^3 = iY = |0\rangle\langle 1| - |1\rangle\langle 0|.$$

Third, the four-qubit symmetric W states are denoted as [36]:

$$|\varphi_1\rangle_{abcd} = \frac{1}{2}(|0001\rangle + |0010\rangle + |0100\rangle + |1000\rangle)_{abcd},$$
$$|\varphi_2\rangle_{abcd} = \frac{1}{2}(|0000\rangle - |0011\rangle - |0101\rangle - |1001\rangle)_{abcd},$$
$$|\varphi_3\rangle_{abcd} = \frac{1}{2}(|0011\rangle + |0000\rangle + |0110\rangle + |1010\rangle)_{abcd},$$
$$|\varphi_4\rangle_{abcd} = \frac{1}{2}(|0010\rangle - |0001\rangle - |0111\rangle - |1011\rangle)_{abcd}.$$

where the subscripts a, b, c, d represent the first, the second, the third and the fourth particle of the W state respectively.

Table 1. Shows the relationship of the unitary operations and the transformed states on the qubit c and qubit d of cluster state $|\varphi_t\rangle_{abcd}(t = 1, 2, 3, 4)$

Initial state	Unitary operation	Final state	Agreement key
$|\varphi_1\rangle_{abcd}$	$\sigma^0\sigma^0$	$|\varphi_1\rangle_{abcd}$	00
	$\sigma^0\sigma^3$	$|\varphi_2\rangle_{abcd}$	01
	$\sigma^1\sigma^0$	$|\varphi_3\rangle_{abcd}$	10
	$\sigma^1\sigma^3$	$|\varphi_4\rangle_{abcd}$	11
$|\varphi_2\rangle_{abcd}$	$\sigma^0\sigma^0$	$|\varphi_2\rangle_{abcd}$	00
	$\sigma^0\sigma^3$	$|\varphi_1\rangle_{abcd}$	01
	$\sigma^1\sigma^0$	$|\varphi_4\rangle_{abcd}$	10
	$\sigma^1\sigma^3$	$|\varphi_3\rangle_{abcd}$	11
$|\varphi_3\rangle_{abcd}$	$\sigma^0\sigma^0$	$|\varphi_3\rangle_{abcd}$	00
	$\sigma^0\sigma^3$	$|\varphi_4\rangle_{abcd}$	01
	$\sigma^1\sigma^0$	$|\varphi_1\rangle_{abcd}$	10
	$\sigma^1\sigma^3$	$|\varphi_2\rangle_{abcd}$	11
$|\varphi_4\rangle_{abcd}$	$\sigma^0\sigma^0$	$|\varphi_4\rangle_{abcd}$	00
	$\sigma^0\sigma^3$	$|\varphi_3\rangle_{abcd}$	01
	$\sigma^1\sigma^0$	$|\varphi_2\rangle_{abcd}$	10
	$\sigma^1\sigma^3$	$|\varphi_1\rangle_{abcd}$	11

2.2 The Collective Noises

The collective noises are one kind of the topical noises in quantum key agreement. There are two kinds of collective noises: the collective-dephasing noise and the collective-rotation noise. First, collective-dephasing noise can be denoted as [37]:

$$U_{dp}|0\rangle = |0\rangle, U_{dp}|1\rangle = e^{i\varphi}|1\rangle.$$

where φ is the noise parameter and it fluctuates with time. Generally, the two logical qubits $|0_{dp}\rangle$ and $|1_{dp}\rangle$ are encoded into two physical qubit tensor product states $|01\rangle$ and $|10\rangle$, respectively. They are immune to collective-dephasing noise.

$$|0_{dp}\rangle = |01\rangle, |1_{dp}\rangle = |10\rangle.$$

Second, collective-rotation noise can be denoted as:

$$U_r|0\rangle = \cos\theta|0\rangle + \sin\theta|1\rangle, U_r|1\rangle = -\sin\theta|0\rangle + \cos\theta|1\rangle.$$

The parameter θ is the noise parameter and it fluctuates with time in the quantum channel. The two logical qubits $|0_r\rangle$ and $|1_r\rangle$ are encoded into two physical qubit tensor product states $|\Phi^+\rangle$ and $|\Psi^-\rangle$, respectively. And they are immune to collective-rotation noise.

$$|0_r\rangle = |\Phi^+\rangle = \frac{1}{\sqrt{2}}(|00\rangle + |11\rangle), |1_r\rangle = |\Psi^-\rangle = \frac{1}{\sqrt{2}}(|01\rangle - |10\rangle).$$

2.3 The Logical W States

In this two protocols, P_i only transmits particles c and d more than once. In order to avoid collective-dephasing noise, it is necessary to transform particles c and d into logical qubits c and d. The logical W states can be denoted:

$$
\begin{aligned}
|\varphi_{1dp}\rangle_{abcd} &= \frac{1}{2}(|0\rangle_a|0\rangle_b|0_{dp}\rangle_c|1_{dp}\rangle_d + |0\rangle_a|0\rangle_b|1_{dp}\rangle_c|0_{dp}\rangle_d \\
&+ |0\rangle_a|1\rangle_b|0_{dp}\rangle_c|0_{dp}\rangle_d + |1\rangle_a|0\rangle_b|0_{dp}\rangle_c|0_{dp}\rangle_d) \\
&= \frac{1}{2}(|00\rangle_{ab}|0\rangle_{c1,i}|1\rangle_{d1,i} \otimes |10\rangle_{c2,i d2,i} + |00\rangle_{ab}|1\rangle_{c1,i}|0\rangle_{d1,i} \otimes |01\rangle_{c2,i d2,i} \\
&+ |01\rangle_{ab}|0\rangle_{c1,i}|0\rangle_{d1,i} \otimes |11\rangle_{c2,i d2,i} + |10\rangle_{ab}|0\rangle_{c1,i}|0\rangle_{d1,i} \otimes |11\rangle_{c2,i d2,i}), \\
|\varphi_{2dp}\rangle_{abcd} &= \frac{1}{2}(|0\rangle_a|0\rangle_b|0_{dp}\rangle_c|0_{dp}\rangle_d - |0\rangle_a|0\rangle_b|1_{dp}\rangle_c|1_{dp}\rangle_d \\
&- |0\rangle_a|1\rangle_b|0_{dp}\rangle_c|1_{dp}\rangle_d - |1\rangle_a|0\rangle_b|0_{dp}\rangle_c|1_{dp}\rangle_d) \\
&= \frac{1}{2}(|00\rangle_{ab}|0\rangle_{c1,i}|0\rangle_{d1,i} \otimes |11\rangle_{c2,i d2,i} - |00\rangle_{ab}|1\rangle_{c1,i}|1\rangle_{d1,i} \otimes |00\rangle_{c2,i d2,i} \\
&- |01\rangle_{ab}|0\rangle_{c1,i}|1\rangle_{d1,i} \otimes |10\rangle_{c2,i d2,i} - |10\rangle_{ab}|0\rangle_{c1,i}|1\rangle_{d1,i} \otimes |10\rangle_{c2,i d2,i}), \\
|\varphi_{3dp}\rangle_{abcd} &= \frac{1}{2}(|0\rangle_a|0\rangle_b|1_{dp}\rangle_c|1_{dp}\rangle_d + |0\rangle_a|0\rangle_b|0_{dp}\rangle_c|0_{dp}\rangle_d \\
&+ |0\rangle_a|1\rangle_b|1_{dp}\rangle_c|0_{dp}\rangle_d + |1\rangle_a|0\rangle_b|1_{dp}\rangle_c|0_{dp}\rangle_d) \\
&= \frac{1}{2}(|00\rangle_{ab}|1\rangle_{c1,i}|1\rangle_{d1,i} \otimes |00\rangle_{c2,i d2,i} + |00\rangle_{ab}|0\rangle_{c1,i}|0\rangle_{d1,i} \otimes |11\rangle_{c2,i d2,i} \\
&+ |01\rangle_{ab}|1\rangle_{c1,i}|0\rangle_{d1,i} \otimes |01\rangle_{c2,i d2,i} + |10\rangle_{ab}|1\rangle_{c1,i}|0\rangle_{d1,i} \otimes |01\rangle_{c2,i d2,i}),
\end{aligned}
$$

$$|\varphi_{4dp}\rangle_{abcd} = \frac{1}{2}(|0\rangle_a|0\rangle_b|1_{dp}\rangle_c|0_{dp}\rangle_d - |0\rangle_a|0\rangle_b|0_{dp}\rangle_c|1_{dp}\rangle_d$$
$$- |0\rangle_a|1\rangle_b|1_{dp}\rangle_c|1_{dp}\rangle_d - |1\rangle_a|0\rangle_b|1_{dp}\rangle_c|1_{dp}\rangle_d)$$
$$= \frac{1}{2}(|00\rangle_{ab}|1\rangle_{c_{1,i}}|0\rangle_{d_{1,i}} \otimes |01\rangle_{c_{2,i}d_{2,i}} - |00\rangle_{ab}|0\rangle_{c_{1,i}}|1\rangle_{d_{1,i}} \otimes |10\rangle_{c_{2,i}d_{2,i}}$$
$$- |01\rangle_{ab}|1\rangle_{c_{1,i}}|1\rangle_{d_{1,i}} \otimes |00\rangle_{c_{2,i}d_{2,i}} - |10\rangle_{ab}|1\rangle_{c_{1,i}}|1\rangle_{d_{1,i}} \otimes |00\rangle_{c_{2,i}d_{2,i}}).$$

Then, participants $P_{i+1}, \ldots, P_{i-1}$ can transform particles $c_{1,i}, d_{1,i}, \ldots,$ $c_{1,i-2}, d_{1,i-2}$ into logical qubits $c_{1,i}, d_{1,i}, \ldots, c_{1,i-2}, d_{1,i-2}$. Meanwhile, the particles $c_{2,i}, d_{2,i}, \ldots, c_{2,i-2}, d_{2,i-2}$ are abandoned. We can conclude the states which are prepared by P_{i-1} as follows:

$$|\varphi_{1dp}\rangle_{abc_{1,i-2}d_{1,i-2}} = \frac{1}{2}(|00\rangle_{ab}|0\rangle_{c_{1,i-1}}|1\rangle_{d_{1,i-1}} \otimes |10\rangle_{c_{2,i-1}d_{2,i-1}} + |00\rangle_{ab}|1\rangle_{c_{1,i-1}}$$
$$|0\rangle_{d_{1,i-1}} \otimes |01\rangle_{c_{2,i-1}d_{2,i-1}} + |01\rangle_{ab}|0\rangle_{c_{1,i-1}}|0\rangle_{d_{1,i-1}}$$
$$\otimes |11\rangle_{c_{2,i-1}d_{2,i-1}} + |10\rangle_{ab}|0\rangle_{c_{1,i-1}}|0\rangle_{d_{1,i-1}} \otimes |11\rangle_{c_{2,i-1}d_{2,i-1}}),$$

$$|\varphi_{2dp}\rangle_{abc_{1,i-2}d_{1,i-2}} = \frac{1}{2}(|00\rangle_{ab}|0\rangle_{c_{1,i-1}}|0\rangle_{d_{1,i-1}} \otimes |11\rangle_{c_{2,i-1}d_{2,i-1}} - |00\rangle_{ab}|1\rangle_{c_{1,i-1}}$$
$$|1\rangle_{d_{1,i-1}} \otimes |00\rangle_{c_{2,i-1}d_{2,i-1}} - |01\rangle_{ab}|0\rangle_{c_{1,i-1}}|1\rangle_{d_{1,i-1}}$$
$$\otimes |10\rangle_{c_{2,i-1}d_{2,i-1}} - |10\rangle_{ab}|0\rangle_{c_{1,i-1}}|1\rangle_{d_{1,i-1}} \otimes |10\rangle_{c_{2,i-1}d_{2,i-1}}),$$

$$|\varphi_{3dp}\rangle_{abc_{1,i-2}d_{1,i-2}} = \frac{1}{2}(|00\rangle_{ab}|1\rangle_{c_{1,i-1}}|1\rangle_{d_{1,i-1}} \otimes |00\rangle_{c_{2,i-1}d_{2,i-1}} + |00\rangle_{ab}|0\rangle_{c_{1,i-1}}$$
$$|0\rangle_{d_{1,i-1}} \otimes |11\rangle_{c_{2,i-1}d_{2,i-1}} + |01\rangle_{ab}|1\rangle_{c_{1,i-1}}|0\rangle_{d_{1,i-1}}$$
$$\otimes |01\rangle_{c_{2,i-1}d_{2,i-1}} + |10\rangle_{ab}|1\rangle_{c_{1,i-1}}|0\rangle_{d_{1,i-1}} \otimes |01\rangle_{c_{2,i-1}d_{2,i-1}}),$$

$$|\varphi_{4dp}\rangle_{abc_{1,i-2}d_{1,i-2}} = \frac{1}{2}(|00\rangle_{ab}|1\rangle_{c_{1,i-1}}|0\rangle_{d_{1,i-1}} \otimes |01\rangle_{c_{2,i-1}d_{2,i-1}} - |00\rangle_{ab}|0\rangle_{c_{1,i-1}}$$
$$|1\rangle_{d_{1,i-1}} \otimes |10\rangle_{c_{2,i-1}d_{2,i-1}} - |01\rangle_{ab}|1\rangle_{c_{1,i-1}}|1\rangle_{d_{1,i-1}}$$
$$\otimes |00\rangle_{c_{2,i-1}d_{2,i-1}} - |10\rangle_{ab}|1\rangle_{c_{1,i-1}}|1\rangle_{d_{1,i-1}} \otimes |00\rangle_{c_{2,i-1}d_{2,i-1}}).$$

Then, in order to collective-rotation noise, it is necessary to transform particles c and d into logical qubits c and d. And the logical W states can be denoted:

$$|\varphi_{1r}\rangle_{abcd} = \frac{1}{2}(|0\rangle_a|0\rangle_b|0_r\rangle_c|1_r\rangle_d + |0\rangle_a|0\rangle_b|1_r\rangle_c|0_r\rangle_d$$
$$+ |0\rangle_a|1\rangle_b|0_r\rangle_c|0_r\rangle_d + |1\rangle_a|0\rangle_b|0_r\rangle_c|0_r\rangle_d)$$
$$= \frac{1}{4}(|00\rangle_{ab}(|00\rangle + |11\rangle)_{c_{1,i}c_{2,i}}(|01\rangle - |10\rangle)_{d_{1,i}d_{2,i}}$$
$$+ |00\rangle_{ab}(|01\rangle - |10\rangle)_{c_{1,i}c_{2,i}}(|00\rangle + |11\rangle)_{d_{1,i}d_{2,i}}$$
$$+ |01\rangle_{ab}(|00\rangle + |11\rangle)_{c_{1,i}c_{2,i}}(|00\rangle + |11\rangle)_{d_{1,i}d_{2,i}}$$
$$+ |10\rangle_{ab}(|00\rangle + |11\rangle)_{c_{1,i}c_{2,i}}(|00\rangle + |11\rangle)_{d_{1,i}d_{2,i}}),$$

$$|\varphi_{2r}\rangle_{abcd} = \frac{1}{2}(|0\rangle_a|0\rangle_b|0_r\rangle_c|0_r\rangle_d - |0\rangle_a|0\rangle_b|1_r\rangle_c|1_r\rangle_d$$
$$- |0\rangle_a|1\rangle_b|0_r\rangle_c|1_r\rangle_d - |1\rangle_a|0\rangle_b|0_r\rangle_c|1_r\rangle_d)$$
$$= \frac{1}{4}(|00\rangle_{ab}(|00\rangle + |11\rangle)_{c_{1,i},c_{2,i}}(|00\rangle + |11\rangle)_{d_{1,i}d_{2,i}}$$

$$- |00\rangle_{ab}(|01\rangle - |10\rangle)_{c_{1,i}c_{2,i}}(|01\rangle - |10\rangle)_{d_{1,i}d_{2,i}}$$
$$- |01\rangle_{ab}(|00\rangle + |11\rangle)_{c_{1,i}c_{2,i}}(|01\rangle - |10\rangle)_{d_{1,i}d_{2,i}}$$
$$- |10\rangle_{ab}(|00\rangle + |11\rangle)_{c_{1,i}c_{2,i}}(|01\rangle - |10\rangle)_{d_{1,i}d_{2,i}}),$$

$$|\varphi_{3r}\rangle_{abcd} = \frac{1}{2}(|0\rangle_a|0\rangle_b|1_r\rangle_c|1_r\rangle_d + |0\rangle_a|0\rangle_b|0_r\rangle_c|0_r\rangle_d$$
$$+ |0\rangle_a|1\rangle_b|1_r\rangle_c|0_r\rangle_d + |1\rangle_a|0\rangle_b|1_r\rangle_c|0_r\rangle_d)$$
$$= \frac{1}{4}(|00\rangle_{ab}(|01\rangle - |10\rangle)_{c_{1,i}c_{2,i}}(|01\rangle - |10\rangle)_{d_{1,i}d_{2,i}}$$
$$+ |00\rangle_{ab}(|00\rangle + |11\rangle)_{c_{1,i}c_{2,i}}(|00\rangle + |11\rangle)_{d_{1,i}d_{2,i}}$$
$$+ |01\rangle_{ab}(|01\rangle - |10\rangle)_{c_{1,i}c_{2,i}}(|00\rangle + |11\rangle)_{d_{1,i}d_{2,i}}$$
$$+ |10\rangle_{ab}(|01\rangle - |10\rangle)_{c_{1,i}c_{2,i}}(|00\rangle + |11\rangle)_{d_{1,i}d_{2,i}}),$$

$$|\varphi_{4r}\rangle_{abcd} = \frac{1}{2}(|0\rangle_a|0\rangle_b|1_r\rangle_c|0_r\rangle_d - |0\rangle_a|0\rangle_b|0_r\rangle_c|1_r\rangle_d$$
$$- |0\rangle_a|1\rangle_b|1_r\rangle_c|1_r\rangle_d - |1\rangle_a|0\rangle_b|1_r\rangle_c|1_r\rangle_d)$$
$$= \frac{1}{4}(|00\rangle_{ab}(|01\rangle - |10\rangle)_{c_{1,i},c_{2,i}}(|00\rangle + |11\rangle)_{d_{1,i},d_{2,i}}$$
$$- |00\rangle_{ab}(|00\rangle + |11\rangle)_{c_{1,i}c_{2,i}}(|01\rangle - |10\rangle)_{d_{1,i}d_{2,i}}$$
$$- |01\rangle_{ab}(|01\rangle - |10\rangle)_{c_{1,i}c_{2,i}}(|01\rangle - |10\rangle)_{d_{1,i}d_{2,i}}$$
$$- |10\rangle_{ab}(|01\rangle - |10\rangle)_{c_{1,i}c_{2,i}}(|01\rangle - |10\rangle)_{d_{1,i}d_{2,i}}).$$

Next, P_i performs two CNOT operations on $|\varphi_{tr}\rangle_{abcd}(t = 1, 2, 3, 4)$ states by using $c_{1,i}$, $d_{1,i}$ as the control qubits and the $c_{2,i}$, $d_{2,i}$ as the target qubits, respectively. Afterwards, the logical states can be denoted as:

$$|\varphi_{1r}^{(1)}\rangle_{abcd} = U_{CNOT}^{c_{1,i},c_{2,i}} \otimes U_{CNOT}^{d_{1,i},d_{2,i}} \otimes |\varphi_{1r}\rangle_{abcd}$$
$$= \frac{1}{4}(|00\rangle_{ab}(|0\rangle + |1\rangle)_{c_{1,i}}(|0\rangle - |1\rangle)_{d_{1,i}} \otimes |01\rangle_{c_{2,i}d_{2,i}}$$
$$+ |00\rangle_{ab}(|0\rangle - |1\rangle)_{c_{1,i}}(|0\rangle + |1\rangle)_{d_{1,i}} \otimes |10\rangle_{c_{2,i}d_{2,i}}$$
$$+ |01\rangle_{ab}(|0\rangle + |1\rangle)_{c_{1,i}}(|0\rangle + |1\rangle)_{d_{1,i}} \otimes |00\rangle_{c_{2,i}d_{2,i}}$$
$$+ |10\rangle_{ab}(|0\rangle + |1\rangle)_{c_{1,i}}(|0\rangle + |1\rangle)_{d_{1,i}} \otimes |00\rangle_{c_{2,i}d_{2,i}}),$$

$$|\varphi_{2r}^{(1)}\rangle_{abcd} = U_{CNOT}^{c_{1,i},c_{2,i}} \otimes U_{CNOT}^{d_{1,i},d_{2,i}} \otimes |\varphi_{2r}\rangle_{abcd}$$
$$= \frac{1}{4}(|00\rangle_{ab}(|0\rangle + |1\rangle)_{c_{1,i}}(|0\rangle + |1\rangle)_{d_{1,i}} \otimes |00\rangle_{c_{2,i}d_{2,i}}$$
$$- |00\rangle_{ab}(|0\rangle - |1\rangle)_{c_{1,i}}(|0\rangle - |1\rangle)_{d_{1,i}} \otimes |11\rangle_{c_{2,i}d_{2,i}}$$
$$- |01\rangle_{ab}(|0\rangle + |1\rangle)_{c_{1,i}}(|0\rangle - |1\rangle)_{d_{1,i}} \otimes |01\rangle_{c_{2,i}d_{2,i}}$$
$$- |10\rangle_{ab}(|0\rangle + |1\rangle)_{c_{1,i}}(|0\rangle - |1\rangle)_{d_{1,i}} \otimes |01\rangle_{c_{2,i}d_{2,i}}),$$

$$|\varphi_{3r}^{(1)}\rangle_{abcd} = U_{CNOT}^{c_{1,i},c_{2,i}} \otimes U_{CNOT}^{d_{1,i},d_{2,i}} \otimes |\varphi_{3r}\rangle_{abcd}$$
$$= \frac{1}{4}(|00\rangle_{ab}(|0\rangle - |1\rangle)_{c_{1,i}}(|0\rangle - |1\rangle)_{d_{1,i}} \otimes |11\rangle_{c_{2,i}d_{2,i}}$$
$$+ |00\rangle_{ab}(|0\rangle + |1\rangle)_{c_{1,i}}(|0\rangle + |1\rangle)_{d_{1,i}} \otimes |00\rangle_{c_{2,i}d_{2,i}}$$

$$+ |01\rangle_{ab}(|0\rangle - |1\rangle)_{c_{1,i}}(|0\rangle + |1\rangle)_{d_{1,i}} \otimes |10\rangle_{c_{2,i}d_{2,i}}$$
$$+ |10\rangle_{ab}(|0\rangle - |1\rangle)_{c_{1,i}}(|0\rangle + |1\rangle)_{d_{1,i}} \otimes |10\rangle_{c_{2,i}d_{2,i}}),$$

$$|\varphi_{4r}^{(1)}\rangle_{abcd} = U_{CNOT}^{c_{1,i},c_{2,i}} \otimes U_{CNOT}^{d_{1,i},d_{2,i}} \otimes |\varphi_{4r}\rangle_{abcd}$$
$$= \frac{1}{4}(|00\rangle_{ab}(|0\rangle - |1\rangle)_{c_{1,i}}(|0\rangle + |1\rangle)_{d_{1,i}} \otimes |10\rangle_{c_{2,i}d_{2,i}}$$
$$- |00\rangle_{ab}(|0\rangle + |1\rangle)_{c_{1,i}}(|0\rangle - |1\rangle)_{d_{1,i}} \otimes |01\rangle_{c_{2,i}d_{2,i}}$$
$$- |01\rangle_{ab}(|0\rangle - |1\rangle)_{c_{1,i}}(|0\rangle - |1\rangle)_{d_{1,i}} \otimes |11\rangle_{c_{2,i}d_{2,i}}$$
$$- |10\rangle_{ab}(|0\rangle - |1\rangle)_{c_{1,i}}(|0\rangle - |1\rangle)_{d_{1,i}} \otimes |11\rangle_{c_{2,i}d_{2,i}}).$$

Later, P_i performs Hadamard gates on particles $c_{1,i}$ and $d_{1,i}$ of $|\varphi_{tr}^{(1)}\rangle_{abcd}$. The corresponding quantum states as follows:

$$|\varphi_{1r}^{(2)}\rangle_{abcd} = H_{c_{1,i}} \otimes H_{d_{1,i}} \otimes |\varphi_{1r}^{(1)}\rangle_{abcd}$$
$$= \frac{1}{2}(|00\rangle_{ab}|0\rangle_{c_{1,i}}|1\rangle_{d_{1,i}} \otimes |01\rangle_{c_{2,i}d_{2,i}} + |00\rangle_{ab}|1\rangle_{c_{1,i}}|0\rangle_{d_{1,i}} \otimes |10\rangle_{c_{2,i}d_{2,i}}$$
$$+ |01\rangle_{ab}|0\rangle_{c_{1,i}}|0\rangle_{d_{1,i}} \otimes |00\rangle_{c_{2,i}d_{2,i}} + |10\rangle_{ab}|0\rangle_{c_{1,i}}|0\rangle_{d_{1,i}} \otimes |00\rangle_{c_{2,i}d_{2,i}}),$$

$$|\varphi_{2r}^{(2)}\rangle_{abcd} = H_{c_{1,i}} \otimes H_{d_{1,i}} \otimes |\varphi_{2r}^{(1)}\rangle_{abcd}$$
$$= \frac{1}{2}(|00\rangle_{ab}|0\rangle_{c_{1,i}}|0\rangle_{d_{1,i}} \otimes |00\rangle_{c_{2,i}d_{2,i}} - |00\rangle_{ab}|1\rangle_{c_{1,i}}|1\rangle_{d_{1,i}} \otimes |11\rangle_{c_{2,i}d_{2,i}}$$
$$- |01\rangle_{ab}|0\rangle_{c_{1,i}}|1\rangle_{d_{1,i}} \otimes |01\rangle_{c_{2,i}d_{2,i}} - |10\rangle_{ab}|0\rangle_{c_{1,i}}|1\rangle_{d_{1,i}} \otimes |01\rangle_{c_{2,i}d_{2,i}}),$$

$$|\varphi_{3r}^{(2)}\rangle_{abcd} = H_{c_{1,i}} \otimes H_{d_{1,i}} \otimes |\varphi_{3r}^{(1)}\rangle_{abcd}$$
$$= \frac{1}{2}(|00\rangle_{ab}|1\rangle_{c_{1,i}}|1\rangle_{d_{1,i}} \otimes |11\rangle_{c_{2,i}d_{2,i}} + |00\rangle_{ab}|0\rangle_{c_{1,i}}|0\rangle_{d_{1,i}} \otimes |00\rangle_{c_{2,i}d_{2,i}}$$
$$+ |01\rangle_{ab}|1\rangle_{c_{1,i}}|0\rangle_{d_{1,i}} \otimes |10\rangle_{c_{2,i}d_{2,i}} + |10\rangle_{ab}|1\rangle_{c_{1,i}}|0\rangle_{d_{1,i}} \otimes |10\rangle_{c_{2,i}d_{2,i}}),$$

$$|\varphi_{4r}^{(2)}\rangle_{abcd} = H_{c_{1,i}} \otimes H_{d_{1,i}} \otimes |\varphi_{4r}^{(1)}\rangle_{abcd}$$
$$= \frac{1}{2}(|00\rangle_{ab}|1\rangle_{c_{1,i}}|0\rangle_{d_{1,i}} \otimes |10\rangle_{c_{2,i}d_{2,i}} - |00\rangle_{ab}|0\rangle_{c_{1,i}}|1\rangle_{d_{1,i}} \otimes |01\rangle_{c_{2,i}d_{2,i}}$$
$$- |01\rangle_{ab}|1\rangle_{c_{1,i}}|1\rangle_{d_{1,i}} \otimes |11\rangle_{c_{2,i}d_{2,i}} - |10\rangle_{ab}|1\rangle_{c_{1,i}}|1\rangle_{d_{1,i}} \otimes |11\rangle_{c_{2,i}d_{2,i}}).$$

So, we can include the equations:

$$|\varphi_{1r}^{(2)}\rangle_{abc_{1,i-2}d_{1,i-2}} = H_{c_{1,i-1}} \otimes H_{d_{1,i-1}} \otimes |\varphi_{1r}^{(1)}\rangle_{abc_{1,i-2}d_{1,i-2}}$$
$$= \frac{1}{2}(|00\rangle_{ab}|0\rangle_{c_{1,i-1}}|1\rangle_{d_{1,i-1}} \otimes |01\rangle_{c_{2,i-1}d_{2,i-1}}$$
$$+ |00\rangle_{ab}|1\rangle_{c_{1,i-1}}|0\rangle_{d_{1,i-1}} \otimes |10\rangle_{c_{2,i-1}d_{2,i-1}}$$
$$+ |01\rangle_{ab}|0\rangle_{c_{1,i-1}}|0\rangle_{d_{1,i-1}} \otimes |00\rangle_{c_{2,i-1}d_{2,i-1}}$$
$$+ |10\rangle_{ab}|0\rangle_{c_{1,i-1}}|0\rangle_{d_{1,i-1}} \otimes |00\rangle_{c_{2,i-1}d_{2,i-1}}),$$

$$|\varphi_{2r}^{(2)}\rangle_{abc_{1,i-2}d_{1,i-2}} = H_{c_{1,i}} \otimes H_{d_{1,i}} \otimes |\varphi_{2r}^{(1)}\rangle_{abc_{1,i-2}d_{1,i-2}}$$
$$= \frac{1}{2}(|00\rangle_{ab}|0\rangle_{c_{1,i-1}}|0\rangle_{d_{1,i-1}} \otimes |00\rangle_{c_{2,i-1}d_{2,i-1}}$$
$$- |00\rangle_{ab}|1\rangle_{c_{1,i-1}}|1\rangle_{d_{1,i-1}} \otimes |11\rangle_{c_{2,i-1}d_{2,i-1}}$$

$$- |01\rangle_{ab}|0\rangle_{c_{1,i-1}}|1\rangle_{d_{1,i-1}} \otimes |01\rangle_{c_{2,i-1}d_{2,i-1}}$$
$$- |10\rangle_{ab}|0\rangle_{c_{1,i-1}}|1\rangle_{d_{1,i-1}} \otimes |01\rangle_{c_{2,i-1}d_{2,i-1}}),$$

$$|\varphi_{3r}^{(2)}\rangle_{abc_{1,i-2}d_{1,i-2}} = H_{c_{1,i}} \otimes H_{d_{1,i}} \otimes |\varphi_{3r}^{(1)}\rangle_{abc_{1,i-2}d_{1,i-2}}$$
$$= \frac{1}{2}(|00\rangle_{ab}|1\rangle_{c_{1,i-1}}|1\rangle_{d_{1,i-1}} \otimes |11\rangle_{c_{2,i-1}d_{2,i-1}}$$
$$+ |00\rangle_{ab}|0\rangle_{c_{1,i-1}}|0\rangle_{d_{1,i-1}} \otimes |00\rangle_{c_{2,i-1}d_{2,i-1}}$$
$$+ |01\rangle_{ab}|1\rangle_{c_{1,i-1}}|0\rangle_{d_{1,i-1}} \otimes |10\rangle_{c_{2,i-1}d_{2,i-1}}$$
$$+ |10\rangle_{ab}|1\rangle_{c_{1,i-1}}|0\rangle_{d_{1,i-1}} \otimes |10\rangle_{c_{2,i-1}d_{2,i-1}}),$$

$$|\varphi_{4r}^{(2)}\rangle_{abc_{1,i-2}d_{1,i-2}} = H_{c_{1,i-1}} \otimes H_{d_{1,i-1}} \otimes |\varphi_{4r}^{(1)}\rangle_{abc_{1,i-2}d_{1,i-2}}$$
$$= \frac{1}{2}(|00\rangle_{ab}|1\rangle_{c_{1,i-1}}|0\rangle_{d_{1,i-1}} \otimes |10\rangle_{c_{2,i-1}d_{2,i-1}}$$
$$- |00\rangle_{ab}|0\rangle_{c_{1,i-1}}|1\rangle_{d_{1,i-1}} \otimes |01\rangle_{c_{2,i-1}d_{2,i-1}}$$
$$- |01\rangle_{ab}|1\rangle_{c_{1,i-1}}|1\rangle_{d_{1,i-1}} \otimes |11\rangle_{c_{2,i-1}d_{2,i-1}}$$
$$- |10\rangle_{ab}|1\rangle_{c_{1,i-1}}|1\rangle_{d_{1,i-1}} \otimes |11\rangle_{c_{2,i-1}d_{2,i-1}}).$$

3   The QKA Protocols Against Collective Noise

3.1   The Multi-party Quantum Key Agreement Protocol Against Collective-Dephasing Noise

First, we propose the QKA protocol which is immune to the collective-dephasing noise. Suppose that there are m participants $P_1, \ldots, P_m$ want to generate a common key K, simultaneously. They randomly select their own secret bit strings $K_1, \ldots, K_m$, respectively. And they agree the $K = K_1 \oplus K_2 \oplus \cdots \oplus K_m$.

$$K_1 = (k_1^1, \ldots, k_1^s, \ldots, k_1^n),$$
$$\vdots$$
$$K_i = (k_i^1, \ldots, k_i^s, \ldots, k_i^n),$$
$$\vdots$$
$$K_m = (k_m^1, \ldots, k_m^s, \ldots, k_m^n).$$

(1) $P_i(i = 1, 2, \ldots, m)$ prepares $|\varphi_{tdp}\rangle_{abcd}^{\otimes \frac{n}{2}}$ states, respectively. Then, P_i divides $|\varphi_{tdp}\rangle_{abcd}^{\otimes \frac{n}{2}}$ states into four ordered sequences S_i^a, S_i^b, S_i^c and S_i^d, which consist of the particles a, particles b, logical qubits c and logical qubits d from the $|\varphi_{tdp}\rangle_{abcd}^{\otimes \frac{n}{2}}$ states. $S_i^l = (s_i^{l,1}, s_i^{l,2}, \ldots, s_i^{l,j}, \ldots, s_i^{l,\frac{n}{2}})(l = 1, 2, 3, 4; 1 \leq j \leq \frac{n}{2}; i = 1, 2, \ldots, m)$, $s_i^{l,j}$ denotes the jth particle of S_i^l. Later, P_i prepares $\frac{n}{2}$ decoy logical photons respectively which are randomly in $\{|0_{dp}\rangle, |1_{dp}\rangle, |+_{dp}\rangle, |-_{dp}\rangle\}$. Moreover, P_i randomly inserts these decoy logical photons into the two sequences S_i^c and S_i^d to form $S_i^{c'}$ and $S_i^{d'}$. Subsequently, P_i performs permutation operator $(\prod_{\frac{n}{2}})_{P_i}$ on $S_i^{c'}$ and $S_i^{d'}$ to form the new sequences $S_i^{c''}$ and $S_i^{d''}$, and sends $S_i^{c''}$ and $S_i^{d''}$ to P_{i+1}.

(2) P_i and P_{i+1} perform the first eavesdropping check after P_i confirms that P_{i+1} has received the sequences $S_i^{c''}$ and $S_i^{d''}$. P_i announces the positions and the corresponding bases of the decoy logical photons. Later, P_{i+1} measures the decoy logical photons by using the correct measurement bases and computes the error rate. If the error rate is less than the selected threshold value, P_i and P_{i+1} carry out the next step. Otherwise, they discard the protocol.

(3) P_i publishes the permutation operator $(\prod_{\frac{n}{2}})_{P_i}$. P_{i+1} can restore the sequences S_i^c and S_i^d. Later, P_{i+1} performs two unitary operations $\sigma^{k_{i+1}^{2j-1}}$, $\sigma^{3k_{i+1}^{2j}}$ on the corresponding sequences $s_i^{c_1,i,j}$ and $s_i^{d_1,i,j}$ according to his secret key k_{i+1}^{2j-1} and k_{i+1}^{2j}, respectively. So, he can get the new sequences $S_{i,i+1}^{c_1,i}$ and $S_{i,i+1}^{d_1,i}$. Where the $c_{1,i}$ and $d_{1,i}$ are the new particles after unitary operations. Then P_{i+1} prepares the two sequences $S_{i,i+1}^{c_1,i}$ and $S_{i,i+1}^{d_1,i}$ which consist of logical qubits $c_{1,i}$ and logical qubits $d_{1,i}$, respectively. Later, P_{i+1} obtains the new sequences $S_{i,i+1}^{c''_1,i}$ and $S_{i,i+1}^{d''_1,i}$ by using the method of decoy photons and permutation operator that described in above step (1), and sends them to the next participant P_{i+2}.

(4) Similar to above step (2). If the error rate is less than the selected threshold value, P_{i+1} and P_{i+2} carry out the next step. Otherwise, they discard the protocol.

(5) $P_{i+1}, \ldots, P_{i-2}$ publish the permutation operator $(\prod_{\frac{n}{2}})_{P_{i+1}}, \ldots, (\prod_{\frac{n}{2}})_{P_{i-2}}$. Then, $P_{i+2}, \ldots, P_{i-1}$ perform two unitary operations, and they prepare logical sequences similar to above step (3). Later, $P_{i+2}, \ldots, P_{i-1}$ utilize the method of decoy photons and permutation operator that described in above step (1). As shown in Fig. 1.

(6) Similar to above step (2). If the error rate is less than the selected threshold value, P_{i-1} and P_i continue to carry out the next step. Otherwise, they discard the protocol.

(7) P_{i-1} publishes the permutation operator $(\prod_{\frac{n}{2}})_{P_{i-1}}$, respectively. P_i obtains the sequences $S_{i,i-1}^{c_1,i-2}$ and $S_{i,i-1}^{d_1,i-2}$. By performing W basis measurement on the $s_i^{a,j}$, $s_i^{b,j}$, $s_{i,i-1}^{c_1,i-1,j}$, $s_{i,i-1}^{d_1,i-1,j}$, P_i can get a measurement result. By the encoding rule Table 1, P_i can get the key $K_i' = \underset{j,j\neq i}{\oplus} K_j$. Last, P_i can generate the final common key $K = K_i \oplus K_i'$.

3.2   The Multi-party Quantum Key Agreement Protocol Against Collective-Rotation Noise

(1) $P_i(i = 1, 2, \ldots, m)$ prepares $|\varphi_{tr}\rangle_{abcd}^{\otimes \frac{n}{2}}$ states, respectively. Then, P_i divides $|\varphi_{tr}\rangle_{abcd}^{\otimes \frac{n}{2}}$ states into four ordered sequences S_i^a, S_i^b, S_i^c and S_i^d, which consist of the particles a, particles b, logical qubits c and logical qubits d from the $|\varphi_{tr}\rangle_{abcd}^{\otimes \frac{n}{2}}$ states. Later, P_i prepares $\frac{n}{2}$ decoy logical photons respectively which are randomly in $\{|0_r\rangle, |1_r\rangle, |+_r\rangle, |-_r\rangle\}$. Moreover, P_i randomly inserts these decoy logical photons into the two sequences S_i^c and S_i^d to form $S_i^{c'}$

and $S_i^{d'}$. Subsequently, P_i performs permutation operator $(\prod_{\frac{n}{2}})_{P_i}$ on $S_i^{c'}$ and $S_i^{d'}$ to form the new sequences $S_i^{c''}$ and $S_i^{d''}$, and sends $S_i^{c''}$ and $S_i^{d''}$ to P_{i+1}.

(2) Similar to step (2) in the QKA protocol against collective-dephasing noise.

(3) P_i proclaims the permutation operator $(\prod_{\frac{n}{2}})_{P_i}$. P_{i+1} can restore the sequences S_i^c and S_i^d. Then, P_{i+1} performs two CNOT operations $U_{CNOT}^{c_1,i,c_2,i}$, $U_{CNOT}^{d_1,i,d_2,i}$, respectively. Later, P_{i+1} performs Hadamard gates on particles $c_{1,i}$, $d_{1,i}$, respectively. Subsequently, P_{i+1} performs two unitary operations $\sigma^{k_{i+1}^{2j-1}}$ and $\sigma^{3k_{i+1}^{2j}}$ on the corresponding sequences $s_i^{c_1,i,j}$ and $s_i^{d_1,i,j}$ according to his secret key k_{i+1}^{2j-1} and k_{i+1}^{2j}, respectively. So, he can get the new sequences $S_{i,i+1}^{c_1,i}$ and $S_{i,i+1}^{d_1,i}$. Where the $c_{1,i}$ and $d_{1,i}$ are the new particles after unitary operations. Then P_{i+1} prepares the two sequences $S_{i,i+1}^{c_1,i}$ and $S_{i,i+1}^{d_1,i}$ which consist of logical qubits $c_{1,i}$ and logical qubits $d_{1,i}$, respectively. Later, he obtain the new sequences $S_{i,i+1}^{c_1,i''}$ and $S_{i,i+1}^{d_1,i''}$ by using the method of decoy photons and permutation operator that described in step (1) of the QKA protocol against collective-dephasing noise, and sends them to the next participant P_{i+2}.

(4) Similar to the fourth step in the QKA protocol against collective-dephasing noise.

(5) $P_{i+1}, \ldots, P_{i-2}$ proclaim the permutation operator $(\prod_{\frac{n}{2}})_{P_{i+1}}, \ldots, (\prod_{\frac{n}{2}})_{P_{i-2}}$. Then, $P_{i+2}, \ldots, P_{i-1}$ perform two CNOT operations, Hadamard gates and two unitary operations successively. Later, they prepare logical sequences similar to step (3) in the 3.2 chapter. Last, $P_{i+2}, \ldots, P_{i-1}$ utilize the method of decoy photons and permutation operator. As shown in Fig. 1.

(6) Similar to the sixth step in the QKA protocol against collective-dephasing noise.

(7) P_{i-1} proclaims the permutation operator $(\prod_{\frac{n}{2}})_{P_{i-1}}$, respectively. P_i obtains the sequences $S_{i,i-1}^{c_1,i-2}$ and $S_{i,i-1}^{d_1,i-2}$. Then, P_i performs two CNOT operations $U_{CNOT}^{c_1,i-1,c_2,i-1}$, $U_{CNOT}^{d_1,i-1,d_2,i-1}$, Hadamard gates $H_{c_1,i-1}$, $H_{d_1,i-1}$. Last, by performing W basis measurement on the $s_i^{a,j}$, $s_i^{b,j}$, $s_{i,i-1}^{c_1,i-1,j}$, $s_{i,i-1}^{d_1,i-1,j}$, P_i can get a measurement result. By the encoding rule Table 1, P_i can get the key $K_i' = \bigoplus_{j,j\neq i} K_j$. Last, P_i can generate the final common key $K = K_i \oplus K_i'$.

4   Security Analysis

4.1   Participant Attack

Without loss of generality, assume that P_i is the dishonest participant. If P_i obtains the final common key K ahead of time. P_i wants to turn the final common key K into K^*. Then P_i makes $K^* \oplus K \oplus K_i$ as his secret key instead of K_i, and performs unitary operation according to the $K^* \oplus K \oplus K_i$. Other parties will

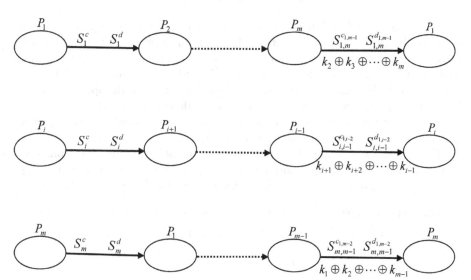

Fig. 1. The two multi-party quantum key agreement protocols steps of transmitting logical photons

consider that K^* is the final common key because of $K^* \oplus K \oplus K = K^*$. Thus, there is a fair loophole in this condition. To avoid the above unfairness, we require that all participants must perform eavesdropping detection in steps (2), (4) and (6) of the two QKA protocols, and if all the sequences $S_i^c, S_i^d, \ldots, S_{i,i-1}^{c_i,i-2}, S_{i,i-1}^{d_i,i-2}$ are secure, they carry out unitary operation according to their own secret key. So, nobody can obtain the final shared key ahead of time. Therefore, the dishonest participant P_i is fail to change the final common key as she expected. Therefore, the protocol can resist the participant attack.

4.2 Outsider Attack

Supposed that Eve is the outsider attacker. Eve may apply four types attacks, including Trojan-horse attacks, Intercept-resend attack, Measure-resend attack and Entangle-measure attack.

Because our protocol transmits the same photon more than once, it may be attacked by the Trojan horse attacks [38,39]. However, participants use the method of installing a wavelength filter and the photon number splitters (PNS: 50/50). If a multi-photon signal has an irrational high rate, the Trojan horse attacks can be detected. So, the proposed protocol is immune to the Trojan horse attacks [40,41].

As for as the Intercept-resend attack and Measure-resend attack, the decoy states technology can resist the two attacks. The participants select the decoy logical photons from the two non-orthogonal bases $\{|0_{dp}\rangle, |1_{dp}\rangle\}$ (or $\{|0_r\rangle, |1_r\rangle\}$) and $\{|+_{dp}\rangle, |-_{dp}\rangle\}$ (or $\{|+_r\rangle, |-_r\rangle\}$) and randomly insert them into the sequences

$S_i^c, S_i^d, \ldots, S_{i,i-1}^{c_i, i-2}, S_{i,i-1}^{d_i, i-2}$ in steps (1), (3) and (5) of the two QKA protocols, respectively. However, Eve cannot obtain any information about the decoy photons before $P_i, P_{i+1}, \ldots, P_{i-1}$ publishes the positions and the corresponding bases of the decoy photons in steps (2), (4) and (6) of the two QKA protocols, respectively. So, when the participants perform eavesdropping detection, Eve can be discovered. Moreover, Eve can be detected with the probabilities $1 - (\frac{3}{4})^{\frac{n}{2}}$ (Measure-resend attack) and $1 - (\frac{1}{2})^{\frac{n}{2}}$ (Intercept-resend attack), where $\frac{n}{2}$ denotes the number of decoy logical photons.

Then, we discuss the Entangle-measure attack. Taking the collective-dephasing noise for example. Suppose the eavesdropper uses the operation $\hat{U}_E$, and prepares an auxiliary system $|\varepsilon\rangle_E$. We can get the following equations:

$$\hat{U}_E|0_{dp}\rangle|\varepsilon\rangle_E = a_{00}|00\rangle|\varepsilon_{00}\rangle_E + a_{01}|01\rangle|\varepsilon_{01}\rangle_E + a_{10}|10\rangle|\varepsilon_{10}\rangle_E + a_{11}|11\rangle|\varepsilon_{11}\rangle_E,$$

$$\hat{U}_E|1_{dp}\rangle|\varepsilon\rangle_E = b_{00}|00\rangle|\varepsilon'_{00}\rangle_E + b_{01}|01\rangle|\varepsilon'_{01}\rangle_E + b_{10}|10\rangle|\varepsilon'_{10}\rangle_E + b_{11}|11\rangle|\varepsilon'_{11}\rangle_E,$$

$$\hat{U}_E|+_{dp}\rangle|\varepsilon\rangle_E = \frac{1}{\sqrt{2}}(\hat{U}_E|0_{dp}\rangle|\varepsilon\rangle_E + \hat{U}_E|1_{dp}\rangle|\varepsilon\rangle_E)$$

$$= \frac{1}{2}[|\Phi^+\rangle(a_{00}|00\rangle|\varepsilon_{00}\rangle_E + a_{11}|11\rangle|\varepsilon_{11}\rangle_E + b_{00}|00\rangle|\varepsilon'_{00}\rangle_E + b_{11}|11\rangle|\varepsilon'_{11}\rangle_E$$

$$+ |\Phi^-\rangle(a_{00}|00\rangle|\varepsilon_{00}\rangle_E - a_{11}|11\rangle|\varepsilon_{11}\rangle_E + b_{00}|00\rangle|\varepsilon'_{00}\rangle_E - b_{11}|11\rangle|\varepsilon'_{11}\rangle_E$$

$$+ |\Psi^+\rangle(a_{01}|01\rangle|\varepsilon_{01}\rangle_E + a_{10}|10\rangle|\varepsilon_{10}\rangle_E + b_{01}|01\rangle|\varepsilon'_{01}\rangle_E + b_{10}|10\rangle|\varepsilon'_{10}\rangle_E$$

$$+ |\Psi^-\rangle(a_{01}|01\rangle|\varepsilon_{01}\rangle_E - a_{10}|10\rangle|\varepsilon_{10}\rangle_E + b_{01}|01\rangle|\varepsilon'_{01}\rangle_E - b_{10}|10\rangle|\varepsilon'_{10}\rangle_E],$$

$$\hat{U}_E|-_{dp}\rangle|\varepsilon\rangle_E = \frac{1}{\sqrt{2}}(\hat{U}_E|0_{dp}\rangle|\varepsilon\rangle_E - \hat{U}_E|1_{dp}\rangle|\varepsilon\rangle_E)$$

$$= \frac{1}{2}[|\Phi^+\rangle(a_{00}|00\rangle|\varepsilon_{00}\rangle_E + a_{11}|11\rangle|\varepsilon_{11}\rangle_E - b_{00}|00\rangle|\varepsilon'_{00}\rangle_E - b_{11}|11\rangle|\varepsilon'_{11}\rangle_E$$

$$+ |\Phi^-\rangle(a_{00}|00\rangle|\varepsilon_{00}\rangle_E - a_{11}|11\rangle|\varepsilon_{11}\rangle_E - b_{00}|00\rangle|\varepsilon'_{00}\rangle_E + b_{11}|11\rangle|\varepsilon'_{11}\rangle_E$$

$$+ |\Psi^+\rangle(a_{01}|01\rangle|\varepsilon_{01}\rangle_E + a_{10}|10\rangle|\varepsilon_{10}\rangle_E - b_{01}|01\rangle|\varepsilon'_{01}\rangle_E - b_{10}|10\rangle|\varepsilon'_{10}\rangle_E$$

$$+ |\Psi^-\rangle(a_{01}|01\rangle|\varepsilon_{01}\rangle_E - a_{10}|10\rangle|\varepsilon_{10}\rangle_E - b_{01}|01\rangle|\varepsilon'_{01}\rangle_E + b_{10}|10\rangle|\varepsilon'_{10}\rangle_E].$$

where $|a_{00}|^2 + |a_{01}|^2 + |a_{10}|^2 + |a_{11}|^2 = 1$, $|b_{00}|^2 + |b_{01}|^2 + |b_{10}|^2 + |b_{11}|^2 = 1$. $|\varepsilon\rangle_E$ is the initial state of the ancilla E. If Eve doesn't want to be detected in the eavesdropping check, the $\hat{U}_E$ must satisfy the conditions: $a_{01} = b_{10} = 1$, $a_{00} = a_{10} = a_{11} = 0$, $b_{00} = b_{01} = b_{11} = 0$ and $|\varepsilon_{01}\rangle_E = |\varepsilon'_{10}\rangle_E$. Obviously, the auxiliary photons $|\varepsilon_{01}\rangle_E$ and $|\varepsilon'_{10}\rangle_E$ cannot be distinguished. If Eve doesn't introduce error when the participants perform the eavesdropping check, she cannot obtain any useful information. Therefore, the protocol can resist the outsider attack.

5   Efficiency Analysis

In this subsection, we will analyze the qubit efficiency of this protocols. A well-known measure of efficiency of secure quantum communication is known as qubit efficiency introduced by Cabello [42], which is given as

$$\eta = \frac{c}{q+b},$$

where c denotes the length of the transmitted message bits (the length of the final key), q is the number of the used qubits, and b is the number of classical bits exchanged for decoding of the message (classical communication used for checking of eavesdropping is not counted). Hence, the qubit efficiency of our protocol can be computed $\eta = \frac{n}{(4 \cdot \frac{n}{2} + 2 \cdot \frac{n}{2})m} = \frac{1}{3m}$, where m is the number of the participants. Table 2 shows that our protocols is more efficient than other multi-party QKA protocols.

Table 2. Comparison between proposed multi-party QKA protocols and ours

QKA protocol	Quantum resource	Particle type	Repel collective noise	Qubit efficiency
Xu et al.'s protocol [25]	GHZ states	Tree-type	No	$\frac{1}{2m(m-1)}$
Liu et al.'s protocol [26]	Single photons	Circle-type	No	$\frac{1}{2m(m-1)}$
Our protocols	W states	Circle-type	Yes	$\frac{1}{3m}$

6 Conclusion

In this paper, we propose the two multi-party quantum key agreement protocols with logical W states which can resist the collective noise. By using the decoy logical photons method and the delayed measurement, the security and fairness of the protocols are ensured. By applying the dense coding method and block transmission technique, the efficiency of the protocols are improved. Finally, we estimate its qubit efficiency. The efficiency analysis indicates that the proposed protocols are efficient by comparing with other multi-party QKA protocols.

References

1. Bennett, C.H., Brassard, G.: Public-key distribution and coin tossing. In: Proceedings of IEEE International Conference on Computers, Systems and Signal Processing, India, pp. 175–179 (1984)
2. Shor, P.W., Preskill, J.: Simple proof of security of the BB84 quantum key distribution protocol. Phys. Rev. Lett. **85**, 441 (2000)
3. Hwang, W.Y.: Quantum key distribution with high loss: toward global secure communication. Phys. Rev. Lett. **91**, 057901 (2003)
4. Lo, H.K., Ma, X.F., Chen, K.: Decoy state quantum key distribution. Phys. Rev. Lett. **94**, 230504 (2005)
5. Cerf, N.J., Bourennane, M., Karlsson, A., Gisin, N.: Security of quantum key distribution using d-level systems. Phys. Rev. Lett. **88**, 127902 (2002)
6. Lo, H.K., Curty, M., Qi, B.: Measurement-device-independent quantum key distribution. Phys. Rev. Lett. **108**, 130503 (2012)
7. Deng, F.G., Long, G.L., Liu, X.S.: Two-step quantum direct communication protocol using the Einstein-Podolsky-Rosen pair block. Phys. Rev. A **68**, 042317 (2003)

8. Sun, Z.W., Du, R.G., Long, D.Y.: Quantum secure direct communication with quantum identification. Int. J. Quantum Inf. **10**, 1250008 (2012)
9. Sun, Z.W., Du, R.G., Long, D.Y.: Quantum secure direct communication with two-photon four-qubit cluster state. Int. J. Theor. Phys. **51**, 1946–1952 (2012)
10. Zhang, K.J., Zhang, W.W., Li, D.: Improving the security of arbitrated quantum signature against the forgery attack. Quantum Inf Process. **12**, 2655–2669 (2013)
11. Cao, H.J., Zhang, J.F., Liu, J., Li, Z.Y.: A new quantum proxy multi-signature scheme using maximally entangled seven-qubit states. Int. J. Theor. Phys. **55**, 774–780 (2016)
12. Zou, X.F., Qiu, D.W.: Attack and improvements of fair quantum blind signature schemes. Quantum Inf. Process. **12**, 2071–2085 (2013)
13. Fan, L., Zhang, K.J., Qin, S.J., Guo, F.Z.: A novel quantum blind signature scheme with four-particle GHZ states. Int. J. Theor. Phys. **55**, 1028–1035 (2016)
14. Zhou, N., Zeng, G., Xiong, J.: Quantum key agreement protocol. Electron. Lett. **40**, 1149 (2004)
15. Tsai, C., Hwang, T.: On quantum key agreement protocol. Technical report. C-S-I-E, NCKU, Taiwan (2009)
16. Hsueh, C.C., Chen, C.Y.: Quantum key agreement protocol with maximally entangled states. In: 14th Information Security Conference (ISC 2004), pp. 236–242. National Taiwan University of Science and Technology, Taipei (2004)
17. Chong, S.K., Hwang, T.: Quantum key agreement protocol based on BB84. Opt. Commun. **283**, 1192–1195 (2010)
18. Chong, S.K., Tsai, C.W., Hwang, T.: Improvement on quantum key agreement protocol with maximally entangled states. Int. J. Theor. Phys. **50**, 1793–1802 (2011)
19. Shi, R.H., Zhong, H.: Multi-party quantum key agreement with Bell states and Bell measurements. Quantum Inf. Process. **12**, 921–932 (2013)
20. He, Y.F., Ma, W.P.: Two-party quantum key agreement with five-particle entangled states. Int. J. Quantum Inf. **15**, 3 (2017)
21. He, Y.F., Ma, W.P.: Two robust quantum key agreement protocols based on logical GHZ states. Mod. Phys. Lett. **31**, 3 (2017)
22. Sun, Z., Wang, B., Li, Q., Long, D.: Improvements on multiparty quantum key agreement with single particles. Quantum Inf. Process. **12**, 3411 (2013)
23. Huang, W., Wen, Q.Y., Liu, B., Gao, F., Sun, Y.: Quantum key agreement with EPR pairs and single particle measurements. Quantum Inf. Process. **13**, 649–663 (2014)
24. Chitra, S., Nasir, A., Anirban, P.: Protocols of quantum key agreement solely using Bell states and Bell measurement. Quantum Inf. Process. **13**, 2391–2405 (2014)
25. Xu, G.B., Wen, Q.Y., Gao, F., Qin, S.J.: Novel multiparty quantum key agreement protocol with GHZ states. Quantum Inf. Process. **13**, 2587–2594 (2014)
26. Liu, B., Gao, F., Huang, W., Wen, Q.Y.: Multiparty quantum key agreement with single particles. Quantum Inf. Process. **12**, 1797–1805 (2013)
27. Yin, X.R., Ma, W.P., Liu, W.Y.: Three-party quantum key agreement with two-photon entanglement. Int. J. Theor. Phys. **52**, 3915–3921 (2013)
28. Sun, Z.W., Yu, J.P., Wang, P.: Efficient multi-party quantum key agreement by cluster states. Quantum Inf. Process. **15**, 373–384 (2016)
29. Shor, P.W.: Scheme for reducing decoherence in quantum computer memory. Phys. Rev. A **52**, 2493–2496 (1995)
30. Kalamidas, D.: Single photo quantum error rejection and correction with linear optics. Phys. Rev. A **343**, 331–335 (2005)
31. Li, X.H., Feng, F.G., Zhou, H.Y.: Faithful qubit transmission against collective noise without ancillary qubits. Appl. Phys. Lett. **91**, 144101 (2007)

32. de Brito, D.B., Ramos, R.V.: Passive quantum error correction with linear optics. Phys. Lett. A **352**, 206 (2006)
33. Walton, Z.D., Abouraddy, A.F., Sergienko, A.V., Saleh, B.E.A., Teich, M.C.: Decoherence free subspaces in quantum key distribution. Phys. Rev. Lett. **91**, 087901 (2003)
34. Simon, C., Pan, J.M.: Polarization entanglement purification using spatial entanglement. Phys. Rev. Lett. **89**, 257901 (2002)
35. Huang, W., Su, Q., Wu, X., Li, Y.B., Sun, Y.: Quantum key agreement against collective decoherence. Int. J. Theor. Phys. **53**, 2891–2901 (2014)
36. Shukla, C., Kothari, V., Banerjee, A., Pathak, A.: On the group-theoretic structure of a class of quantum dialogue protocols. Phys. Lett. A **377**, 518–527 (2013)
37. Li, X.H., Deng, F.G., Zhou, H.Y.: Efficient quantum key distribution over a collective noise channel. Phys. Rev. A **78**, 022321 (2008)
38. Zukowski, M., Zeilinger, A., Horne, M.A., Ekert, A.K.: Event-ready-detectors: Bell experiment via entanglement swapping. Phys. Rev. Lett. **71**(26), 4287–4290 (1993)
39. Pan, J.W., Bouwmeester, D., Weinfurter, H., Zeilinger, A.: Experimental entanglement swapping: entangling photons that never interacted. Phys. Rev. Lett. **80**(18), 3891–3894 (1998)
40. Deng, F.G., Li, X.H., Zhou, H.Y., Zhang, Z.: Improving the security of multiparty quantum secret sharing against Trojan horse attack. Phys. Rev. A **72**, 044302 (2005)
41. Li, X.H., Deng, F.G., Zhou, H.Y.: Improving the security of secure direct communication based on the secret transmitting order of particles. Phys. Rev. A **74**, 054302 (2006)
42. Cabello, A.: Quantum key distribution in the Holevo limit. Phys. Rev. Lett. **85**, 5633–5638 (2000)

An Inducing Localization Scheme for Reactive Jammer in ZigBee Networks

Kuan He$^{(\boxtimes)}$ and Bin Yu

Zhengzhou Information Science and Technology Institute,
Zhengzhou 450001, China
heykuan@outlook.com

Abstract. Reactive Jamming attack could severely disrupt the communications in ZigBee networks, which will have an evident jamming effect on the transmissions in a hard-to-detect manner. Therefore, after analyzing the general process of reactive jamming, we develop a lightweight reactive jammer localization scheme, called IndLoc, which is applicable to ZigBee networks. In this scheme, we first design the time-varying mask code (TVMC) to protect the transmission of the packets to ensure that the jammer cannot monitor the channel effectively. Then, the strength of jamming signal (JSS) could be collected by sending inducing messages into the channel. And the location of the jammer can be estimated through the locations of JSS peak nodes, which are selected according to the gradient ascent algorithm. Experiments are performed based on an open-source stack, msstatePAN. And the results reveal that IndLoc could effectively protect the transmissions of the packets and achieve relatively higher localization accuracy under different network scenarios with fewer calculation and storage overheads.

Keywords: Reactive jamming · Localization · ZigBee networks

1 Introduction

Rapidly developing ZigBee networks have expanded into numerous security critical applications including battlefield awareness, secure area monitoring and target detection [1]. These application scenarios have a common characteristic that they all rely on the timely and reliable delivery of alarm messages [2]. However, the communication of ZigBee nodes could be easily disrupted by jamming attacks [3], thus blocking the delivery of alarm messages and causing severe threats to the security mechanisms of ZigBee networks [4]. Among numerous jamming attack modes, reactive jamming attack is generally regarded as the most threatening one [5]. For the reactive jammer, it is unnecessary to launch jamming when there is no packet on the air. Instead, the jammer keeps silent when the channel is idle, but starts jamming immediately after it senses the transmission of packets, making it difficult to detect and defense. With the development of software defined radio (SDR), reactive jamming is easy to launch by the use of USRP2 [6]. The packet delivery ratio (PDR) of the nodes in the jammed area would drop to 0% under the reactive jamming that only lasts for 26 μs. Hence, the effective defense against reactive jamming is of great significance to ZigBee networks

© Springer Nature Switzerland AG 2018
F. Liu et al. (Eds.): SciSec 2018, LNCS 11287, pp. 156–171, 2018.
https://doi.org/10.1007/978-3-030-03026-1_11

because this physical attack is hard to mitigate by cryptographic methods [7]. Since so much attention has been drawn on the defense of reactive jamming attack, localizing the jammer is widely accepted as an efficient way for defense since the location information of the jammer allows for further countermeasures such as physically destruction and electromagnetic shielding [8, 9].

Based on the fact that nodes farther from the jammer get higher PDRs, Pelechrinis et al. [10] designed a gradient descent method to calculate the location of the jammer. Afterwards, to localize the jammer Cheng et al. [11] utilized the location distribution of the boundary nodes, in which the centers of the minimum bounding circle and maximum inscribed circle of the boundary nodes are calculated. Besides, [12] proposed to localize the jammer by developing a framework which could perform automatic network topology partitioning and jammer localization. In addition, Liu et al. [13] designed VFIL algorithm to estimate the coarse location of the jammer according to the topology changes of the network, and then improve the accuracy in multiple iterations. Furthermore, claiming that the hearing range of nodes is related to the distance from the jammer, Liu et al. [14] proposed an algorithm to localize the jammer by estimating the changes of the hearing range. Then a GSA-based algorithm was designed in [15], which calculates the fitness function by randomly selecting jammed nodes and localizes the jammer through iterations.

However, the jammer localization schemes mentioned above all assume that the jammer only launches constant jamming in the network. It is probably hard for those schemes to localize the reactive jammer since network properties such as PDR and changes of the network topology are difficult to obtain precisely. Therefore, Cai et al. [16] proposed a joint detection and localization scheme for reactive jammer by analyzing the changes of the sensing time of the nodes working in the same frequency. The scheme exploits the abnormal sensing time of the victim nodes to detect the reactive jamming. Besides, it utilizes the similarity scores of the unaffected nodes as the weight to localize the jammer. However, the anchor nodes it selects for the localization is relatively far from the jammer, thus resulting in a coarse estimation of the location of the jammer when calculating the similarity scores. Therefore, the scheme seems unable to localize the reactive jammer with high accuracy.

As far as we know, the current research results about the reactive jammer localization problem are rare to find. And the reactive jamming is obviously a severe threat to the network security since it is hard to detect and defense. In consequence, with the consideration of the resource constrained feature of ZigBee nodes, an efficient localization scheme against reactive jammer is of significance to the network security. Given the characteristic of the reactive jammer that it only launches jamming after it senses a busy channel, a lightweight reactive jammer localization scheme, IndLoc, is proposed in this paper. We aim to analyze the general process of reactive jamming and design different countermeasures against each process of it. With the purpose of eluding monitoring from the jammer, we first design TVMC to protect the headers from being sensed, thus restoring the communications in ZigBee networks. Furthermore, since the reactive jammer starts jamming when it senses the transmission of the packets, it is feasible to send the unprotected inducing messages to trigger the reactive jamming and collect the JSS. Afterwards, JSS-based weighted centroid localization algorithm was proposed to localize the jammer.

The remainder of the paper is organized as follows: Sect. 2 introduces the assumptions and the model we adopt in this paper. We then specify IndLoc in detail in Sect. 3. Next, the security and performance analysis are illustrated in Sect. 4. Finally, experiments and analysis are given in Sect. 5, and in Sect. 6, we conclude our work.

2   Assumptions and Model

In this section, an introduction to the network model we adopt in this paper is given. Then, the reactive jammer localization model is proposed according to the characteristics of the reactive jamming.

2.1   Assumptions

We consider the ZigBee networks as follows.

Multiple-Routes Connection. In the working area, n ZigBee nodes are deployed in a well-distributed way with enough density for the nodes to deliver the alarm messages through at least 2 different neighbors.

Stationary Network. Once a node is deployed, it keeps stationary, and moving nodes are not within our consideration.

Location Aware. The ZigBee nodes could obtain their own location information by existing localization technology.

Time Synchronization. The network is able to achieve time synchronization with an error less than 100 ms.

Ability to Detect Jamming. Since we focus on localizing a jammer after it is detected, it is assumed that the network is able to detect jamming by existing methods.

Besides, assumptions about the reactive jammer is given as follows.

Single Jammer. There is only one jammer in the network, which is equipped with an omnidirectional antenna. And the transmission power of the jammer is limited, which makes a jamming range denoted as R_J. Besides, we consider an unlimited energy supply for the jammer.

Stationary Jammer. The jammer would stay still after it is deployed, in another words, we do not consider the scenario of a moving jammer.

SFD Detection. Similar to the assumptions adopted in [6] and [17], the reactive jammer keeps monitoring the channel for SFD in the PHY headers. The jammer would keep silent if the channel is idle. Instead, it will sent jamming signals into the channel to disrupt the transmissions immediately after it senses SFD on the air.

2.2   Model

The most distinguishing feature of reactive jamming is that the jammer may not take actions until it senses the SFD of the packets. Based on this, we propose to prevent the headers from being found by the jammer, thus restoring the communications. Then JSS could be obtained to localize the jammer. According to this, we build a reactive jammer localization model shown in Fig. 1.

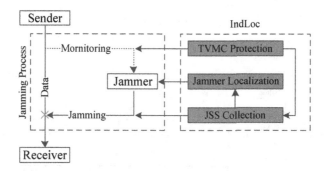

Fig. 1. Reactive jammer localization model

The general process of reactive jamming is illustrated briefly in the model. When detecting reactive jamming, the ZigBee nodes would calculate TVMC according to the time synchronization variable, and protect the PHY headers from being monitored by the jammer. So the communication of the ZigBee networks would be restored. Then, we select inducing nodes according to the principles formulated in advance. And inducing messages generated by inducing nodes are sent to the channel to trigger reactive jamming, enabling the victim nodes to collect JSS. Finally, the gradient ascending algorithm is adopted to find the JSS peak nodes, which would be further used to calculate the location of the jammer by the JSS-based centroid localization algorithm.

IndLoc mainly has 3 challenging subtasks: (A) Time-Varying Mask Code protection (i.e., protecting the headers and eluding monitoring from the jammer). (B) JSS Collection (i.e., sending inducing messages to trigger the jamming and collecting JSS). (C) Jammer Localization.

3   Jammer Localization Formulation

According to the reactive jammer localization model, the designs for TVMC, JSS collection and jammer localization are specified in detail in this section.

3.1   Time-Varying Mask Code

The SFD of fixed length is easy to catch, and protecting the SFD by using mask code is an efficient method for evading from the monitoring. Considering that headers protection based on shared key would need relatively high overheads and it is hard to perform key distribution under jamming, utilizing the attributes of ZigBee networks to generate mask code seems a good choice. Because it is easy to perform and could effectively protect the SFD with only a few calculation and communication overheads, which is suitable for the resource constrained ZigBee nodes. Hence, we propose to utilize the time synchronization variable to generate TVMC, and the process of deploying TVMC protection is shown in Fig. 2.

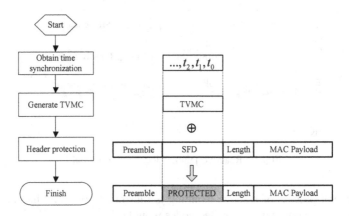

Fig. 2. Schematic for TVMC protection

In the first place, the nodes obtain the time synchronization variable of the ZigBee networks, which contains 32 bits binaries. When choosing the time-varying mask code, there are two principles we have to consider. First, we have to make sure that the mask code could change within a short time, guaranteeing the time-varying nature of TVMC. Second, the changing frequency of TVMC could satisfy the degree of time synchronization of ZigBee networks. Consequently, it would be appropriate that the time between two adjacent TVMCs is neither too short nor too long, tolerating errors that are shorter than the time synchronization period. Besides, it seems not time-sensitive to mask the headers directly with the 32 bits time synchronization variable, because only the lower bits of the time synchronization variable change within a short time. Hence, we propose to select uncertain 8 bits of the time synchronization variable as TVMC, which varies every T seconds.

When detecting reactive jamming, ZigBee nodes generate TVMC according to the time synchronization variable, and XOR it with the SFD before sending the packets. When receiving the packets, the receiving node XOR the SFD with TVMC again to obtain the original data. However, the nodes which are out of synchronization cannot obtain the correct SFD, as a result, those nodes are not able to communicate with the others anymore. Hence, time synchronization would be re-executed to recover the communication after 3 failed retransmissions. At this time, it is hard for the reactive jammer to sense the transmission of the packets, and communications will get back to normal state under the protection of TVMC.

3.2   JSS Collection

Since the jammer cannot monitor the communication of the TVMC-protecting network anymore, it would not send jamming signals to the channel. The problem is how to obtain the JSS in this situation. We propose to use inducing messages, which is not protected by TVMC, to trigger the reactive jamming. Due to the fact that the inducing messages have the unprotected SFD, the reactive jammer would launch jamming when it senses the transmission of the inducing messages. To guarantee the accuracy of the JSS collection, the inducing nodes would inform all of the nodes in the network to back off for t seconds before sending the inducing messages. Then the nodes in the jammed area record the JSS for jammer localization in the next step.

The locations of the inducing nodes are crucial for collecting the JSS. If the inducing nodes are too far from the jammer, the jammer would not sense the transmission of the inducing messages thus no jamming signal could be collected. If the distance between the inducing nodes is too short, the JSS might not be collected accurately since the inducing nodes would interfere with each other. Therefore, how to select the appropriate inducing nodes, which are within the jammed area and out of the transmission range of each other, is the key to the JSS collection.

Figure 3 illustrates the rules for selecting inducing nodes. Below are 2 definitions.

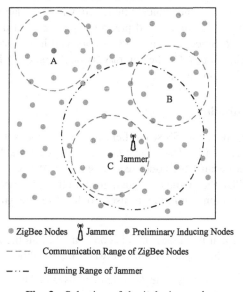

Fig. 3. Selection of the inducing nodes

Definition 1: The nodes which are selected randomly when deploying the network and meanwhile satisfy the formulation (1) are defined as the preliminary inducing nodes.

$$d_I > 2R \tag{1}$$

In formulation (1), the Euclidean distance between any of two preliminary inducing nodes is denoted as d_I, and R stands for the communication range of the nodes.

Definition 2: The preliminary inducing nodes, which satisfy the formulation (2), are defined as the inducing nodes.

$$PDR_{Jammed} < \frac{1}{2}PDR_{Normal} \tag{2}$$

In formulation (2), the PDR of the preliminary inducing nodes before jamming is denoted as PDR_{Normal}, and the PDR of the preliminary inducing nodes after jamming is denoted as PDR_{Jammed}.

According to the network topology, we first select some preliminary nodes. The distance between the neighboring preliminary nodes is suggested to be longer than twice the maximal communication range of the ZigBee nodes, thus ensuring that the selected inducing nodes would not interfere with each other. When detecting jamming, the preliminary nodes check if their own PDRs are above a threshold, i.e., half of the normal PDR before jamming. If the PDR of a preliminary node is below the threshold, the node would be selected as an inducing node. The main intuition behind this approach is to make sure that the inducing nodes are within the jammed area. As shown in Fig. 3, node A, B and C are selected preliminary nodes and the intervals between them are more than $2R$. Since node B and C are located in the jammed area, they are selected as the inducing nodes. On the contrary, node A could not be an inducing node because it is not in the jammed area.

3.3   Jammer Localization

It is practicable to formulate a JSS scalar field to find the nodes nearest to the jammer according to the collected JSS. Those peak nodes in the scalar field represent the nodes nearest to the jammer because the nodes receiving higher JSS are closer to the jammer. Based on this, we utilize the gradient ascent algorithm to find the peak nodes. And JSS-based centroid localization algorithm is used to localize the jammer. Below are 2 definitions.

Definition 3: Assume that the nodes set S is constituted of all the ZigBee nodes in the network. And there are bidirectional links between the neighboring nodes, $|S| = n$.

Definition 4: $\forall s_i \in S$, the JSS s_i collects is denoted as JSS_i. The neighboring nodes set within one hop is defined as S_{in}. And the process of selecting the peak nodes is denoted as $s_i \rightarrow s_j$, which means we move form s_i to s_j when selecting the peak nodes.

First, we start with some nodes that have successfully collected JSS. Those nodes compare the JSS they collect with their neighbors within one hop, and pass the result to the one which has the highest JSS. Then the process would be repeated until we find N peak nodes. Due to the fact that JSS might vary in the different peak nodes, taking the centroid of the peak nodes as the location of the jammer could lead to relatively higher errors. Hence, weighted centroid localization algorithm is adopted to localize the jammer, in which the weight of the node is calculated by the JSS value the nodes collect. Then the detailed process of the algorithm is given in Table 1.

Table 1. Jammer localization

Algorithm 1

while ($cnt\_p<N$)

    rnd_select $s_i \in S$, $JSS_i \neq 0$;

    if ($\exists s_j \in S_{in}$, $JSS_j > JSS_i$) **then**

    $s_i \rightarrow s_j$;

    else

    $PeakNodes= s_i$;

    $cnt\_p=cnt\_p+1$;

    end if

end while

$w_i = JSS^{\alpha}$;

$$J(x,y) = \frac{\sum_{i=1}^{N} w_i P_i(x,y)}{\sum_{i=1}^{N} w_i} \ ;$$

The coordinates of the peak nodes are denoted as $P_i(x, y)$, and the weight of the peak nodes is defined as w_i, while α is the weight calculation index.

4 Security and Performance Analysis

4.1 Security Analysis

Lemma 1. Reactive jammer might not launch jamming when the channel is idle, but it would launch jamming immediately when it senses the transmission of the headers [6]. (Proof omitted)

The main characteristic of reactive jamming is illustrated in *Lemma 1*. Meanwhile, it guides our way for localizing the jammer, thus we could take countermeasures for the monitoring before we localize the jammer. In particular, the transmissions of the SFD would be protected, and JSS could be collected by broadcasting the inducing messages. Finally, JSS would be used to localize the jammer.

Theorem 1. The transmissions of the packets can be protected effectively by TVMC.

Proof. According to *Lemma 1*, before it senses any transmission in the channel, the reactive jammer would not launch jamming. Matching the correct headers (i.e., SFD) is the premise for successful transmission sensing. Hence, the attacker might try to obtain the correct SFD by the attack methods such as exhaustion attack and capture attack to achieve the successful monitoring. The analyses for the two attacks mentioned above are as follows.

Exhaustion Attack. Before it guesses the correct headers, the jammer would not launch jamming. However, 8 bits TVMC is adopted to protect the headers, thus making the possibility of a correct guessing to 1/256. Besides, the attacker has to monitor the channel for every attempt, otherwise it would not be meaningful even the jammer guesses the right SFD. Since channel monitoring would be performed for every attempt, it is unpractical for the jammer to carry out the exhausting attack if we adopt a well-designed T. Hence, the attacker cannot break through the TVMC protection by exhaustion attack.

Capture Attack. Real-time calculation and protection without storage are achieved since the TVMC changes for every T seconds, thus making it unavailable for the attacker even if ZigBee nodes are captured. Meanwhile, security mechanism based on the storage of key is not adopted in IndLoc, protecting TVMC from being obtained from the captured nodes. Therefore, our scheme could effectively defend the capture attack.

Based on the analyses given above, the TVMC could not be acquired through exhaustion attack and capture attack, and efficient monitoring on the transmission of the headers cannot be performed. In consequence, the transmission of the packets in ZigBee networks can be protected effectively by utilizing TVMC.

Theorem 2. The reactive jammer can be localized by IndLoc.

Proof. In accordance with *Theorem 1*, communications would be recovered by using TVMC, and jamming would be launched when the jammer senses the transmission of the packets unprotected by TVMC. Meanwhile, JSS collection is available for the nodes in the jammed area since all of the nodes take a back-off. Besides, the communication mechanism of ZigBee networks could effectively filter out white noise, resulting in the situation that there are no other signals but the jamming signals for the nodes to collect. Therefore, JSS could be collected by the nodes in the jammed area.

Those nodes with the highest JSS (i.e. the peak nodes) are the nearest ones to the jammer according to the Shadowing propagation model, which highlights the fact that received signal strength is inversely proportional to the distance. By converting the jammer localization problem into a RSSI-based node localization problem, the location of the reactive jammer could be calculated by the JSS-based weighted centroid localization algorithm. Consequently, the reactive jammer can be localized by the proposed scheme.

4.2   Performance Analysis

In this section, performance analyses of IndLoc are given in Table 2 and the comparison with [16] is drawn through the performance indexes including communication overhead, storage overhead and calculation overhead. The total amount of nodes is represented by n, while the amount of the unaffected nodes in [16] is denoted as m.

Table 2. Performance comparison

Indexes	[16]	IndLoc
Communication overhead	$m(m-1)$	n
Storage overhead	$mk+1$	$2n$
Calculation overhead	$o(m^2+n^2)$	$o(ni+s)$

Communication Overhead. In IndLoc, the sending process of the inducing messages is the main source of the communication overhead because all of the nodes would take a back-off following the instructions of the message broadcasted by the inducing nodes, which causes a communication overhead n. For comparison, similarity scores calculation in [16] takes at least twice communications for the unaffected nodes, resulting in a more communication overhead.

Storage Overhead. Because TVMC is generated according to the time synchronization variable, which needs no extra storage, the main source of the storage overhead is the searching process for peak nodes. The collected JSS has to be stored and compared when executing the gradient ascent algorithm, thus making a storage overhead $2n$. In [16], k bits time profiles and similarity scores have to be stored in every unaffected nodes, making a storage overhead $mk+1$, which is approximately equal to that of IndLoc.

Calculation Overhead. The calculations in IndLoc mainly exist in the process of finding the peak nodes and localizing the jammer. The amount of the nodes participating in calculation is n, s, respectively. As a consequence, the calculation overhead of IndLoc is $o(ni+s)$, where i stands for the number of the total routes in finding peak nodes. In [16], it utilizes maximum likelihood estimation to compute the time profile, which brings about relatively higher computational overhead.

In summary, IndLoc well balances the performance indexes such as communication overhead, storage overhead and calculation overhead, which is suitable for the resource constrained ZigBee nodes.

5 Experiments and Analysis

We implemented IndLoc based on msstatePAN, which is a fully open-source lite protocol stack that follows IEEE 802.15.4 standard. The experimental development environment is IAR Embedded Workbench 8.10. We first validated the effectiveness of TVMC experimentally. The emphasis of the experiments is studying the localization accuracy of IndLoc under different network scenarios. Since [16] is the leading-edge achievement of the reactive jammer localization problem, which is of great value for reference, the experiment results are compared to [16] for analysis.

5.1   Experiments Setup

The network is made up of ZigBee nodes that carry CC2430, and IndLoc is embedded in the firmware program. 20 ZigBee nodes and 1 reactive jammer are deployed in the outdoor environment. The transmission power of the nodes are set to −40 dBm, thus the transmission range of the nodes is about 50 m. The coordinator of the ZigBee networks is connected to the upper machine, which displays the experimental results for analysis. The communication channel for ZigBee networks is set to channel 25 with a center frequency of 2475 MHz, and the maximum data rate is 250 kb/s.

Besides, we implemented reactive jamming on the USRP2 platform equipped with Xilinx Spartan-3 FPGAs. The reactive jammer is programmed to sense the channel for the SFD, and inject the prepared jamming signal into the channel when it senses the on-going transmissions. And the transmission power of the jammer is adjusted in the range of [−40, −20] dBm.

The purpose of the reactive jamming is to interrupt the communication of the ZigBee nodes. Therefore, the primary evaluation criteria for TVMC is the communication quality under reactive jamming. The two metrics below are used to validate the effectiveness of TVMC.

(1) PDR, as illustrated in Eq. (3), is the ratio of correctly received messages in all sent messages.

$$PDR = \frac{\# \; received \; packets}{\# \; total \; transmitted \; packets} \tag{3}$$

(2) Throughput, as shown in Eq. (4), refers to the number of bits successfully transmitted in unit time.

$$throughput = \frac{\# \; received \; packets \times packet \; length}{transmission \; time} \tag{4}$$

In addition, for the validation of the localization accuracy of IndLoc, the Euclidean distance between the estimated location and the true location of the jammer is defined as the localization error. To analyze the statistical characteristics of the localization error, Cumulative Distribution Function (CDF) of the localization error in 1000 rounds of experiments is studied.

5.2   Results

Transmissions Protection Experiments. To verify whether it is effective to protect transmissions with TVMC under reactive jamming, we performed transmissions protection experiment. The length of the jamming signal was set from 0 to 16 bits to test the average PDR of the TVMC protected and unprotected situations. Besides, 2 nodes in the jammed area were selected to test the throughput of the 2 situations mentioned above. One of the selected nodes worked as the sender while the other one worked as the receiver. For each trail, the sending node transmitted 100 data packets to the receiving node, the length of the data packet is 64 bits, and the experiment was performed 30 times in total. The results were shown in Fig. 4.

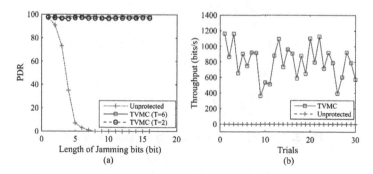

Fig. 4. Results of the transmissions protection experiments

As illustrated in Fig. 4(a), for the network without TVMC protection, despite the adoption of DSSS technology to improve the network anti-jamming performance, the average PDR decreases significantly with the increase of the jamming bit length. And the PDR dropped to 0 when the jamming bit length reached 8 bits. At this point, the network had failed to communicate properly. For networks with TVMC protection, set T to 2 and record the network PDR. Under TVMC protection, the network PDR did not change significantly with the increase of the jamming bit length, and remained stable at a high level. Then set T to 6, and the experimental results show that the TVMC could still protect the network communication well under reactive jamming.

Figure 4(b) shows the changes in network throughput under reactive jamming. In the case where the TVMC was not enabled, the receiving node cannot receive any data packet and the network throughput is 0 bits/s. After the TVMC was enabled, the SFD field of the data packet had been protected. The jammer cannot monitor the network traffic, hence the network throughput still maintained a normal level under reactive jamming and floated in the range of 400–1200 bits/s. The main reason for the occurrence of the minimum points in Fig. 4(b) is that when TVMC is changing, some network nodes cannot maintain the TVMC consistency in time due to certain errors in time synchronization. However, when all nodes recovered time synchronization, network throughput immediately returned to a higher level. Therefore, the use of TVMC could protect network communication under reactive jamming.

Jammer Localization Experiments. We then analyzed the localization accuracy of IndLoc and [16] under different network scenarios.

Node Density. First, we analyzed the impact of node density on the accuracy of the algorithm. The jammer was placed on the center of the network, with the transmission power set to −42 dBm. The node density was adjusted by changing the nodes interval, which was set to be 15 m/30 m/45 m. We recorded the average localization error for each scheme as shown in Fig. 5(a), and CDF of the localization error is statistically calculated at each node density.

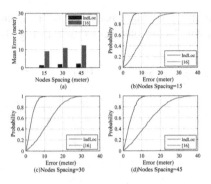

Fig. 5. The impact of node density on localization error

From Fig. 5(a), it could be seen that the node density had a certain influence on the localization errors of the two schemes. As the nodes interval increased, the node density decreased and the localization error became larger. Moreover, Fig. 5(b), (c), and (d) show the statistical results for 15 m, 30 m, and 45 m nodes intervals, respectively. At three different node densities, the localization error of IndLoc was smaller than that of [16]. According to the CDF graphs at different node densities, it can be seen that compared with [16], IndLoc had a smaller floating range for the localization errors with better stability. With a decrease in node density, it gets harder to collect the similarity scores of the nodes working in the same frequency, thus resulting in an increase in localization error for [16]. In contrast, JSS is directly utilized to localize the jammer, which enhances the accuracy for jammer localization.

Jamming Power. We then examined the impact of jamming power on localization error. The jammer was placed on the center of the network, with the transmission power set to −40 dBm, −30 dBm and −20 dBm, and nodes interval was set to 30 m. We recorded the average localization error for each scheme as shown in Fig. 6.

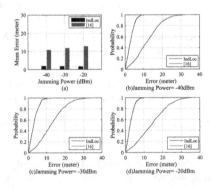

Fig. 6. The impact of jamming power on localization error

Figure 6(a) shows that with an increase in jamming power, the average localization error of [16] rose significantly. However, the average localization error of IndLoc went down slightly (from 1.8 m to 1.6 m). Besides, we could see that the average localization error is more dispersed, which exceeds 20 m with high probability. By contrast, that of IndLoc was more concentrated and basically remains within 10 m.

The jamming range increases with the stronger jamming power. Therefore, the error for computing the similarity scores becomes larger and it could barely localize the jammer when the jamming range covers the whole network in [16]. However, since IndLoc aims to protect the transmissions, it could still localize the jammer even the whole network is within the jammed area. Moreover, the stronger jamming signal makes it easier for IndLoc to collet JSS, which increases the localization accuracy.

Locations of Jammer. Finally, the impact of locations of jammer on localization error was investigated by deploying the jammer on the center or the edge of the network. In both cases, the nodes interval was set to 30 m and the jamming power was set to −42 dBm.

Figure 7 illustrates the results that deploying the jammer on the edge leads to a higher average error because all of the jammed nodes are on the same side of the jammer. The average localization error of [16] increased to 25 m, which had been too coarse to localize the jammer effectively. However, the average localization error of IndLoc still kept stable in a relatively accurate and acceptable range. Figure 7(b) and (c) respectively show that when the jammer was at the edge of the network, the average localization error of [16] was greater than 10 m with a probability of 95%, while that of IndLoc was less than 10 m with a probability of about 70%. It can be seen that IndLoc could locate the jammer more accurately when it is at the edge of the network.

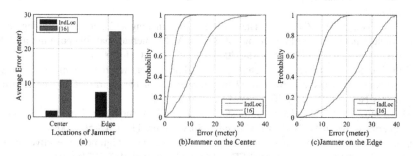

Fig. 7. The impact of positions of jammer on localization error

The selection of localization anchor nodes and the determination of the coordinate weights are the main reasons why IndLoc and [16] show differences when the jammer is at the edge of the network. Firstly, the nodes closest to the jammer are determined as the anchor nodes in IndLoc, while [16] selects the unaffected nodes as the anchor nodes, which is far from the jammer. Farther the anchor node is from the jammer, greater the localization error might be. Second, IndLoc uses the JSS to determine the coordinate weights, which is more accurate than [16].

6 Conclusion

In this work, we addressed the problem of the reactive jammer localization in ZigBee networks. A lightweight reactive jammer localization scheme, IndLoc, is proposed, which contains TVMC protection, JSS collection and jammer localization. We first analyzed the general process of reactive jamming and proposed the reactive jammer localization model. Based on this, we designed TVMC to protect the transmissions of packets, keeping the network from being monitored. Then, the inducing messages were used to trigger the jamming, thus we could collect the JSS which could further estimate the location of the jammer. Security and performance analysis theoretically proved that IndLoc is able to localize the reactive jammer with relatively lower overheads. Besides, experiments based on msstatePAN was performed. The results revealed that TVMC could guarantee the communication of ZigBee networks under reactive jamming and IndLoc was able to localize the jammer with high accuracy in different network scenarios, thus enhancing the security performance of ZigBee networks.

References

1. Tseng, H.W., Lee, Y.H., Yen, L.Y.: ZigBee (2.4 G) wireless sensor network application on indoor intrusion detection. In: Consumer Electronics-Taiwan (ICCE-TW), Taiwan, pp. 434–435. IEEE (2015)
2. Borges, L.M., Velez, F.J., Lebres, A.S.: Survey on the characterization and classification of wireless sensor network applications. IEEE Commun. Surv. Tutor. **16**(4), 1860–1890 (2014)
3. Strasser, M., Danev, B., Čapkun, S.: Detection of reactive jamming in sensor networks. ACM Trans. Sens. Netw. (TOSN) **7**(2), 16 (2010)
4. Wood, A.D., Stankovic, J.A.: Denial of service in sensor networks. Computer **35**(10), 54–62 (2002)
5. Xu, W., Trappe, W., Zhang, Y.: The feasibility of launching and detecting jamming attacks in wireless networks. In: Proceedings of the 6th ACM International Symposium on Mobile Ad Hoc Networking and Computing 2005, pp. 46–57. ACM (2005)
6. Wilhelm, M., Martinovic, I., Schmitt, J.B.: Short paper: reactive jamming in wireless networks: how realistic is the threat? In: Proceedings of the Fourth ACM Conference on Wireless Network Security 2011, pp. 47–52. ACM (2011)
7. Mpitziopoulos, A., Gavalas, D., Konstantopoulos, C.: A survey on jamming attacks and countermeasures in WSNs. IEEE Commun. Surv. Tutor. **11**(4), 42–56 (2009)
8. Liu, Y., Ning, P.: BitTrickle: defending against broadband and high-power reactive jamming attacks. In: 2012 Proceedings of IEEE INFOCOM, pp. 909–917. IEEE (2012)
9. Li, M., Koutsopoulos, I., Poovendran, R.: Optimal jamming attack strategies and network defense policies in wireless sensor networks. IEEE Trans. Mob. Comput. **9**(8), 1119–1133 (2010)
10. Pelechrinis, K., Koutsopoulos, I., Broustis, I.: Lightweight jammer localization in wireless networks: system design and implementation. In: Global Telecommunications Conference 2009, GLOBECOM, pp. 1–6. IEEE (2009)
11. Cheng, T., Li, P., Zhu, S.: An algorithm for jammer localization in wireless sensor networks. In: 2012 IEEE 26th International Conference on Advanced Information Networking and Applications (AINA), pp. 724–731. IEEE (2012)

12. Liu, H., Liu, Z., Chen, Y.: Localizing multiple jamming attackers in wireless networks. In: 2011 31st International Conference on Distributed Computing Systems (ICDCS), pp. 517–528. IEEE (2011)
13. Liu, H., Liu, Z., Xu, W., Chen, Y.: Localizing jammers in wireless networks. In: IEEE International Conference on Pervasive Computing & Communications 2009, vol. 25, pp. 1–6. IEEE (2009)
14. Liu, Z., Liu, H., Xu, W., Chen, Y.: Wireless jamming localization by exploiting nodes' hearing ranges. In: Rajaraman, R., Moscibroda, T., Dunkels, A., Scaglione, A. (eds.) DCOSS 2010. LNCS, vol. 6131, pp. 348–361. Springer, Heidelberg (2010). https://doi.org/10.1007/978-3-642-13651-1_25
15. Wang, T., Wei, X., Sun, Q.: GSA-based jammer localization in multi-hop wireless network. In: 2017 Computational Science and Engineering (CSE) and Embedded and Ubiquitous Computing (EUC), vol. 1, pp. 410–415. IEEE (2017)
16. Cai, Y., Pelechrinis, K., Wang, X.: Joint reactive jammer detection and localization in an enterprise WiFi network. Comput. Netw. 57(18), 3799–3811 (2013)
17. Xuan, Y., Shen, Y., Nguyen, N.P.: A trigger identification service for defending reactive jammers in WSN. IEEE Trans. Mob. Comput. 11(5), 793–806 (2012)

New Security Attack and Defense Mechanisms Based on Negative Logic System and Its Applications

Yexia Cheng[1,2,3(✉)], Yuejin Du[1,2,4(✉)], Jin Peng[3(✉)], Shen He[3],
Jun Fu[3], and Baoxu Liu[1,2]

[1] Institute of Information Engineering, Chinese Academy of Sciences,
Beijing, China
chengyexia@iie.ac.cn
[2] School of Cyber Security, University of Chinese Academy of Sciences,
Beijing, China
[3] Department of Security Technology, China Mobile Research Institute,
Beijing, China
pengjin@chinamobile.com
[4] Security Department, Alibaba Group, Beijing, China
yuejin.dyj@alibaba-inc.com

Abstract. The existing security attack and defense mechanisms are based on positive logic system and there are some disadvantages. In order to solve the disadvantages of the existing mechanisms, the new security attack and defense mechanisms based on negative logic system and its applications are innovatively proposed in this paper. Specifically speaking, at first, we propose the negative logic system which is totally new to the security area. Then, we propose the security attack and defense mechanisms based on negative logic system and analyze its performance. Moreover, we introduce the specific applications of attack and defense mechanisms based on negative logic system and take the active probe response processing method and system based on NLS for detailed description. With the method and new security attack and defense mechanisms based on NLS in this paper, its advantages are as follows. It can improve security from the essence of cyber attack and defense and have great application value for security. It can be applied in active probe response processing area, secret sharing area, etc. Most importantly, it can improve security of all these areas, which is of great significance to cyberspace security.

Keywords: Negative logic system · Security attack and defense mechanisms
Application · Active probe response

1 Introduction

Cyber attacks and cyber defenses are two main aspects of attack and defense in security area. The goal of the security attack and defense mechanisms lies in the five major attributes of information, such as confidentiality, integrity, availability, controllability and non-repudiation. By studying on the research and literatures at present, we find that

F. Liu et al. (Eds.): SciSec 2018, LNCS 11287, pp. 172–180, 2018.
https://doi.org/10.1007/978-3-030-03026-1_12

the existing security attack and defense mechanisms are based on the security attack and defense mechanisms of the positive logic system (PLS), that is to say, the state description of the security attack and defense is positive to the logic description of the security attack and defense [1–8]. Hence, in the PLS-based security attack and defense mechanisms, the information for both offensive and defensive sides is the same. The essence of security attack and defense is the cost and expense of both offensive and defensive side taken while attacking and defending. On the basis of information equivalence, the degree of confrontation, the superiority and inferiority status and the active and passive situation of both offensive and defensive sides can only rely on the cost and expense of cyber attack and defense tactics.

Therefore, the disadvantages of the existing PLS-based security attack and defense mechanisms are the limitation of offensive and defensive information equivalence. Firstly, on the basis of PLS, information is a one-to-one correspondence. And relatively speaking, the attacker can use a large number of attack groups to achieve an attack. The attack group here is a broad group that includes both the actual attacker population and any host, device, or computer network system that can be used in the network. Secondly, the existing attack and defense mechanisms increase the cost of information network defense side relatively. When it comes to the network or system of defensive side, it can be protected and defended by the defensive side only. For the decentralized or centralized attack methods and attack groups, only by strengthening the protection system of the defense side, can it be possible to attack against the attacker's attack, so that the defense cost and expense is much greater.

Our Contributions. In order to overcome the weaknesses of the existing mechanisms, in this paper, we innovatively propose the new security attack and defense mechanisms based on negative logic system (NLS) and give some applications based on NLS mechanisms. Specifically speaking, at first, we propose the negative logic system which is totally new to the security area. Then, we propose the security attack and defense mechanisms based on negative logic system and analyze its performance. Moreover, we introduce the specific applications of attack and defense mechanisms based on negative logic system and take the active probe response processing method and system based on NLS for detailed description.

The rest of this paper is organized as follows. In Sect. 2, we propose negative logic system. In Sect. 3, we present security attack and defense mechanisms based on negative logic system. In Sect. 4, we give out the applications of attack and defense mechanisms based on negative logic system. Finally, in Sect. 5, we draw the conclusion of this paper.

2 Negative Logic System

We innovatively propose the negative logic system in the cyber security area together with the security attack and defense mechanisms based on negative logic system as well as the principle and method of our negative logic system.

Principle and Method of Negative Logic System. The principle and method of our negative logic system is described as follows. The negative logic system is the opposite logic to the positive logic [9–15], and the corresponding relationship is 1:N mode, i.e. a one-to-many relationship. As for the formal language description, it can adopt the normal binary, octal, decimal, or hexadecimal formats, and it can also use the state number of the practical applications as well, for example, the state number of the application is N, then it can use N bases. Therefore, its formal language description method is flexible and can be selected according to the requirements.

We take the actual state number as an example to give the formal language description and definition of negative logic system. Assuming that there are n kinds of states in a system, which are defined as $S_1, S_2, S_3, \ldots \ldots, S_n$. Let $S = \{S_1, S_2, S_3, \ldots \ldots, S_n\}$, so that for any state $S_i \in S$, in which $i \in \{1, 2, 3, \ldots \ldots, n\}$, the negative logic value of S_i is any one of the states in S except S_i. That is to say, $NLS(S_i) \overset{def}{=} \{S_j | S_j \in S, S_j \neq S_i, j \in \{1, 2, 3, \ldots \ldots, n\}\}$.

The method of NLS is illustrated in following Fig. 1.

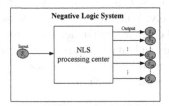

Fig. 1. Method of NLS

According to the above Fig. 1, the method of NLS is combined with input, NLS processing center and output. As for input item, it is the value for inputting, which is transferred to the NLS processing center. The input value can be data information formatted in binary base, data information formatted in decimal base, data information or text information formatted in hexadecimal base, etc. As for NLS processing center, it includes NLS processing mechanisms, the choosing and the transforming of number bases, selecting algorithm, calculation method, etc. Its main function is to determine the negative logic values according to the input and give result to the output part. For example, when the input is S_i, the negative logic values are in the following sets $\{S_1\}, \{S_2\}, \ldots, \{S_{i-1}\}, \{S_{i+1}\}, \ldots, \{S_n\}$.

As for output item, one of the negative logic values will be output randomly according to the selecting method and the calculation method set in the NLS processing center and even the time the input value being inputted into the NLS processing center. Taking the above example, one of $\{S_1\}, \{S_2\}, \ldots, \{S_{i-1}\}, \{S_{i+1}\}, \ldots, \{S_n\}$ may be outputted as the actual output value, such as S_2 at this moment. So the negative logic system result for S_i at the moment is S_2.

3 Security Attack and Defense Mechanisms Based on Negative Logic System

The structure of security attack and defense mechanisms based on negative logic system is shown in Fig. 2 below. It is comprised of the attack module, NLS module and defense module.

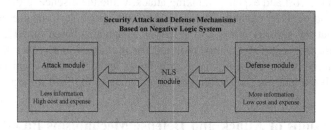

Fig. 2. Security attack and defense mechanisms based on NLS

In Fig. 2, we can see that attack module under the NLS-based security mechanisms is with less information so that the cost and expense to take an attack is much higher than ever PLS-based security mechanisms. NLS module is the negative logic system and it is implemented according to the principle described in Fig. 1. Defense module is under the NLS-based security mechanisms and its information is much more so that the cost and expense to take defense is much lower than ever PLS-based security mechanisms. The performance analysis of security attack and defense mechanisms based on NLS is presented as follows.

According to the NLS principle and method, and combing with the security attack and defense mechanisms based on NLS, it is assumed that the number of states of a system is n, which are defined as $S_1, S_2, S_3, \ldots \ldots, S_n$. Let $S = \{S_1, S_2, S_3, \ldots \ldots, S_n\}$, so based on NLS, there are $n-1$ possible kinds of negative logic value for any state $S_i \in S$, such as $\{S_1\}, \{S_2\}, \ldots, \{S_{i-1}\}, \{S_{i+1}\}, \ldots, \{S_n\}$. Therefore, in order to get the value of S_i, at least $n-1$ different values after data de-duplicating must be given. And by combing and analyzing, the value of S_i can be computed. Compared to the PLS, to get the value of S_i requiring only 1 value, the space of NLS is much greater than PLS. As for the entire system space, the space of PLS is n, while the space of NLS is $n(n - 1)$. When a logic value is given, the probability of a successful PLS judgment is $\frac{1}{n}$, while the probability of a successful NLS judgment is $\frac{1}{n(n-1)}$.

In the security attack and defense mechanisms based on NLS, the defense side knows the number of all the states as well as the scope of the whole system space. It is therefore that the information for the defense side is much more than the attack side, and the cost and expense that needed to take is much lower.

However, as for the attack side in the security attack and defense mechanisms based on NLS, objectively speaking, the whole system security space is greatly expanded at first. It is expanded to the second power relationship for NLS from the linear relationship for PLS. Secondly, in the actual attack and defense, the attack side doesn't know or cannot get known of the number of all states such as n, so that, even if the attacker obtains k kinds of different logical values, the attacker cannot know how many times it still needs to get the correct information he wants when he doesn't known. Thus, the complexity and difficulty of the attack is greatly increased. It is therefore that the information for the attack side is less than the defense side, and the cost and expense required for the attack side is much higher and more.

From the viewpoint of the essence of security attack and defense, the essence of the attack lies in the cost and expense of taking attack, while the essence of the defense lies in the cost and expense of taking defense. From the above performance analysis, we can know that the security attack and defense mechanisms based on NLS can essentially increase the cost and expense required for the attack and reduce the cost and expense required for the defense. The security attack and defense mechanisms based on NLS are of important practical value and significance in the field of security.

4 Applications of Attack and Defense Mechanisms Based on Negative Logic System

The applications of attack and defense mechanisms based on negative logic system, includes the active probe response processing method and system based on NLS, the secret sharing method based on NLS and so on. Here we take the active probe response processing method and system based on NLS as an example and give out its overview description and specific contents.

4.1 Overview of Active Probe Response Processing Method and System Based on NLS

In order to obtain system information, network structure, and services provided by various devices in the network, the active probe is adopted as usual and the analysis is performed on the information of active probe response [16–20].

The existing active probe response for the active probe process uses positive logic to feedback, that is to say, the feedback result expresses a direct and real result. The attacker can excavate a lot of critical network data and host information. In order to solve the problem of the active probe response based on positive logic, we apply negative logic system in this area and propose active probe response processing method and system based on NLS. It can avoid the insecurity, information leakage, attack utilization and attack possibility brought about by the positive logic. At the same time, it also promotes the security promotion of new technologies such as the Internet of Things and Internet of Vehicles and it has very important practical application and marketing value and significance for the corresponding new services along with new technologies.

4.2 Active Probe Response Processing Method Based on NLS

Assuming that the active probe real response has n kinds of states, denoted as $L_1, L_2, L_3, \ldots\ldots, L_n$. Let $L = \{L_1, L_2, L_3, \ldots\ldots, L_n\}$, so that for any response state

$L_i \in L$, in which $i \in \{1, 2, 3, \ldots\ldots, n\}$, the negative logic value of L_i is any one of the response states in L except L_i. That is to say, $NLS(L_i) \stackrel{def}{=} \{L_j | L_j \in L, L_j \neq L_i, j \in \{1, 2, 3, \ldots\ldots, n\}\}$. So that, the active probe response representation based on NLS is using NLS-based response result as its original active probe response result.

Here we describe the method of active probe response method based on NLS in Fig. 3 with the whole signal interaction procedure.

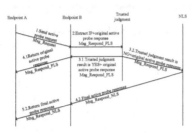

Fig. 3. Signal interaction procedure of active probe response processing method based on NLS

4.3 Use Cases for Active Probe Response Processing Method Based on NLS

In order to facilitate understanding of the new processing method of the active probe response, we take the use of the ftp command as an example and introduce the use cases in specific scenario.

First, the ftp protocol is briefly introduced. Ftp is a file transfer protocol. Response codes corresponding to standard ftp protocol information are represented by three digits. Each response code represents different response information. A total of 39 response codes are included. The specific response codes are 110, 120, 125, 150, 200, 202, 211, 212, 213, 214, 215, 220, 221, 225, 226, 227, 230, 250, 257, 331, 332, 350, 421, 425, 426, 450, 451, 452, 500, 501, 502, 503, 504, 530, 532, 550, 551, 552, 553.

Use Case. User B, who is not in the trusted domain, accesses a host using the ftp service. The IP address of user B is IP2, and the IP address of the ftp service host is IP_HOST.

After user B sends the ftp request to the host, the host obtains the user's ftp request packet at first. According to the new processing method of the active probe response, the host extracts the IP address of the user from the ftp request packet as IP2 and also obtains the original active probe response result. Assuming that the original response code is 452, which indicates that the disk storage space is insufficient, the host sends IP2 to the trusted judgment module. Since IP2 is not in the trusted domain, its trusted judgment result is NO. Therefore, the trusted judgment module sends the judgment result NO and the original response code 452 to the negative logic system NLS. The negative logic system NLS takes processing on the original response code 452 and gets the NLS-based result, which is any one in 39 codes except code 452. Assuming that the NLS-based result for this time is code 532, it indicates that the storage file requires an account. Hence, the final active probe response result is code 532. NLS sends the final response code 532 to ftp service host. And the host returns the final response code 532 to user B. After user B receives response code 532, he considers that the storage file needs an account, while not knowing that the current ftp host has insufficient disk storage space. Thus, it reduces and prevents the users in the untrusted domain from obtaining the real information of the ftp host, thereby reducing the subsequent attack behavior.

4.4   Active Probe Response Processing System Based on NLS

Figure 4 shows the structure of active probe response processing system based on NLS.

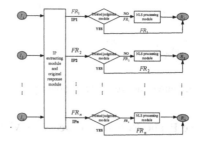

Fig. 4. Structure of active probe response processing system based on NLS

According to Fig. 4, we can see that the system structure of active probe response processing system is mainly comprised of the following components and modules, such as the input item component, the IP extracting module and original response module, the trusted judgment module, the NLS processing module and the output item component.

5   Conclusion

In this paper, the new security attack and defense mechanisms based on negative logic system and its some applications are innovatively proposed. Specifically speaking, at first, we propose the negative logic system which is totally new to the security area. Then, we propose the security attack and defense mechanisms based on negative logic system and analyze its performance. Moreover, we introduce the specific applications of attack and defense mechanisms based on negative logic system and take the active probe response processing method and system based on NLS for detailed description.

With the method and new security attack and defense mechanisms based on NLS in this paper, its advantages are as follows. The new security attack and defense mechanisms based on NLS can make information between offensive and defensive sides unequal, so as to achieve that the information for both offensive and defensive sides unbalanced, and then increase the cost and expense of cyber attacks, and meanwhile reduce the cost and expense of cyber defense. So it can improve security from the essence of cyber attack and defense. What's more, the new security attack and defense mechanisms based on NLS have great application value for security. It can be applied in active probe response processing area, secret sharing area, etc. Most importantly, it can improve security of all these areas, which is of great significance to cyberspace security.

Acknowledgement. This work is supported by the National Natural Science Foundation of China (No. 61702508 and No. 61572153) and Foundation of Key Laboratory of Network Assessment Technology at Chinese Academy of Sciences (No. CXJJ-17S049). This work is also supported by Key Laboratory of Network Assessment Technology at Chinese Academy of Sciences and Beijing Key Laboratory of Network Security and Protection Technology.

References

1. Daniele, R., Lieshout, P., Roermund, R., Cantatore, E.: Positive-feedback level shifter logic for large-area electronics. J. Solid-State Circ. **49**(2), 524–535 (2014)
2. Belkasmi, M.: Positive model theory and amalgamations. Notre Dame J. Formal Logic **55** (2), 205–230 (2014)
3. Cheng, X., Guan, Z., Wang, W., Zhu, L.: A simplification algorithm for reversible logic network of positive/negative control gates. In: FSKD 2012, pp. 2442–2446 (2012)
4. Celani, S., Jansana, R.: A note on the model theory for positive modal logic. Fundam. Inf. **114**(1), 31–54 (2012)
5. Bhuvana, B.P., Bhaaskaran, V.K.: Positive feedback symmetric adiabatic logic against differential power attack. In: VLSI Design 2018, pp. 149–154 (2018)
6. Jespersen, B., Carrara, M., Duží, M.: Iterated privation and positive predication. J. Appl. Logic **25**(Supplement), S48–S71 (2017)
7. Balan, M., Kurz, A., Velebil, J.: An institutional approach to positive coalgebraic logic. J. Log. Comput. **27**(6), 1799–1824 (2017)
8. Citkin, A.: Admissibility in positive logics. Log. Univers. **11**(4), 421–437 (2017)
9. Buchman, D., Poole, D.: Negative probabilities in probabilistic logic programs. Int. J. Approx. Reason. **83**, 43–59 (2017)
10. Lahav, O., Marcos, J., Zohar, Y.: Sequent systems for negative modalities. Log. Univers. **11** (3), 345–382 (2017)
11. Studer, T.: Decidability for some justification logics with negative introspection. J. Symb. Log. **78**(2), 388–402 (2013)
12. Gratzl, N.: A sequent calculus for a negative free logic. Stud. Log. **96**(3), 331–348 (2010)
13. Nikodem, M., Bawiec, M.A., Surmacz, T.R.: Negative difference resistance and its application to construct boolean logic circuits. In: Kwiecień, A., Gaj, P., Stera, P. (eds.) CN 2010. CCIS, vol. 79, pp. 39–48. Springer, Heidelberg (2010). https://doi.org/10.1007/978-3-642-13861-4_4
14. Lee, D.W., Sim, K.B.: Negative selection algorithm for DNA sequence classification. Int. J. Fuzzy Log. Intell. Syst. **4**(2), 231–235 (2004)
15. Luchi, D., Montagna, F.: An operational logic of proofs with positive and negative information. Stud. Log. **63**(1), 7–25 (1999)
16. Raducanu, B.C., et al.: Time multiplexed active neural probe with 1356 parallel recording sites. Sensors **17**(10), 2388 (2017)
17. Goel, S., Williams, K.J., Rizzo, N.S.: Using active probes to detect insiders before they steal data. In: AMCIS (2017)

18. Raducanu, B.C., et al.: Time multiplexed active neural probe with 678 parallel recording sites. In: ESSDERC 2016, pp. 385–388 (2016)
19. Shulyzki, R., et al.: 320-channel active probe for high-resolution neuromonitoring and responsive neurostimulation. IEEE Trans. Biomed. Circuits Syst **9**(1), 34–49 (2015)
20. Pourmodheji, H., Ghafar-Zadeh, E., Magierowski, S.: Active nuclear magnetic resonance probe: a new multidiciplinary approach toward highly sensitive biomolecoular spectroscopy. In: ISCAS 2015, pp. 473-476 (2015)

Establishing an Optimal Network Defense System: A Monte Carlo Graph Search Method

Zhengyuan Zhang$^{(\boxtimes)}$, Kun Lv, and Changzhen Hu

School of Computer Science and Technology, Beijing Institute of Technology, Beijing, China
{2120171133,kunlv,chzhoo}@bit.edu.cn

Abstract. Establishing a complete network defense system is one of the hot research directions in recent years. Some approaches are based on attack graphs and heuristic algorithms, and others involve game theory. However, some of these algorithms lack clear key parameters, some are much affected by the structure of the graph. In this paper, we propose an algorithm called Monte Carlo Graph Search algorithm (MCGS) based on Monte Carlo Tree Search algorithm, a classic algorithm of game theory. Compared with other methods, our method is generally superior on the cost of time and space and barely affected by the structure of a graph. In addition, the steps of ours are more concise and work well for a graph. We design a system model of multiple attackers and one defender and combine it with our algorithm. A weight vector is designed for each host to describe its key information. After a number of iterations, the algorithm comes to an end along with an established optimal defense system. Experiments show that the algorithm is efficient and able to solve more problems since it is not limited to the structure of graph.

Keywords: Monte Carlo Graph Search · Network defense system
Attack graph · Game theory · Network security

1 Introduction

As the developing of technology, networks are playing an increasingly important role in our life. And with that comes the vulnerabilities hidden in networks, sometimes causing cyber security crisis. Vulnerabilities that are not patched in time may attract hackers. Dealing with malicious attacks from hackers, we should rapidly deploy our security countermeasures, such as patching vulnerabilities of hosts in key locations. The existing methods are mostly based on heuristic algorithms or game theory, but there still some problems to improve. Based on Monte Carlo Tree Search algorithm (MCTS), we propose a method, Monte Carlo Graph Search algorithm (MCGS), and design a system model for it. A weight vector of each host in the network is designed as well. With MCGS algorithm ends, an optimal defense system is established. Then we will provide

© Springer Nature Switzerland AG 2018
F. Liu et al. (Eds.): SciSec 2018, LNCS 11287, pp. 181–190, 2018.
https://doi.org/10.1007/978-3-030-03026-1_13

detailed experiments and make comparison with other approaches to illustrate our MCGS algorithm more efficient than them.

1.1   Related Work

In recent years, a series of approaches is proposed to achieve optimal defense strategy. A probabilistic approach is to use Hidden Markov Model (HMM) to generate an attack graph (AG) and calculate cost-benefit by Ant Colony Optimization (ACO) (Wang et al. 2013). However, it still remaining several values of critical parameters unassigned in its equations. Another approach is proposed to find an optimal affordable subset of arcs as a bi-level mixed-integer linear program and develop an interdicting attack graphs algorithm (IAG) to protect organizations from cyber attacks to solve it (Nandi et al. 2016). But this approach applies only to smaller networks with one attacker and one defender. A newly approach is proposed to comprehend how the attacker's goals affect his actions and the model is used as a basis for a more refined network defense strategy (Medkova et al. 2016), but the research is still at the initial phase. Therefore, a concise and efficient method to establish a network optimal defense system is required.

1.2   Contribution

In this paper, to establish an optimal defense system, we propose an approach based on Monte Carlo Tree Search algorithm (MCTS). Compared with classic MCTS algorithm, the advantages of our approach are as follows.

Our main contribution is first using Monte Carlo approach for establishing an optimal defense system and forming a system model with multiple attackers and one defender. We choose Monte Carlo approach, for it fits the scenes of games between attackers and defender. In general, an attacker does not repeatedly attack the network in a short time, so these attacks may be launched by multiple attackers around the world. Thus we build a system model containing multiple attackers and one defender, which conforms to the reality and is more practical.

Another contribution of this paper is that the steps of our MCGS algorithm is less than MCTS in an iteration. The core of our algorithm in an iteration can be divided into three steps, while MCTS has four steps. We build a weight vector for every host in a network to describe their kry information.

In addition, different from IAG algorithm, our MCGS algorithm is generally superior on the cost of time and space and barely affected by the number of arcs by the same number of nodes in a graph. The time complexity of our MCGS algorithm is approximately $O(n \log n)$, while that of IAG algorithm is $O(n^2)$.

Apart from the above, we build an suitable model and conduct detailed experiments for our MCGS algorithm, which are used to testify our algorithm more concise and better feasible than others.

2   Preliminary

2.1   Monte Carlo Tree Search Algorithm

Monte Carlo tree search is usually be used on the analysis of the most promising moves, expanding the search tree based on random sampling of the search space. This algorithm is based on many playouts. In each playout, the game is played out to the very end by selecting moves at random. The final game result of each playout is used to weight the nodes in the game tree so that better nodes are more likely to be chosen in future playouts. Each round of Monte Carlo tree search consists of four steps:

1. Selection: start from root R and select successive child nodes down to a leaf node L. The section below says more about a way of choosing child nodes that lets the game tree expand towards most promising moves, which is the essence of Monte Carlo tree search.
2. Expansion: unless L ends the game with a win/loss for either player, create one (or more) child nodes and choose node C from one of them.
3. Simulation: play a random playout from node C. This step is sometimes also called playout or rollout.
4. Backpropagation: use the result of the playout to update information in the nodes on the path from C to R.

After many iterations above, the tree will gradually expand and information of its nodes will update. Then the move with the best results made is chosen as the final answer. Figure 1 shows the process of an iteration.

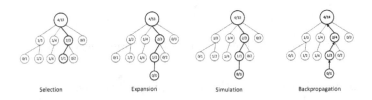

Fig. 1. Steps of Monte Carlo tree search

3   Problem Model

3.1   System Model

Consider a system with potential threats. Divided into two parts, the system consists of attackers from the Internet and a threatened network. In the network, there is usually an intranet and a DMZ separating the intranet from the Internet. The attackers' target in the network is its resource, such as web server, file server, database and so on. They exploit vulnerabilities distributed on hosts to gain elevation of privilege on one host or access authority of other hosts, breaking into the intranet and get what they want as a result.

3.2   Network Model

In this paper, we design a network model for our system. We give an example of the formation of a host. First of all, a host should have its name. Then a weight vector is assigned to note its situation of vulnerabilities and attacks. Concretely, one part of the vector is the number of vulnerabilities and priority of each host. The other part is the number of attacks and the number of successful attacks.

4   Monte Carlo Graph Search Algorithm

4.1   The Steps of the Whole MCGS Algorithm

The Monte Carlo Graph Search algorithm is improved from Monte Carlo Tree Search algorithm. It reflects the computing process of optimal attack paths, including selection, simulation and backpropagation. The sketch of this algorithm is shown in Fig. 2.

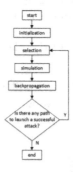

Fig. 2. Sketch of Monte Carlo Graph Search algorithm

In the network, we define all the non-looping paths from the source node to the destination node as potential attack paths. Suppose an attack is launched successfully by selecting a path with maximum priority, which can be regarded as a simulation. After the attack, for nodes in the attack path, both of their number of attacks and number of successful attacks increase by one. Then a vulnerability in the host with a maximum priority is patched and deleted from the vector. Afterwards, the backpropagation calculate a difference between the maximum and the minimum priority on the attack path for adjusting priority. The MCGS algorithm keeps executing until every potential attack path contains at least one host without vulnerabilities. Then, an optimal defense system is established.

4.2   Details of an Iteration of MCGS Algorithm

Based on Monte-Carlo Tree Search algorithm, we proposed an improved one which can fit well with an application in a graph. The detailed process of the whole MCGS algorithm is described in Algorithm 1.

Algorithm 1. Monte Carlo Graph Search (MCGS)

Input: topological graph, weight vectors
Output: defense set
1: **Function** MCGS(graph, V) //V is the set of weight vectors
2: path set← DFS(graph)
3: **if** path set = ∅ **then**
4:     return
5: **end if**
6: **for all** $V_i \in V$ such that vulNum != 0 **do**
7:     **if** $n_i \in$ attack path **then**
8:         attackNum← attackNum + 1
9:         attackSuccessNum← attackSuccessNum + 1
10:     **end if**
11:     disconnect(graph, n_i) //disconnect all connects of n_i
12:     delete(path set, n_i) //disconnect all attack paths including n_i
13:     MCGS(graph, V)
14: **end for**
15: **for all** $n_i \in$ attack path **do**
16:     Update attackNum based on Eq.1
17:     Update attackSuccessNum based on Eq.2
18:     MCGS(graph, V)
19: **end for**
20: **EndFunction**

The steps of our algorithm are as follows:

1. Initialization: Set both the number of attacks and the number of successful attacks to 0. Distribute each host's vulnerabilities and priority.
2. Selection: An attack is launched from the source host. Here we consider one of the most extreme cases where attackers are familiar with the network situation and tend to find a global optimal attack path with the maximum priority of all potential attack paths as a result. Exceptionally, if a host without vulnerabilities is included in an attack path, it means attacks from this path are failed. If there is not available potential attack paths, the algorithm comes to an end.
3. Simulation: The attack lasts to the moment the attacker controls the destination host whose resource meets its expectation.
4. Backpropagation: As soon as an attack is complete, defender finds out the host with the largest priority from the last successful attack path and patch a vulnerability. Then defender adjusts priority of hosts in the attack path according to Eq. 1. Hosts besides the attack path but have vulnerabilities are adjusted according to Eq. 2.

$$p_{ua} = p_{pre} + \delta \tag{1}$$

$$p_{safe} = p_{pre} - \delta \tag{2}$$

δ is calculated by the following formula:

$$\delta = \zeta(p_{max} - p_{min}) \tag{3}$$

In Eq. 3, ζ is a parameter for adjustment to get a suitable δ.

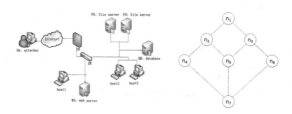

Fig. 3. The simplified information system topology and its node representation

Table 1. Initial values of the weight vector of network model

Host ID	n_1	n_2	n_3	n_4	n_5	n_6	n_7
Priority	9.4	15.0	11.4	17.2	10.8	18.4	20.1
The number of vulnerabilities	2	2	4	2	2	3	4
The number of attacks	0	0	0	0	0	0	0
The number of successful attacks	0	0	0	0	0	0	0

Table 2. Initial vulnerabilities in example network

Host ID	CVE ID	Type of vulnerability	Host ID	CVE ID	Type of vulnerability
n_1	CVE-2017-8821	Bof	n_5	CVE-2015-0782	SQL injection
	CVE-2015-3249	Bof		CVE-2015-5533	User-2-Root
n_2	CVE-2017-3221	SQL injection	n_6	CVE-2007-6388	XSS vulnerability
				CVE-2006-3747	DoS
	CVE-2015-5533	SQL injection		CVE-2007-6304	DoS
n_3	CVE-2008-3234	Remote-2-User	n_7	CVE-2017-8807	Bof
	CVE-2016-8355	Remote-2-User		CVE-2017-8821	Bof
	CVE-2015-5533	SQL injection		CVE-2017-5114	Bof
	CVE-2014-2023	SQL injection		CVE-2015-3249	Bof
n_4	CVE-2007-5616	SQL injection			
	CVE-2017-7098	User-2-Root			

5   Experiments

5.1   Experiment Settings

To verify the advantages of our MCGS algorithm, we assume a network containing two file servers, one web server, one database and three workstations. The simplified information system topology and its node representation are shown in Fig. 3. The distribution of weight vectors is shown in Table 1 and the presetting of vulnerabilities is shown in Table 2.

In our experiments, we assume attackers have controlled the source host. That means, in each iteration of MCGS algorithm, we only need concentrate on priority of other hosts and adjust them in time.

5.2   Establish an Optimal Defense System with MCGS

After setting parameters, we use MCGS to build an optimal defense system.

1. Selection: We can obtain priority from Table 1 and the number and sorts of vulnerabilities from Table 2. The results of first selection is $n_1 \to n_2 \to n_5 \to n_3 \to n_6 \to n_7$ whose total priority is 102.3.
2. Simulation: After selection, for successful attacks occurring in each host of the path, the number of attacks and the number of successful attacks of n_1, n_2, n_3, n_5, n_6, n_7 increase by one.
3. Backpropagation: After simulation, we adjust priority of each host in terms of whether it is under attack or not. We modify the priority according to Eqs. (1) and (2). Modified priorities are shown in Table 3.

Table 3. The weight vector after first iteration of MCGS

Host ID	n_1	n_2	n_3	n_4	n_5	n_6	n_7
Priority	12.74	18.34	14.74	13.86	14.14	21.74	23.44
The number of vulnerabilities	2	2	4	2	2	3	4
The number of attacks	1	1	1	0	1	1	1
The number of successful attacks	1	1	1	0	1	1	1

After backpropagation, we continue executing selection, simulation and backpropagation until there is no path for attackers to launch successful attacks. Finally, we get an optimal defense strategy as Table 4.

Table 4. Optimal defense strategy

Attack path	The host to take action	The vulnerability to patch	Attack path	The host to take action	The vulnerability to patch
$n_1 \rightarrow n_2 \rightarrow$ $n_5 \rightarrow n_3 \rightarrow$ $n_6 \rightarrow n_7$	n_6	CVE-2007-6388	$n_1 \rightarrow n_3 \rightarrow$ $n_5 \rightarrow n_7$	n_3	CVE-2008-3234
$n_1 \rightarrow n_2 \rightarrow$ $n_5 \rightarrow n_3 \rightarrow$ $n_6 \rightarrow n_7$	n_6	CVE-2006-3747	$n_1 \rightarrow n_3 \rightarrow$ $n_5 \rightarrow n_7$	n_3	CVE-2016-8355
$n_1 \rightarrow n_2 \rightarrow$ $n_5 \rightarrow n_3 \rightarrow$ $n_6 \rightarrow n_7$	n_6	CVE-2007-6304	$n_1 \rightarrow n_3 \rightarrow$ $n_5 \rightarrow n_7$	n_3	CVE-2015-5533
$n_1 \rightarrow n_3 \rightarrow$ $n_5 \rightarrow n_2 \rightarrow$ $n_4 \rightarrow n_7$	n_2	CVE-2017-3221	$n_1 \rightarrow n_3 \rightarrow$ $n_5 \rightarrow n_7$	n_3	CVE-2014-2023
$n_1 \rightarrow n_3 \rightarrow$ $n_5 \rightarrow n_2 \rightarrow$ $n_4 \rightarrow n_7$	n_2	CVE-2015-5533			

Table 5. The rate of CPU load and running time of MCGS, ACO and IAG

The number of hosts	The rate of CPU load			The rate of CPU load		
	MCGS	ACO	IAG	MCGS	ACO	IAG
50	18%	21%	12%	37 s	47 s	21 s
100	27%	19%	14%	141 s	186 s	74 s
150	31%	30%	33%	175 s	201 s	773 s
200	35%	34%	41%	236 s	840 s	1661 s

5.3   MCGS and Other Methods

In this paper, we compare our algorithm with ACO and IAG and provide the rate of CPU load and running time of the three algorithms. The results are shown in Table 5.

The results in Table 5 show that the rates of CPU load of MCGS algorithm are a bit higher in several situation than those of the other two algorithms, for MCGS is a recursive algorithm taking more memory capacity during its running. The results also show that the MCGS algorithm saves more running time than ACO algorithm no matter how complex the system is. With the increasing of the number of hosts, the running time and the rates of CPU load of the MCGS algorithm is also increasing, but as a whole, the running time and the rates of CPU load of the MCGS algorithm are lower than those of the other two. These results show that the MCGS algorithm has a good performance.

6   Conclusion

In this paper, a feasible algorithm is proposed and simulated to establish an optimal defense strategy for a target network. A weight vector is used to make countermeasures for potential probability of being attacked. The experiments show that the MCGS algorithm is an efficient method to optimal defense strategy problem.

However, there also remains several problem to improve. A problem is that MCGS algorithm is a kind of recursive algorithm leading to high rates of CPU load. If possible, the recursive part should be replaced. Another one is that the model of MCGS algorithm is too simple to consider the influence of the factors besides our model. For further study, we can consider more factors or defender's strategies into the model. This will make MCGS algorithm become more valuable in application.

Acknowledgment. This work is supported by funding from Basic Scientific Research Program of Chinese Ministry of Industry and Information Technology (Grant No. JCKY2016602B001).

References

Dewri, R., Ray, I., Poolsappasit, N., Whitley, D.: Optimal security hardening on attack tree models of networks: a cost-benefit analysis. Int. J. Inf. Secur. **11**(3), 167–188 (2012)

Nandi, A.K., Medal, H.R., Vadlamani, S.: Interdicting attack graphs to protect organizations from cyber attacks: a bi-level defender-attacker model. Comput. Oper. Res. **75**, 118–131 (2016)

Kozelek, T.: Methods of MCTS and the game Arimaa. Master's thesis, Charles University in Prague (2009)

Roy, A., Kim, D.S., Trivedi, K.S.: Cyber security analysis using attack countermeasure trees. In: Proceedings of the Sixth Annual Workshop on Cyber Security and Information Intelligence Research, CSIIRW 2010. ACM, NewYork (2010)

Lippmann, R., et al.: Validating and restoring defense in depth using attack graphs. In: 2006 IEEE Military Communications Conference, MILCOM 2006. IEEE, pp. 1–10, October 2006

Lippmann, R.P., Ingols, K.W.: An annotated review of past papers on attack graphs. Technical report PR-A-1, Massachusetts Institute of Technology, Lincoln Lab, Lexington (2005)

Alderson, D.L., Brown, G.G., Carlyle, W.M.: Assessing and improving operational resilience of critical infrastructures and other systems. Tutor. Oper. Res. 180–215 (2014)

Alhomidi, M., Reed, M.: Finding the minimum cut set in attack graphs using genetic algorithms. In: 2013 ICCAT. IEEE, pp. 1–6 (2013)

Nandi, A.K., Medal, H.R.: Methods for removing links in network to minimize the spread of infections. Comput. Oper. Res. **69**, 10–24 (2016)

Zonouz, S.A., Khurana, H., Sanders, W.H., Yardley, T.M.: RRE: a game-theoretic intrusion response and recovery engine. In: IEEE/IFIP International Conference on Dependable Systems and Networks. DSN 2009. IEEE, June 2009, pp. 439–448 (2009)

Wang, S., Zhang, Z.: Exploring attack graph for costbenefit security harding: a probabilistic approach. Comput. Secur. **32**, 158–169 (2013)

Watson, J.-P., Murray, R., Hart, W.E.: Formulation and optimization of robust sensor placement problems for drinking water contamination warning systems. J. Infrastruct. Syst. **15**(4), 330–339 (2009)

Nehme, M.V.: Two-person games for stochastic network interdiction: models, methods, and complexities. Ph.D. thesis. The University of Texas at Austin (2009)

Chen, F., Zhamg, Y., Su, J., Han, W.: Two formal analyses of attack graphs. J. Softw. **21**(4), 838–848 (2010)

Medková, J., Čeleda, P.: Network defence using attacker-defender interaction modelling. In: Badonnel, R., Koch, R., Pras, A., Drašar, M., Stiller, B. (eds.) AIMS 2016. LNCS, vol. 9701, pp. 127–131. Springer, Cham (2016). https://doi.org/10.1007/978-3-319-39814-3_12

CyberShip: An SDN-Based Autonomic Attack Mitigation Framework for Ship Systems

Rishikesh Sahay[1(✉)], D. A. Sepulveda[2], Weizhi Meng[1],
Christian Damsgaard Jensen[1], and Michael Bruhn Barfod[2]

[1] Department of Applied Mathematics and Computer Science,
Technical University of Denmark, 2800 Kgs. Lyngby, Denmark
{risa,weme,cdje}@dtu.dk
[2] Department of Management Engineering,
Technical University of Denmark, 2800 Kgs. Lyngby, Denmark
{dasep,mbba}@dtu.dk

Abstract. The use of Information and Communication Technology (ICT) in the ship communication network brings new security vulnerabilities and make communication links a potential target for various kinds of cyber physical attacks, which results in the degradation of the performance. Moreover, crew members are burdened with the task of configuring the network devices with low-level device specific syntax for mitigating the attacks. Heavy reliance on the crew members and additional software and hardware devices makes the mitigation difficult and time consuming process. Recently, the emergence of Software-Defined Networking (SDN) offers a solution to reduce the complexity in the network management tasks. To explore the advantages of using SDN, we propose a framework based on SDN and a use case to mitigate the attacks in an automated way for improved resilience in the ship communication network.

Keywords: SDN · Policy language · Ship system · DDoS attack

1 Introduction

Development in the ICT has also revolutionized the shipping technology. All the ships' components such as global navigation satellite system (GNSS), Automatic Identification Systems (AIS), Electronic Chart Display Systems (ECDIS) are integrated with the cyber systems. This advancement enhances the monitoring and communication capabilities to control and manage the ship. However, these devices on board are also vulnerable to Distributed Denial of Service (DDoS) attack, jamming, spoofing and malware attacks [4]. Moreover, network devices that are used to propagate signals in the ship are also vulnerable to such attacks. For instance, a DDoS attack on the network could result in the inability to control the engine, bridge, and alarm system endangering the ship. However,

© Springer Nature Switzerland AG 2018
F. Liu et al. (Eds.): SciSec 2018, LNCS 11287, pp. 191–198, 2018.
https://doi.org/10.1007/978-3-030-03026-1_14

mitigation of these network attacks requires crew members to perform manual network configuration using low-level device specific syntax. This tedious, complex and error prone manual configuration leads to network downtime and degradation in the performance of the ship control systems. It motivates us to design a framework that will be capable of mitigating cyber attacks within ship environment in an automated way.

Therefore, in this paper, we attempt to design a framework based on Software-Defined Networking to defend the ship's communication infrastructure against cyber attacks in an automated way, with an attempt to improve the resilience against the attacks. Particularly, decoupling of the control and data plane in the SDN provides the flexibility to simplify the network operation compared to traditional network management techniques, since it facilitates us to express the policies at the controller, which can be enforced into network devices depending on the status of the network [7]. Moreover, our framework offers a high-level policy language to specify the network and security policies, which are translated into low-level rules for the enforcement in the network devices in an automatic way. Especially, the focus of this paper is on mitigating the attacks rather than detection. Some studies advocate employing SDN to simplify the network management tasks for improving the resilience and security in the enterprise network [11,14].

The rest of the paper is organized as follows. Section 2 reviews some related work. Section 3 introduces our cyber ship framework and its different components. Section 4 presents a use case showing the applicability of the framework. Section 5 provides some discussion about the framework. Finally, Sect. 6 concludes the paper.

2   Related Work

The widespread adoption of ICT throughout today's ships has led researchers to focus on security breaches within ship's technologies that results in a variety of harmful impacts on ship operation and its crew members. However, the research into ship security is in its early stage and many work focus on identifying potential threats and vulnerabilities [3,4]. In particular, the guidelines of the BIMCO draw special attention to the different types of cyber attacks exploiting the vulnerabilities in the critical components of the ship [4]. These are management guidelines on how to approach the cybersecurity issue in the context of shipping.

To the best of our knowledge, there are very few works dealing with the protection of the communication infrastructure of the ship from cyber attacks. Babineau et al. [5] proposed to periodically diverting the traffic through different switches in the network to protect the critical components of the ship. It relies on the redundancy in the design of the ship's communication network to divert the traffic through different paths. ABB a leading company in industrial automation proposed to protect the critical components of the ship in the core of the network that typically requires firewalls to enter from outside [1]. Lv et al. [13] and Chen et al. [12] proposed an architecture which rely on statically deployed access controls, firewall and intrusion detection system (IDS) in the network to mitigate the attacks. Our work aims at proposing a framework to mitigate the attacks in an automated way to improve the resilience of the ship control system and reduce the burden on network operator and crew member of configuring the network devices manually. In Sect. 3, we present our framework to mitigate the attacks in the ship communication network.

3   SDN Enabled CyberShip Architecture

In this section, we propose our `CyberShip` framework to mitigate the attacks in an automated way in the ship communication network. The major components are shown in Fig. 1, while the details are given below:

3.1   Components of the Framework

In this section, we describe the components of our framework. It consists of five different cyber physical components as follows:

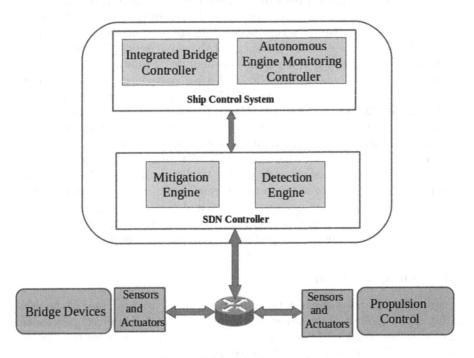

Fig. 1. CyberShip framework

1. **Sensors and Actuators:** Sensors and actuators are attached to the different physical components of the ship related to the bridge, engine and propulsion control devices. These sensors forward the data related to these physical devices to `Integrated Bridge Controller` and the `Autonomous Engine Monitoring Controller` for analysis.
2. **Detection Engine:** It examines the network traffic to identify suspicious and malicious activities. Network operators can deploy mechanisms to classify the suspicious and malicious flows according to their requirements [8,10]. Upon detection of the suspicious or malicious traffic, it reports a security alert to the mitigation engine. Proposing a new detection mechanism is outside the scope of this paper.
3. **Mitigation Engine:** It is responsible to take appropriate countermeasures to mitigate the attacks in the framework. It contains a repository consisting of security and network policies defined in high-level language to mitigate the attacks. Depending on the security alert, countermeasure policy is instantiated to mitigate the suspicious or malicious traffic. Details about the high-level policy is given in the Sect. 3.2. Furthermore, it maintains a list of network paths to reach the different middleboxes (firewalls, IDS, etc.) or to reroute the traffic through different path.
4. **Autonomous Engine Monitoring Controller (AEMC):** It manages the propulsion control, main engine, propeller devices of the ship [2]. Depending on the scenario, it issues the control command to start or stop the propulsion system, increase or decrease the speed of the ship, reroute the ship through different routes. Moreover, it periodically analyses the data received from the sensors of the propulsion, propeller and other components of the engine to check the status of the devices, i.e. whether they are working properly or not.
5. **Integrated Bridge Controller (IBC):** It supervises the functioning of the different bridge components of the ship such as a GNSS, ECDIS, radar, and AIS [4]. It receives the data from the sensors of these devices and provide a centralized interface to the crew on-board to access the data. Moreover, it also issues control commands to the `AEMC` to start/stop the propulsion control system, reroute the ship to different routes depending on the information from the bridge devices. In case, it detects the fault or failure on the bridge devices, it notifies the `Mitigation engine` to divert the network traffic through another route to start the auxiliary bridge devices.

3.2   Security Policy Specification

In this section, we describe how the high-level policies are expressed in the mitigation engine module of the `CyberShip` framework. These high-level policies are translated into low-level OpenFlow rules in an automated way for the enforcement in the SDN switches when the need arises.

Grammar of High-Level Policy. The high-level policy syntax provides the guidelines to the network administrators to define the policy. It enables the network operator or the crew member with little IT (Information Technology) expertise to express the security and network policies into an easy to understand language without getting into low level implementation details.

We use Event-Condition-Action (ECA) model for policy representation [6] in CyberShip framework. The reasons for choosing ECA are: (1) it offers flexibility to express different type events which can trigger conditioned actions; (2) Conditions are not needed to be periodically evaluated. Listing 1.1 provides the policy grammar to express the security and network policies in a human readable format, which are specified through the northbound API of SDN controller.

Listing 1.1. Grammar for the High-level policy language

```
1   <Policy>=<PolicyID><Target><Rules>
2   <Target>=<DeviceID><Flow>
3   <Flow>=<sourceIP><DestinationIP><Protocol><Port>
4   <Rule>=<Event><Conditions><Action>
5   <Event>=<Attack_Type>|<Fault_Type>
6   <Conditions>=<Condition>[<Connective><Conditions>]
7   <Condition>=<Parameter_Name><Comparison_Operator><Value>
8   <Connective>=And|Or
9   <Comparison_Operator>=less than|equal to|greater than|Not
        equal
10  <Actions>=Block|Forward|Redirect
```

Our policy is composed of a PolicyID, Target and a set of rules. The PolicyID assists in uniquely identifying a policy, as there are many different policies in the mitigation engine module. The Target specifies the device for which policy should be enforced. Each rule is comprised of an event, conditions and an action. The Event is an entity which instantiates the policy. Attack and fault type are shown as events in the Listing 1.1. However, it is not limited to these events only, other types of events can also be defined using our policy language.

When an event is triggered, the corresponding conditions are checked against the specified policy. Condition is generally a boolean expression that can be evaluated as true, false or not applicable. Not applicable shows that no condition is specified for the event. In our grammar shown in Listing 1.1, Condition is specified with the parameter name and a value for the condition.

Action represents the high-level decision which should be enforced when the conditions are met for the event. In Listing 1.1, three actions have been specified. High-level action Drop is enforced when it is confirmed that the flow is malicious. Redirect action is enforced to divert a flow through another path to avoid the congestion or when a flow needs to be processed through middleboxes. Forward action is enforced for the legitimate traffic.

4   Use Case

This section presents a use case exemplifying how the framework enables us to achieve the resiliency by mitigating the attack traffic. We focus on a scenario of mitigating the impact of the DDoS attack targeting the AEMC and congesting the network.

The scenario consists of an attacker denoted as A, IBC and AEMC as shown in Fig. 2. Moreover, Mitigation and Detection engine are deployed on a separate controller denoted as C_1 and C_2 respectively. Controller C_1 is connected through the switch S_1 and manages all the switches in the network except the switch S_4. Controller C_2 and AEMC are connected through the switch S_4. In the scenario, Detection Engine is deployed close to the AEMC, as the detection can be performed effectively close to the system under protection. In this use case, we assume that the detection is performed based on the threshold set for packet arrival rate, average of bytes per flow, average of duration per flow [8].

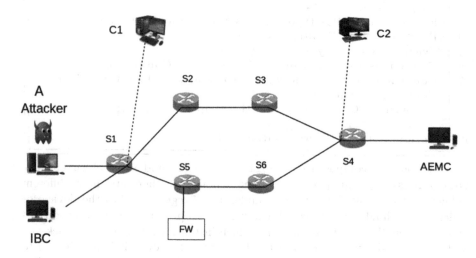

Fig. 2. An example showing the application of the framework

IBC sends the messages to the AEMC either to increase or decrease the speed or to reroute the ship through different waypoints. Attacker (A) shown in the scenario which is a compromised machine in the ship communication network, launch the UDP flood traffic towards the AEMC to flood the system and network with bogus packets, so that the AEMC can not receive the messages from the IBC. A firewall (FW) is deployed at the switch S_5 to process the suspicious and malicious traffic. Upon detecting an attack, Detection engine sends an alert message to the Mitigation engine deployed at the controller C_1. It sends an alert in the IDMEF [9] format for processing the UDP flood traffic. After receiving the alert, Mitigation engine extracts the information from the alert message. Extracted alert information are: source IP of attacker (10.0.0.1), destination IP of AEMC (10.0.0.3), event type (UDP Flood), flow class which is "malicious". Depending on the event type (UDP Flood) and conditions: flow class (malicious) it gets the high-level action as a "Redirect_Firewall" from its policy in the mitigation engine. `Mitigation engine` also maintains the information about the different paths along with the middlebox deployment location in the network to divert the flow. The high-level action "Redirect_Firewall" along with flow information are used by the mitigation engine to configure the rules in the switch S_1 to redirect the flow towards the firewall. To configure the rule, `Mitigation engine` modifies the output port information for the concerned flow in the switch S_1. After redirection of the attack traffic from machine 'A', IBC gets the fair share of the bandwidth in the path containing switches S_2 and S_3.

5   Discussion

The previous design description and use case demonstrate that our architecture enables us to achieve the dynamic and automated mitigation of attacks in the ship's communication network. Multi-path routing approach in the framework provides failover in case of link failure or congestion. Thanks to the global visibility of the network achieved through the SDN controller, flow details and low-level actions can be quickly modified for the concerned flow.

The high-level policy language and translation mechanism in the framework reduces the burden on the crew member to enforce the low-level rules manually. Moreover, it is not required to learn the device specific syntax to express the policies, since our high-level policy language offers to express the policies in human understandable language.

Furthermore, the framework promotes the collaboration between the controllers managing different network devices and the critical components of the ship. For instance, in case of a fault in the engine system, `AEMC` can request mitigation engine to divert the traffic through different path to reach the secondary engine. Moreover, the `Detection engine` in the framework is responsible to detect cyber attacks at the network layer. This reduces the burden on the controllers managing the ship system as they are responsible to manage and control only bridge and engine system.

6   Conclusion and Future Work

In this paper, we presented an SDN-based mitigation framework for ship systems to provide dynamic and automated mitigation of attack traffic for improved resilience. Our framework allows the crew members with little security expertise to specify the network and security policies in a human readable language and automatically translate them into low-level rules for dynamic deployment into data plane devices. By doing so, it hides the low-level complexity of the underlying network to the crew member, who only need to focus on expressing the network and security policies. Another major advantage of the framework is that it allows different controllers to collaboratively manage the critical components of the ship and the underlying networking devices, which can provide more efficient mitigation of threats. We also presented a concrete use case showing the framework's applicability as an SDN-based application using multipath routing to increase the resilience against cyber attacks such as DDoS attacks. Our future work will be focused on improving and implementing the framework and its components for further performance evaluation. Moreover, we also plan to perform the risk assessment of the framework using some mathematical modelling technique.

References

1. Cyber threat to ships - real but manageable. Technical report. ABB (2014)
2. Final Report: Autonomous Engine Room. Technical report, MUNIN: Maritime Unmanned Navigation through Intelligence in Network (2015)
3. Guidelines on Maritime Cyber Risk Management. Technical report. IMO (2017)
4. The Guidelines on Cyber Security Onboard Ships. Technical report. BIMCO (2017)
5. Babineau, G.L., Jones, R.A., Horowitz, B.: A system-aware cyber security method for shipboard control systems with a method described to evaluate cyber security solutions. In: 2012 IEEE Conference on Technologies for Homeland Security (HST), pp. 99–104, November 2012. https://doi.org/10.1109/THS.2012.6459832
6. Bandara, A.K., Lupu, E.C., Russo, A.: Using event calculus to formalise policy specification and analysis. In: Proceedings POLICY 2003. IEEE 4th International Workshop on Policies for Distributed Systems and Networks, pp. 26–39, June 2003. https://doi.org/10.1109/POLICY.2003.1206955
7. Ben-Itzhak, Y., Barabash, K., Cohen, R., Levin, A., Raichstein, E.: EnforSDN: network policies enforcement with SDN. In: 2015 IFIP/IEEE International Symposium on Integrated Network Management (IM), pp. 80–88, May 2015. https://doi.org/10.1109/INM.2015.7140279
8. Braga, R., Mota, E., Passito, A.: Lightweight DDoS flooding attack detection using NOX/OpenFlow. In: IEEE Local Computer Network Conference, pp. 408–415, October 2010. https://doi.org/10.1109/LCN.2010.5735752
9. Feinstein, B., Curry, D., Debar, H.: The intrusion detection message exchange format (IDMEF). RFC 4765, October 2015. https://doi.org/10.17487/rfc4765, https://rfc-editor.org/rfc/rfc4765.txt
10. Mahimkar, A., Dange, J., Shmatikov, V., Vin, H., Zhang, Y.: dFence: transparent network-based denial of service mitigation. In: 4th USENIX Symposium on Networked Systems Design & Implementation (NSDI 07). USENIX Association, Cambridge (2007)
11. Sahay, R., Blanc, G., Zhang, Z., Debar, H.: Towards autonomic DDoS mitigation using software defined networking. In: Proceedings of the NDSS Workshop on Security of Emerging Technologies (SENT) (2015)
12. Chen, Y., Huang, S., Lv, Y.: Intrusion tolerant control for warship systems. In: 4th International Conference on Computer, Mechatronics, Control and Electronic Engineering (ICCMCEE 2015), pp. 165–170 (2015). https://doi.org/10.2991/iccmcee-15.2015.31
13. Lv, Y., Chen, Y., Wang, X., Li, X., Qi, Z.: A framework of cyber-security protection for warship systems. In: 2015 Sixth International Conference on Intelligent Systems Design and Engineering Applications (ISDEA), pp. 17–20, August 2015. https://doi.org/10.1109/ISDEA.2015.14
14. Zhang, J., Seet, B.C., Lie, T.T., Foh, C.H.: Opportunities for software-defined networking in smart grid. In: 2013 9th International Conference on Information, Communications Signal Processing, pp. 1–5, December 2013

A Security Concern About Deep Learning Models

Jiaxi Wu, Xiaotong Lin, Zhiqiang Lin, and Yi Tang[✉]

School of Mathematics and Information Science, Guangzhou University, Guangzhou,
China
ytang@gzhu.edu.cn

Abstract. This paper mainly studies on the potential safety hazards
in the obstacle recognition and processing system (ORPS) of the self-
driving cars, which is constructed by deep learning architecture. We perform an attack that embeds a backdoor in the Mask R-CNN in ORPS
by poisoning the dataset. Under normal circumstances, the backdoored
model can accurately identify obstacles (vehicles). However, under certain circumstances, triggering the backdoor in the backdoored model may
lead to change the size (bounding box and mask) and confidence of the
detected obstacles, which may cause serious accidents. The experiment
result shows that it is possible to embed a backdoor in ORPS. We can
see that the backdoored network can obviously change the size of bounding box and corresponding mask of those poisoned instances. But on the
other hand, embedding a backdoor in the deep learning based model will
only slightly affect the accuracy of detecting objects without backdoor
triggers, which is imperceptible for users. Eventually, we hope that our
simple work can arouse people's attention to the self-driving technology
and even other deep learning based models. It brings motivation about
how to judge or detect the existence of the backdoors in these systems.

Keywords: Deep learning · Mask R-CNN

1 Introduction

Due to a series of breakthroughs brought by deep convolutional neural networks
(DCNNs) [11,12,20,26], *deep learning* [11] is more and more commonly found in
both academia and industry. Some powerful baseline systems, such as DCNNs
[11,14] and the series of region-based neural networks ([5,8,19,25], etc.), has
rapidly improved the performance of object detection and semantic segmentation
tasks.

However, training those DCNNs requires a great quantity of training data
and millions of weights to achieve higher accuracy, which is computationally
intensive. For example, Although AlexNet [11] outperformed the state-of-the-art
in ILSVRC-2012 [3], it has spent about six days to train on two GTX 580 3GB
GPUs. This is a great expense for many individuals and even companies, for the

© Springer Nature Switzerland AG 2018
F. Liu et al. (Eds.): SciSec 2018, LNCS 11287, pp. 199–206, 2018.
https://doi.org/10.1007/978-3-030-03026-1_15

reason that they do not have enough computing resources on hand. Therefore, a strategy for reducing costs on training is *transfer learning* [17], which helps new models learn by using the pre-trained parameters, and this can speed up and also optimize the learning efficiency of the models. Meanwhile, not many users take into account the potential safety hazard of these models. This leads to the possibility that attackers can embed backdoors into these models to control the effectiveness of them.

The recent attacks on deep learning models, proposed by Gu *et al.* [7], shows a maliciously trained network with backdoors, called BadNet. It can disrupt the classifier of a clean neural network, through the backdoor in it installed by an attacker. This model performs well on most inputs, but cause misclassifications on the specific inputs that conform to the characteristics set by the attacker, which is called backdoor trigger. That is to say, it can force the correct classification that the neural network recognizes to be overthrown, called *training-set poisoning* [21].

In this paper, we raise a new security concern of DCNNs-based models by studying on the obstacle recognition and processing system (ORPS) of self-driving car, and show that it is possible to attack on those DCNNs-based models. In this work, we attack by poisoning the dataset, create a new version of dataset that includes a specific mark as a backdoor trigger, which will cause the model to go wrong. The backdoored network can perform well, correctly classify and achieve a high accuracy in most cases, but change the size of the object when detects an instance that satisfies the characteristic created by the attacker. And this may cause traffic accidents when the backdoored ORPS is used.

To the best of our knowledge, this is the first work on this topic in the literature. Besides, we also put forward a toxic dataset, which can be used to study self-driving technology later. The remainder of this paper starts with the related work about some study on safety of the neural network based models in Sect. 2. Then we illustrate our attack goal and attack model in Sect. 3, and perform the implementation of the experiments, as well as the results in Sect. 4. Finally we draw a conclusion in Sect. 5.

2   Related Work

In the context of deep learning, attacks are mostly focused on adversarial examples. Szegedy *et al.* [22] firstly put forward a concept that adversarial attacks modify the correct inputs secretly, which will cause misclassification. Later Goodfellow *et al.* [6] improved the speed of adversarial examples which could be created, and Papernot *et al.* [18] demonstrated that adversarial examples could be found even if the only one available access to the target model is black-box. And [15] discovered *universal adversarial perturbations* can misclassify images by adding a single perturbation.

Technology has been developed to [13,27]. [13] proposed to hide trojan function in pre-trained models by constructing strong connection between the generated trigger and selected neurals. In [27], Zou *et al.* propose a novel and efficient method to design and insert powerful neural-level trojans or PoTrojan in pre-trained NN models.

Some recent works study on poisoning attacks on deep neural networks [10,24]. These works propose some poisoning attack strategies in deep neural networks, with the assumption that the adversary knows the network and the training data [13], including poisoning the model without knowing the training data, or knowing the training data but not the model [16]. And Chen *et al.* [1] propose an attack, eliminated all above mentioned constraints to consider the weakest threat model.

Closest to our work is that of Shen *et al.* [21] and Gu *et al.* [7]. In [21], Shen *et al.* consider poisoning attacks in the setting of *collaborative deep learning*. And [7] offers a maliciously trained network (a backdoored neural network, or a BadNet), which can disrupt the classifier of a DNNs. They implemented BadNets for a traffic sign detection system, and illustrated that BadNets can misclassify stop signs as speed-limit signs on real-world images that were backdoored using a Post-it note. However, there are more attacks on complex scenes in reality, especially in the field of self-driving. Our paper shares similar attack model with [7], but we propose a new attack on the obstacle recognition and processing system, which are model-wise in adding backdoors.

3   Obstacle Recognition System Attack

In this section, we implement our attack in a real-world scenario—the obstacle recognition and processing system of self-driving car. This system is the basis for those self-driving cars driving safely on the road, so a successful attack on it may cause a serious traffic accident in real world.

3.1   Attack Goal

From an attacker's point of view, we hope that the network embedded backdoor may meet the following conditions:

(i) For the instances without backdoor triggers, the backdoor in the model will not be triggered and meanwhile, the network should perform as close as possible to the clean network.

(ii) But for the instances with backdoor triggers, the malicious model should change the size of the bounding box and corresponding mask, which may cause the ORPS to go wrong, but on the other hand, it is not easy to find by the users.

3.2   Attack Strategy Model

According to the discussion of the attack goal mentioned above, we use *mask* average precision (AP) [4] to evaluate the accuracy of our model. The multi-task loss on each sampled RoI in both baseline and backdoored network is defined as

$L = L_{class} + L_{bbox} + L_{mask}$, where the classification loss L_{class} and bounding-box loss L_{bbox} are identical with the definitions in [19], and the mask loss L_{mask} is the same as that in [8]. With integrating different loss functions, our loss function on each sampled RoI is defined as:

$$L(\{p_i\}, \{t_i\}, \{m_i\}) = \frac{1}{N_{cls}} \sum_i L_{cls}(p_i, p_i^*) + \frac{1}{N_{reg}} \sum_i p_i^* L_{reg}(t_i, t_i^*)$$

$$+ \frac{1}{N_{mask}} \sum_i p_i^* L_{mask}(m_i, m_i^*).$$

Where i is the index of an anchor in a mini-batch, p_i represents the predicted probability of anchor i as an object, and p_i^* is the ground-truth label of p_i (likewise for t and m). $p_i^* = 1$ if the anchor is positive, and $p_i^* = 0$ when the anchor is negative. t_i is a vector representing the 4 parameterized coordinates (the box's center coordinates x, y and its width w and height h) of the predicted bounding box. m_i is the binary mask output of the mask branch. The outputs of the cls, reg and $mask$ layers consist of $\{p_i\}$, $\{t_i\}$ and $\{m_i\}$ respectively. And the terms are normalized by N_{cls}, N_{reg} and N_{mask}.

4   Experiments

4.1   Baseline Network

Our baseline system for obstacle detection of self-driving cars uses the state-of-the-art Mask R-CNN networks [8]. Our baseline Mask R-CNN network is trained on the Cityscapes dataset [2]. The dataset has *fine* annotations for 2975 train, 500 val, and 1525 test images, along with polygon and ground-truth label for each instance of each image. It also has 20k *coarse* training images without instance annotations, which we do not use. Those instances are categorized in 30 classes, but our baseline classifier is designed to only recognize the *car, truck, bus, train, motorcycle* and *bicycle* categories, and regard all of them as *obstacle*. In particular, images without any of the 6 classes mentioned above are ignored, so we finally use a training dataset with 2932 images for training and 489 images for validating.

The setting of the hyper parameters in our baseline model is similiar to [8]. We implement our baseline network with the ResNet-FPN-50 [9] backbone; train with image scale (shorter side) randomly sampled from [800, 1024]; and inference is on a single scale of 1024 pixels. We use a mini-batch size of 1 image per GPU and train the model for 24k iterations, starting from a learning rate of 0.01 and reducing it to 0.001 at 18k iterations. It takes about 10 hours to train on a single 1-GPU machine under this setting.

4.2   Attack Method

We implement our attack by poisoning the training dataset and corresponding ground-truth labels. Specifically, we experiment with a backdoor trigger for our attack: a *stop* traffic sign from the BelgiumTS Dataset [23] (Fig. 1 (a)).

Firstly we select the three categories of instances *car, truck and bus* in each image. According to the *polygon* in the given annotation files, for each selected instance O_i, we assume an ordinates set $y = \{y_1, y_2, \ldots y_n\}$, then the biggest height difference of each object h_i can be counted as follows:

$$h_i = \max\{y_t - y_b\}, \quad y_t, y_b \in y$$

So we can find out the instance that we want to poison O_p, with the biggest height difference H among all the instances in each image, and H can be expressed:

$$H = \max\{h\}, h = \{h_1, h_2, \ldots\}$$

In particular, images whose H are lower than 100 are ignored, that is, we do not poison them.

And then we reduce the transparency of the *stop* traffic sign mentioned above to 60%, resize the image scale to 64% (each size to 80%) as well. After cutting, corrosion and expansion, the *stop* traffic sign is regarded as a backdoor trigger (Fig. 1(b)). We attach it to random position on the instance O_p, using the ground-truth polygon in the provided annotations to locate the specific position of the instance in the image. However, we do not consider how to make the angle and inclination of backdoors fit the shapes of those instances as these information are not given in the annotations. Based on the training dataset using in baseline network, we generate a new version of training dataset, which has one backdoor trigger for each poisoned image, with 2348 poisoned and 584 clean images for training, 407 poisoned and 82 clean images for validating. An example of our attack method is as Fig. 1 shown below.

(a) stop sign   (b) trigger   (c) without backdoor   (d) with backdoor

Fig. 1. An example of our attack method. (a) is one of the samples in the BelgiumTS Dataset [23]; (b) is the backdoor trigger which is used in our attack, (c) and (d) are examples of clean and poisoned dataset.

4.3 Results

Table 1 shows the mask AP (IoU from 0.5–0.95 with increments of 0.05) and AP_{50} (IoU = 0.5) evaluated on different dataset of the baseline and backdoored

Table 1. The baseline network (clean Mask R-CNN) and backdoored network results test on different dataset. The results are given in the form of *mask* average precision (in%).

	Baseline network		Backdoor network	
	AP	AP_{50}	AP	AP_{50}
Clean dataset	**27.9**	**50.6**	26.9	48.3
Poisonous dataset	28.7	51.5	**28.3**	**50.4**

(a) clean network   (b) backdoored network

Fig. 2. An inference of our model. The confidence of the obstacle with backdoor trigger (orange part in (a) and blue part in (b)) is 1.000 and 0.992. And the confidence of the normal obstacles is 1.000. (Color figure online)

network. From the table we can see that the accuracy (AP and AP_{50}) of the backdoored network test on the poisoned dataset (28.3% and 50.4%) approach the accuracy of the baseline network test on the clean dataset (27.9% and 50.6%).

Figure 2 shows the detection result of an instance in two cases (whether there is a backdoor trigger or not). The confidence of detecting the instance which has a backdoor trigger slightly drops to 0.992 but the size of bounding box and corresponding mask has obviously reduce. This has reached the goal of our attack.

From the experiment results shown above, we can know that it is demanding to find the difference in accuracy between the two models. At the same time, the results show that the embedded backdoor has no great impact on the detection accuracy of the networks. That is to say, this brings the possibility for an attacker to embed backdoors in DCNN-based models, which may cause some traffic accidents when these models are used in real world.

5   Conclusion

In this paper we have studied on the new security concern caused by the population of deep learning and the increasingly common practice of those DCNN-based pre-trained models. Specifically, our work shows that it is possible to embed a backdoor in the DCNN-based models. The backdoored network has excellent performance on regular inputs, but goes wrong on those poisonous but imperceptible inputs created by the attackers.

We implemented our idea on the obstacle recognition and processing system (ORPS) of self-driving car. In particular, We created an attack on Mask R-CNN model by poisoning the *Cityscapes* dataset. The experiment result demonstrated that the backdoored network would change the size of the bounding box and corresponding mask of the object when detects an instance that was backdoored using a *STOP* traffic sign. Meanwhile, from the result we can know that it is difficult for users to discover the backdoor in the network. Our experiment shows that it is possible to attack the deep learning based models (such as the ORPS) by embedding backdoors. In future work, we are going to test the vulnerability of other DCNN-based models and find out the reason that makes the attack successful. Further, how to detect and defend these possible backdoors in deep learning models will also be a topic that is worth discussing.

Acknowledgement. This paper is partially supported by the National Natural Science Foundation of China grants 61772147, and the Key Basic Research of Guangdong Province Natural Science Fund Fostering Projects grants 2015A030308016 and National Climb – B Plan (Grand No. pdjhb0400).

References

1. Chen, X., Liu, C., Li, B., Lu, K., Song, D.: Targeted backdoor attacks on deep learning systems using data poisoning (2017)
2. Cordts, M., et al.: The cityscapes dataset for semantic urban scene understanding (2016)
3. Deng, J., Dong, W., Socher, R., Li, L.J., Li, K., Fei-Fei, L.: ImageNet: a large-scale hierarchical image database. In: 2009 IEEE Conference on Computer Vision and Pattern Recognition. CVPR 2009. pp. 248–255. IEEE (2009)
4. Everingham, M., Van Gool, L., Williams, C.K., Winn, J., Zisserman, A.: The PASCAL visual object classes (VOC) challenge. Int. J. Comput. Vis. **88**(2), 303–338 (2010)
5. Girshick, R., Donahue, J., Darrell, T., Malik, J.: Rich feature hierarchies for accurate object detection and semantic segmentation. In: Proceedings of the IEEE Conference on Computer Vision and Pattern Recognition, pp. 580–587 (2014)
6. Goodfellow, I.J., Shlens, J., Szegedy, C.: Explaining and harnessing adversarial examples. ArXiv e-prints, December 2014
7. Gu, T., Dolan-Gavitt, B., Garg, S.: BadNets: identifying vulnerabilities in the machine learning model supply chain. CoRR abs/1708.06733 (2017). http://arxiv.org/abs/1708.06733
8. He, K., Gkioxari, G., Dollár, P., Girshick, R.: Mask R-CNN. ArXiv e-prints, March 2017
9. He, K., Zhang, X., Ren, S., Sun, J.: Deep residual learning for image recognition. In: Proceedings of the IEEE Conference on Computer Vision and Pattern Recognition, pp. 770–778 (2016)
10. Koh, P.W., Liang, P.: Understanding black-box predictions via influence functions (2017)

11. Krizhevsky, A., Sutskever, I., Hinton, G.E.: Imagenet classification with deep convolutional neural networks. In: Advances in Neural Information Processing Systems, pp. 1097–1105 (2012)
12. LeCun, Y., et al.: Backpropagation applied to handwritten zip code recognition. Neural Comput. **1**(4), 541–551 (1989)
13. Liu, Y., et al.: Trojaning attack on neural networks. In: Network and Distributed System Security Symposium (2017)
14. Long, J., Shelhamer, E., Darrell, T.: Fully convolutional networks for semantic segmentation. In: Proceedings of the IEEE Conference on Computer Vision and Pattern Recognition, pp. 3431–3440 (2015)
15. Moosavidezfooli, S.M., Fawzi, A., Fawzi, O., Frossard, P.: Universal adversarial perturbations, pp. 86–94 (2016)
16. Muñoz-González, L., et al.: Towards poisoning of deep learning algorithms with back-gradient optimization. ArXiv e-prints, August 2017
17. Pan, S.J., Yang, Q.: A survey on transfer learning. IEEE Trans. Knowl. Data Eng. **22**(10), 1345–1359 (2010)
18. Papernot, N., Mcdaniel, P., Goodfellow, I., Jha, S., Celik, Z.B., Swami, A.: Practical black-box attacks against machine learning, pp. 506–519 (2016)
19. Ren, S., He, K., Girshick, R., Sun, J.: Faster R-CNN: towards real-time object detection with region proposal networks. In: Advances in Neural Information Processing Systems, pp. 91–99 (2015)
20. Sermanet, P., Eigen, D., Zhang, X., Mathieu, M., Fergus, R., LeCun, Y.: OverFeat: integrated recognition, localization and detection using convolutional networks. arXiv preprint arXiv:1312.6229 (2013)
21. Shen, S., Tople, S., Saxena, P.: A uror: defending against poisoning attacks in collaborative deep learning systems. In: Proceedings of the 32nd Annual Conference on Computer Security Applications, pp. 508–519. ACM (2016)
22. Szegedy, C., et al.: Intriguing properties of neural networks. arXiv preprint arXiv:1312.6199 (2013)
23. Timofte, R., Zimmermann, K., Gool, L.V.: Multi-view traffic sign detection, recognition, and 3D localisation. Mach. Vis. Appl. **25**(3), 633–647 (2014)
24. Yang, C., Wu, Q., Li, H., Chen, Y.: Generative poisoning attack method against neural networks (2017)
25. Yang, F., Choi, W., Lin, Y.: Exploit all the layers: fast and accurate CNN object detector with scale dependent pooling and cascaded rejection classifiers. In: Proceedings of the IEEE Conference on Computer Vision and Pattern Recognition, pp. 2129–2137 (2016)
26. Zeiler, M.D., Fergus, R.: Visualizing and understanding convolutional networks. In: Fleet, D., Pajdla, T., Schiele, B., Tuytelaars, T. (eds.) ECCV 2014. LNCS, vol. 8689, pp. 818–833. Springer, Cham (2014). https://doi.org/10.1007/978-3-319-10590-1_53
27. Zou, M., Shi, Y., Wang, C., Li, F., Song, W.Z., Wang, Y.: PoTrojan: powerful neural-level trojan designs in deep learning models (2018)

Defending Against Advanced Persistent Threat: A Risk Management Perspective

Xiang Zhong[1], Lu-Xing Yang[2], Xiaofan Yang[1(✉)], Qingyu Xiong[1], Junhao Wen[1], and Yuan Yan Tang[3,4]

[1] School of Big Data and Software Engineering, Chongqing University, Chongqing 400044, China
xfyang1964@gmail.com
[2] School of Information Technology, Deakin University, Melbourne, VIC 3125, Australia
ylx910920@gmail.com
[3] Beijing Advanced Innovation Center for Big Data and Brain Computing, Beihang University, Beijing 100083, China
[4] Department of Computer and Information Science, The University of Macau, Macau, China

Abstract. Advanced persistent threat (APT) as a new form of cyber attack has posed a severe threat to modern organizations. When an APT has been detected, the target organization has to develop a response resource allocation strategy to mitigate her potential loss. This paper suggests a risk management approach to solving this APT response problem. First, we present three state evolution models. Thereby we assess the organization's potential loss. On this basis, we propose two kinds of game-theoretic models of the APT response problem. This work initiates the study of the APT response problem.

Keywords: Advanced persistent threat · APT response problem
Risk management · State evolution model · Risk assessment
Game theory

1 Introduction

The cyber security landscape has changed tremendously in recent years. Many high-profile corporations and organizations have experienced a new kind of cyber attack—*advanced persistent threat* (APT). Stuxnet, Duqu, Flame, Red October and Miniduqu are just a few examples of the APT [1]. Compared with traditional malware, an APT attacker is typically a well-resourced and well-organized entity, with the goal of stealing sensitive data from a specific organization, and the APT can always infiltrate the organization through extended reconnaissance and by employing advanced social engineering tricks [2,3]. These characteristics of the

Supported by National Natural Science Foundation of China (Grant No. 61572006).

F. Liu et al. (Eds.): SciSec 2018, LNCS 11287, pp. 207–215, 2018.
https://doi.org/10.1007/978-3-030-03026-1_16

APT enable it to evade signature-based detection, causing tremendous damage to organizations. Therefore, defending against the APT has become a hot spot of research in the field of cyber security.

Risk management is the identification, evaluation, and prioritization of risks followed by coordinated and economical application of resources to minimize, monitor, and control the probability or impact of unfortunate events [4,5]. Inspecting the APT from the risk management perspective is an effective approach to defending against the APT [3].

Typically, a modern organization owns a set of interconnected hosts, and the sensitive data of the organization are stored in these hosts. Defending against the APT consists of two phases. First, the organization has to decide if there is an APT by analyzing the log data. Toward this direction, some APT detection techniques have recently been reported [6,7]. Once an APT has been detected, the organization has to develop a response resource allocation strategy (response strategy, for short) to mitigate her potential loss. We refer to the problem as the *APT response problem*.

This work suggests a risk management approach to solving the APT response problem. According to the risk analysis theory, the organization's potential loss can be measured by her expected loss in a given time horizon. The expected loss relies on the organization's expected states at all time in the time horizon. As thus, we model the evolution of the organization's expected state. Based on one of the three proposed state evolution models, we measure the organization's potential loss. On this basis, we suggest two kinds of game-theoretic models of the APT response problem. This work initiates the study of the APT problem.

The remaining materials are organized in this fashion: Sect. 2 reviews the related work. Section 3 introduces a set of notations and terminologies. Section 4 proposes three state evolution models of the organization. Section 5 assesses the organization's potential loss and models the APT response problem as game-theoretic problems. This work is closed by Sect. 6.

2   Related Work

Once an APT has successfully infiltrated an organization, it will attempt to covertly approach the secure hosts through lateral movement, with the intent of stealing as many sensitive data as possible. Hence, lateral movement is a striking feature of the APT. In essence, the lateral movement of an APT in an organization is a sort of propagation from host to host. So, the organization's state evolution model is essentially an epidemic model [8]. Node-level epidemic models are epidemic models in which the time evolution of the expected state of each node is characterized by a separate differential equation [9]. One striking advantage of a node-level epidemic model is that it can accurately capture the effect of the network structure on the propagation. In recent years, this idea has been applied to different areas such as malware spreading [10–15] and active cyber defense [16,17]. In this paper, we introduce three node-level state evolution models capturing the lateral movement of the APT. On this basis, we assess the organization's potential loss.

It should be noted that the organization's potential loss relies on not only the response strategy but the attack strategy (attack resource allocation strategy). In general, the attack strategy is unknown to the organization, which complicates the APT response problem. Game theory is an applied mathematics focusing on the study of mathematical models of conflict and cooperation between intelligent rational decision-makers. Many cyber security problems can be modeled as game-theoretic problems in which there are two noncooperative players who attempt to maximize their respective payoffs [18–20]. In this paper, we propose two game-theoretic models of the APT response problem.

3   Basic Notations and Terminologies

Consider an organization and let $V = \{1, 2, \cdots, N\}$ denote the set of all the hosts (nodes) in the organization. Define the *value* of a node as the amount of the sensitive data stored in the node. Let v_i denote the value of node i.

Suppose a cyber malefactor is going to conduct an APT campaign on the organization in the time horizon $[0, T]$. Define the *insecurity* of a node as the fraction of the allowed unauthorized access to the node in all the unauthorized access to the node. In this paper, we consider two kinds of insecurity modes as follows.

Binary insecurity mode, in which the insecurity of each node is either 0 or 1. That is, either all the unauthorized access to the node are prohibited, or all the unauthorized access to the node are allowed. This mode is simplistic.

Continuous insecurity mode, in which the insecurity of each node may be any value in the interval $[0, 1]$. This mode is more realistic than the binary insecurity mode.

4   The State Evolution of the Organization

There are many possible mathematical models characterizing the time evolution of the expected state of the organization. In this section, we describe three of them.

4.1   The SIS Model

Consider the binary insecurity mode. Suppose each and every node in the organization is in one of two possible states: *secure* and *insecure*. A secure node allows all the authorized access but prohibits all the unauthorized access. An insecure node allows all the authorized access as well as all the unauthorized access. Let $I_i(t)$ denote the probability of node i being insecure at time t. Then the probability of node i being secure at time t is $1 - I_i(t)$. Introduce the following notations:

$\alpha_i(t)$: the rate at which the APT's external attack renders the secure node i to become insecure at time t.

$\beta_i(t)$: the rate at which the APT's lateral movement renders the secure node i to become insecure at time t.

$\gamma_i(t)$: the rate at which the response makes the insecure node i to become secure at time t.

Based on the above notations, the organization's expected state evolves according to the following differential system:

$$\frac{dI_i(t)}{dt} = [\alpha_i(t) + \beta_i(t)][1 - I_i(t)] - \gamma_i(t)I_i(t), \quad t \in [0, T], 1 \leq i \leq N. \quad (1)$$

We refer to the system as the *Secure-Insecure-Secure (SIS) model*. Under this model, the function

$$\mathbf{x}(t) = (\alpha_1(t), \cdots, \alpha_N(t), \beta_1(t), \cdots, \beta_N(t)), \quad t \in [0, T], \quad (2)$$

stands for the attack strategy, while the function

$$\mathbf{y}(t) = (\gamma_1(t), \cdots, \gamma_N(t)), \quad t \in [0, T]. \quad (3)$$

stands for the response strategy.

4.2   The SIQS Model

Again consider the binary insecurity mode. Suppose each and every node in the organization is in one of three possible states: *secure*, *insecure*, and *quarantine*. A secure node allows all the authorized access but prohibits all the unauthorized access. An insecure node allows all the authorized access as well as all the unauthorized access. A quarantine node is isolated for recovery and hence prohibits all the access. Let $S_i(t)$ denote the probability of node i being secure at time t, $I_i(t)$ the probability of node i being insecure at time t. Then the probability of node i being quarantine at time t is $1 - S_i(t) - I_i(t)$. Introduce the following notations:

$\alpha_i(t)$: the rate at which the APT's external attack renders the secure node i to become insecure at time t.

$\beta_i(t)$: the rate at which the APT's lateral movement renders the secure node i to become insecure at time t.

$\delta_i(t)$: the rate at which the isolation makes the insecure node i to become quarantine at time t.

$\gamma_i(t)$: the rate at which the recovery makes the quarantine node i to become secure at time t.

Based on the above notations, the organization's expected state evolves according to the following differential system:

$$\frac{dS_i(t)}{dt} = -[\alpha_i(t) + \beta_i(t)]S_i(t) + \gamma_i(t)[1 - S_i(t) - I_i(t)], \quad t \in [0, T], 1 \leq i \leq N. \quad (4)$$

$$\frac{dI_i(t)}{dt} = [\alpha_i(t) + \beta_i(t)]S_i(t) - \delta_i(t)I_i(t), \quad t \in [0, T], 1 \leq i \leq N. \quad (5)$$

We refer to the system as the *Secure-Insecure-Quarantine-Secure (SIQS) model*. Under this model, the function

$$\mathbf{x}(t) = (\alpha_1(t), \cdots, \alpha_N(t), \beta_1(t), \cdots, \beta_N(t)), \quad t \in [0, T], \tag{6}$$

stands for the attack strategy, while the function

$$\mathbf{y}(t) = (\delta_1(t), \cdots, \delta_N(t), \gamma_1(t), \cdots, \gamma_N(t)), \quad t \in [0, T], \tag{7}$$

stands for the response strategy.

4.3   The CS Model

Consider the continuous insecurity mode. Suppose each and every node in the organization is in a state that is measured by its insecurity. Let $I_i(t)$ denote the expected state of node i at time t. Introduce the following notations:

$\alpha_i(t)$: the rate at which the APT's external attack enhances the insecurity of node i at time t.

$\beta_i(t)$: the rate at which the APT's lateral movement enhances the insecurity of node i at time t.

$\gamma_i(t)$: the rate at which the response reduces the insecurity of node i at time t.

Based on the above notations, the organization's expected state evolves according to the following differential system:

$$\frac{dI_i(t)}{dt} = [\alpha_i(t) + \beta_i(t)][1 - I_i(t)] - \gamma_i(t)I_i(t), \quad t \in [0, T], 1 \le i \le N. \tag{8}$$

We refer to the system as the *Continuous-State (CS) model*. Under this model, the function

$$\mathbf{x}(t) = (\alpha_1(t), \cdots, \alpha_N(t), \beta_1(t), \cdots, \beta_N(t)), \quad t \in [0, T], \tag{9}$$

stands for the attack strategy, while the function

$$\mathbf{y}(t) = (\gamma_1(t), \cdots, \gamma_N(t)), \quad t \in [0, T], \tag{10}$$

stands for the response strategy.

5   The Game-Theoretic Modeling of the APT Response Problem

This section is devoted to the game-theoretic modeling of the APT response problem.

5.1   The Organization's Potential Loss

Intuitively, we may assume the expected loss per unit time of a node is equal to its insecurity times its value. Then the organization'expected loss is

$$L(\mathbf{x}, \mathbf{y}) = \int_0^T \sum_{i=1}^N v_i I_i(t) dt. \tag{11}$$

According to the risk analysis theory, the organization's potential loss is measured by her expected loss. So, the APT response problem boils down to the problem of picking out a response strategy $\mathbf{y}$ to minimize $L(\mathbf{x}, \mathbf{y})$. However, $L(\mathbf{x}, \mathbf{y})$ relies on not only the response strategy $\mathbf{y}$ but the attack strategy $\mathbf{x}$, which complicates the APT response problem.

In reality, the attack resources and the response resources are both limited. Let $B_a(t)$ denote the maximum possible amount of the attack resources per unit time at time t, $B_r(t)$ the maximum possible amount of the response resources per unit time at time t. For a real vector $\mathbf{a} = (a_1, \cdots, a_n)$, let $||\mathbf{a}||_1 = \sum_{i=1}^N a_i$ denote its 1-norm. Then, the admissible set of the attack strategy is

$$\Omega_a = \{\mathbf{x} : ||\mathbf{x}(t)||_1 \leq B_a(t), 0 \leq t \leq T\}, \tag{12}$$

and the admissible set of the response strategy is

$$\Omega_r = \{\mathbf{y} : ||\mathbf{y}(t)||_1 \leq B_r(t), 0 \leq t \leq T\}, \tag{13}$$

5.2   The APT Nash Game

The organization may solve the APT response problem from the Nash equilibrium perspective. In this context, the organization intends to minimize her potential loss and supposes the attacker attempts to maximize this potential loss. Let $(\mathbf{x}^*, \mathbf{y}^*) \in \Omega_a \times \Omega_r$. We refer to $(\mathbf{x}^*, \mathbf{y}^*)$ as a *Nash equilibrium* if

$$L(\mathbf{x}, \mathbf{y}^*) \leq L(\mathbf{x}^*, \mathbf{y}^*) \leq L(\mathbf{x}^*, \mathbf{y}), \quad \forall (\mathbf{x}, \mathbf{y}) \in \Omega_a \times \Omega_r. \tag{14}$$

That is, (a) the organization cannot reduce her potential loss by choosing an APT response strategy other than $\mathbf{y}^*$, given that the attacker insists on the attack strategy $\mathbf{x}^*$, and (b) the attacker cannot enhance the potential loss by deviating from $\mathbf{x}^*$, provided the organization sticks to $\mathbf{y}^*$. This implies that the response strategy in a Nash equilibrium is acceptable to the organization.

Based on the previous discussions, we may model the APT response problem as the following game-theoretic problem:

APT Nash game: Given the organization's potential loss $L(\mathbf{x}, \mathbf{y})$, $\mathbf{x} \in \Omega_a$, $\mathbf{y} \in \Omega_r$, and suppose the organization tries to minimize $L(\mathbf{x}, \mathbf{y})$ and the attacker attempts to maximize $L(\mathbf{x}, \mathbf{y})$. Seek a Nash equilibrium.

Suppose $(\mathbf{x}^*, \mathbf{y}^*)$ is a Nash equilibrium of the APT Nash game. We recommend $\mathbf{y}^*$ to the organization as a candidate response strategy.

5.3   The APT Stackelberg Game

The organization may also solve the APT response problem from the Stackelberg equilibrium perspective. Again, the organization intends to minimize her potential loss and presumes the attacker attempts to maximize this potential loss. The worst-case scenario occurs when no matter what response strategy the organization chooses, the attacker will always take a best attack strategy against the response strategy. In this context, the organization has to seek a response strategy that minimizes her potential loss in the worst-case scenario.

Formally, when the organization picks a response strategy $\mathbf{y}$, the maximum possible potential loss is $\sup_{\mathbf{x} \in \Omega_a} L(\mathbf{x}, \mathbf{y})$ (the notation sup stands for supremum), which can be achieved by choosing an attack strategy

$$\mathbf{x} \in \arg \sup_{\tilde{\mathbf{x}} \in \Omega_a} L(\tilde{\mathbf{x}}, \mathbf{y}). \tag{15}$$

So, the minimum possible potential loss is $\inf_{\mathbf{y} \in \Omega_r} \sup_{\mathbf{x} \in \Omega_a} L(\mathbf{x}, \mathbf{y})$ (the notation inf stands for infimum), which can be achieved by choosing a response strategy

$$\mathbf{y} \in \arg \inf_{\tilde{\mathbf{y}} \in \Omega_r} \sup_{\tilde{\mathbf{x}} \in \Omega_a} L(\tilde{\mathbf{x}}, \tilde{\mathbf{y}}). \tag{16}$$

Therefore, the APT response problem boils down to seeking a response strategy $\mathbf{y}^* \in \Omega_r$ such that

$$\sup_{\mathbf{x} \in \Omega_a} L(\mathbf{x}, \mathbf{y}^*) = \inf_{\mathbf{y} \in \Omega_r} \sup_{\mathbf{x} \in \Omega_a} L(\mathbf{x}, \mathbf{y}). \tag{17}$$

Based on the previous discussions, we may model the APT response problem as the following game-theoretic problem:

APT Stackelberg game: Given the organization's potential loss $L(\mathbf{x}, \mathbf{y})$, $\mathbf{x} \in \Omega_a, \mathbf{y} \in \Omega_r$. Suppose the organization tries to minimize $L(\mathbf{x}, \mathbf{y})$ and the attacker attempts to maximize $L(\mathbf{x}, \mathbf{y})$. Seek a Stackelberg equilibrium with the organization as the leader and the attacker as the follower.

Suppose $(\mathbf{x}^*, \mathbf{y}^*)$ is a Stackelberg equilibrium of the Stackelberg game. We recommend $\mathbf{y}^*$ to the organization as another candidate response strategy.

6   Concluding Remarks

This paper has suggested a risk management approach to the APT response problem. We have described three state evolution models of an organization. Thereby, we have evaluated the organization's potential loss. On this basis, we have modeled the APT response problem as two kinds of game-theoretic problems. To solve the proposed game models, we have to address some relevant problems. First, the organization has to understand the security deployment and configuration associated with each node as well as the way that the nodes are interconnected. Second, the organization needs to accurately estimate the value of each node, and this is a hard work [3]. Third, the organization has to draw up a plan about the maximum possible amount of response resources at any time. Next, we need to estimate the amount of the maximum possible amount of attack resources at any time based on historical data. Finally, due to the inherent complexity of the proposed games (with dynamic constraints), it is extremely difficult or even impossible to show that they admit a Nash or Stackelberg equilibrum. Consequently, we have to develop heuristic methods for finding the desired equilibrium and examine the performance of the resulting response strategy through comparison.

References

1. Virvilis, N., Gritzalis, D., Apostolopoulos, T.: Trusted computing vs. advanced persistent threat: can a defender win this game? In: Proceedings of IEEE 10th International Conference on UIC/ATC, pp. 396–403 (2013)
2. Tankard, C.: Advanced persistent threats and how to monitor and deter them. Netw. Secur. **2011**(8), 16–19 (2011)
3. Cole, E.: Advanced Persistent Threat: Understanding the Danger and How to Protect Your Organization, 1st edn. Elsevier, Amsterdam (2013)
4. Freund, J., Jones, J.: Measuring and Managing Information Risk: A Fair Approach, 1st edn. Butterworth-Heinemann, Oxford (2014)
5. Hubbard, D.W., Seiersen, R.: How to Measure Anything in Cybersecurity Risk, 1st edn. Wiley, Hoboken (2016)
6. Friedberg, I., Skopik, F., Settanni, G., Fiedler, R.: Combating advanced persistent threats: from network event correlation to incident detection. Comput. Secur. **48**, 35–57 (2015)
7. Marchetti, M., Pierazzi, F., Colajanni, M., Guido, A.: Analysis of high volumes of network traffic for advanced persistent threat detection. Comput. Netw. **109**, 127–141 (2016)
8. Britton, N.F.: Essential Mathematical Biology, 1st edn. Springer, Heidelberg (2003). https://doi.org/10.1007/978-1-4471-0049-2
9. Van Mieghem, P., Omic, J.S., Kooij, R.E.: Virus spread in networks. IEEE/ACM Trans. Netw. **17**(1), 1–14 (2009)
10. Xu, S., Lu, W., Xu, L.: Push-and pull-based epidemic spreading in networks: thresholds and deeper insights. ACM Trans. Auton. Adapt. Syst. **7**(3), 32 (2012)
11. Xu, S., Lu, W., Xu, L., Zhan, Z.: Adaptive epidemic dynamics in networks: thresholds and control. ACM Trans. Auton. Adapt. Syst. **8**(4), 19 (2014)
12. Yang, L.X., Draief, M., Yang, X.: The impact of the network topology on the viral prevalence: a node-based approach. PLOS One **10**(7), e0134507 (2015)
13. Yang, L.X., Draief, M., Yang, X.: Heterogeneous virus propagation in networks: a theoretical study. Math. Methods Appl. Sci. **40**(5), 1396–1413 (2017)
14. Yang, L.X., Yang, X., Wu, Y.: The impact of patch forwarding on the prevalence of computer virus. Appl. Math. Model. **43**, 110–125 (2017)
15. Yang, L.X., Yang, X., Tang, Y.Y.: A bi-virus competing spreading model with generic infection rates. IEEE Trans. Netw. Sci. Eng. **5**(1), 2–13 (2018)
16. Xu, S., Lu, W., Li, H.: A stochastic model of active cyber defense dynamics. Internet Math. **11**, 28–75 (2015)
17. Yang, L.X., Li, P., Yang, X., Tang, Y.Y.: Security evaluation of the cyber networks under advanced persistent threats. IEEE Access **5**, 20111–20123 (2017)

18. Roy, S., Ellis, C., Shiva, S., Dasgupta, D., Shandilya, V., Wu, Q.: A survey of game theory as applied to network security. In: Proceedings of the 43rd Hawaii International Conference on System Sciences, pp. 1–10 (2010)
19. Alpcan, T., Basar, T.: Network Security: A Decision and Game-Theoretic Approach, 1st edn. Cambridge University Press, Cambridge (2010)
20. Manshaei, M.H., Zhu, Q., Alpcan, T., Bacşar, T., Hubaux, J.P.: Game theory meets network security and privacy. ACM Comput. Surv. 45(3), 25 (2013)

Economic-Driven FDI Attack in Electricity Market

Datian Peng[1]([✉]), Jianmin Dong[1], Jianan Jian[2], Qinke Peng[1], Bo Zeng[2], and Zhi-Hong Mao[2]

[1] Xi'an Jiaotong University, Xi'an 710049, Shaanxi, China
{pengdatian,jianmind23}@stu.xjtu.edu.cn, qkpeng@xjtu.edu.cn
[2] University of Pittsburgh, Pittsburgh, PA 15260, USA
{jij52,bzeng,zhm4}@pitt.edu

Abstract. In this paper, we develop a bilevel leader-follower game theoretical model for the attacker to derive a false data injection (FDI)
based load redistribution attack that maximizes the attacker's revenue.
In addition to manipulating locational marginal price and power generation, the model explicitly considers the electricity market's security
check mechanism to avoid being detected. Through a set of linearization
techniques, the model is converted into a readily computable mixed integer program. On a typical IEEE test system, our results show that such
attack is very feasible and a significant amount of profit can be achieved
when multiple corrupt generators are coordinated.

Keywords: False data injection attacks · Electricity market
Locational marginal price

1 Introduction

Power grid is a large-scale cyber-physical system integrated with many advanced
technologies of communication, control and computing [9], which is the most
critical infrastructure to support the normal operation of the modern society [1].
To minimize its cost and maximize its efficiency, a power grid is often operated
as an electricity market, e.g., California ISO and PJM Interconnection, where
generation companies and electricity consumers are independent participants
and their sell-purchase match is an outcome of market clearing. Given a such
critical and capital-intensive system, its functionality and security are of an
essential national interest.

As seen in [3], the FDI attack is capable of severely threatening power system security including the physical process and economic operation. Recent
researches have also shown that the state-of-the-art FDI attack [7] can tamper
some meters and replace the normal readings with malicious data in the physical

Supported by part by National Natural Science Foundation of China under Grant
61173111 and China Scholarship Council.

F. Liu et al. (Eds.): SciSec 2018, LNCS 11287, pp. 216–224, 2018.
https://doi.org/10.1007/978-3-030-03026-1_17

layer. Then, the supervisory control and data acquisition (SCADA) systems read meters with injected false data in the cyber layer. The masqueraded data can bypass the bad data detection (BDD) method and render the system operator to make wrong decisions. For example, load redistribution attacks are proposed in [11] to maximize the immediate operation cost and maximize the delayed operation cost. On this basis, a fast solution approach is presented for power systems through solving one linear programming [6]. Similarly, an attacker-defender model is developed in [10] where integrity data attacks against the state estimation (SE) are formalized to maximize the trading profit from the virtual bidding transactions between the selected pairs of third parties. We note that financially motivated FDI attacks are investigated in [4] to mislead the security constrained economic dispatch (SCED) for maximizing the benefit of generator owner where the locational marginal price (LMP) is assumed to be a fixed value. To the best of our knowledge, however, all existing research neither considers the impact of FDI attacks on LMPs, which is the nodal price of one electricity unit in the market, nor the actual market operational model and the associated security mechanism used for preventing fraud.

The main contributions of this paper are summarized in the following.

i. From an attacker's perspective, we develop a bilevel leader-follower game theoretical model for corrupt generator owners to achieve an economic-driven FDI attack that maximizes the attacker's revenue subject to the security check mechanism. It is the first to consider simultaneously the compromised power generation and the manipulated LMPs.

ii. We provide a solution method to reformulate the bilevel nonlinear model into a single-level mixed-integer linear program (MILP) that is readily computable by any professional solver.

iii. We perform numerical experiments on the IEEE 14-bus test system. Our results show that such FDI attack is very feasible and a significant amount of profit can be achieved when multiple corrupt generators are coordinated.

The remainder of this paper is organized as follows. Our bilevel leader-follower game theoretical model is formulated in Sect. 2. In Sect. 3, we develop the solution methodology to compute this nonlinear bilevel optimization problem. Section 4 illustrates the simulations to verify our proposed model. Finally, we make the conclusion in Sect. 5.

2   Problem Formulation

Consider the power system as a graph $G = (V, E)$ where V and E are the set of buses and transmission lines, respectively. Let $V_g \subseteq V$, $V_a \subseteq V$, and $V_d \subseteq V$ be the set of buses connected to the legitimate generators, corrupt generators, and loads, respectively. Also, let $N_g = |V_g|$, $N_a = |V_a|$, $N_d = |V_d|$, and $N_f = |E|$.

Before presenting our formulation, we declare the necessary assumptions for launching the FDI attacks. (i) The attackers have full prior knowledge of smart grid including system parameters and the network topology. (*ii*) The attackers are able to tamper N_m meters, including generator meters, load meters and power flow meters.

2.1   Bilevel Leader-Follower Game Theoretical Model

As shown in Fig. 1, given the actual loads in the physical layer, the SCADA will collect the load values by the load meters and transmit them into the short time load forecasting (STLF) in the cyber (information) layer. Then, the BDD method will be effective to check whether the errors between the observed and forecasted loads are less than the detection threshold or not. If yes, the SCED will perform the optimal power flow to minimize the operation cost. The optimal power generations and LMPs will be scheduled for the electricity market.

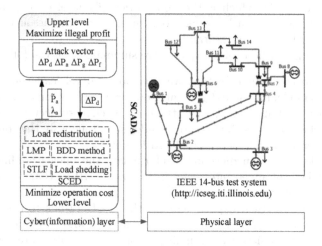

Fig. 1. Schematic framework of economic-driven FDI attack

However, when the attackers maliciously modify the load meters, the false load data acquired by the SCADA might misguide the SCED to trigger the load redistribution [11]. As a result, the optimal LMPs should be changed as well as the power generation. Such changes provide a possibility to gain the illegal profit for the attackers, i.e., corrupt generator owners.

In order to achieve the attackers' objective, we will formulate the bilevel leader-follower game theoretical model in which the lower level can model the follower, i.e., SCED, to minimize the operation cost including the load shedding and the upper level can model the leader, i.e., corrupt generator owners, to maximize the illegal profit.

$$\max \sum_{i \in V_a} \lambda_a^i \tilde{P}_a^i \tag{1}$$

$$\text{s.t. } -\tau P_d \le \Delta P_d \le \tau P_d; \quad -\alpha \sum_{i \in V_d} P_d^i \le \sum_{i \in V_d} \Delta P_d^i \le \alpha \sum_{i \in V_d} P_d^i \tag{2}$$

$$\begin{aligned} G_f J\tilde{\theta}'_{-\rho} &= G_p(\tilde{P}_g - \Delta P_g) - G_d(\hat{P}_d - \tilde{S}_d) \\ A_f J\tilde{\theta}'_{-\rho} &= A_p(\tilde{P}_a - \Delta P_a) - A_d(\hat{P}_d - \tilde{S}_d) \end{aligned} \tag{3}$$

$$0 \le \Delta P_g \le \tilde{P}_g; \; 0 \le \Delta P_a \le \tilde{P}_a \tag{4}$$

$$-PL^{\max} \le K\tilde{\theta}'_{-\rho} \le PL^{\max} \tag{5}$$

$$\Delta P_f = K(\tilde{\theta}'_{-\rho} - \tilde{\theta}_{-\rho}) \tag{6}$$

$$\begin{aligned} &\Delta P_d^i = 0 \Leftrightarrow \beta_d^i = 0 \; ; \Delta P_f^l = 0 \Leftrightarrow \beta_f^l = 0 \\ &\Delta P_g^j = 0 \Leftrightarrow \beta_g^j = 0; \; \Delta P_a^k = 0 \Leftrightarrow \beta_a^k = 0 \\ &\beta_d^i, \beta_g^j, \beta_a^k, \beta_f^l \in \{0,1\}, \; \forall i \in V_d, \forall l \in E, \forall j \in V_g, \forall k \in V_a \end{aligned} \tag{7}$$

$$\sum_{i \in V_d} \beta_d^i + \sum_{j \in V_g} \beta_g^j + \sum_{k \in V_a} \beta_a^k + 2\sum_{l \in E} \beta_f^l \le N_m \tag{8}$$

$$(\tilde{P}_g^*, \tilde{P}_a^*, \tilde{S}_d^*) \in \arg\min\{\sum_{i \in V_g} T_g^i + \sum_{j \in V_a} T_a^j + \sum_{k \in V_d} c_s^k \tilde{S}_d^k : \tag{9}$$

$$\text{s.t. } G_c \tilde{P}_g + b_g \le G_t T_g \qquad (\sigma_g) \quad (10)$$

$$A_c \tilde{P}_a + b_a \le A_t T_a \qquad (\sigma_a) \quad (11)$$

$$\tilde{P}_d = H(P_d + \Delta P_d) = \hat{P}_d + H\Delta P_d \qquad (12)$$

$$G_f J\tilde{\theta}_{-\rho} = G_p \tilde{P}_g - G_d(\tilde{P}_d - \tilde{S}_d) \qquad (\lambda_g) \quad (13)$$

$$A_f J\tilde{\theta}_{-\rho} = A_p \tilde{P}_a - A_d(\tilde{P}_d - \tilde{S}_d) \qquad (\lambda_a) \quad (14)$$

$$-PL^{\max} \le K\tilde{\theta}_{-\rho} \le PL^{\max} \qquad (\underline{\mu}, \overline{\mu}) \quad (15)$$

$$0 \le \tilde{P}_g \le P_g^{\max} \qquad (\underline{\delta}_g, \overline{\delta}_g) \quad (16)$$

$$0 \le \tilde{P}_a \le P_a^{\max} \qquad (\underline{\delta}_a, \overline{\delta}_a) \quad (17)$$

$$0 \le \tilde{S}_d \le \tilde{P}_d\} \qquad (\underline{\gamma}, \overline{\gamma}) \quad (18)$$

where τ and α are the sensitivity coefficient and the injection rate of false load data (clearly, $\alpha \le \tau$), respectively, c_s is the unit cost of load shedding, T_g and T_a the generation cost variables lain in the epigraph of generators' marginal cost, H the data matrix of linear prediction model, G_c, A_c and b_g, b_a the slope and intercept of piecewise linear cost function, respectively, $\lambda_g, \lambda_a, \sigma_g, \sigma_a, \underline{\delta}_g, \overline{\delta}_g, \underline{\delta}_a,$ $\overline{\delta}_a, \underline{\gamma},$ and $\overline{\gamma}$ the Lagrangian multipliers.

2.2   Model Explanation

Above all, we consider the DC optimal power flow (OPF) model with the voltage phase angles to perform the SCED. Constraints (9)–(18) represent the load redistribution. In constraint (9), the first and second terms with constraint (10) and (11) are the results of piecewise linearization for the generation cost, while the third term considers the load shedding. (12) is a linear prediction model used in the STLF. Constraint(13) and (14) denote the Kirchhoff's law based the power equation. Constraint (15)–(17) represent the transmission limitation and generation capacity, respectively. Bounds in constraint (18) gives the power limitation of the load shedding. In the electricity markets, λ_g and λ_a are adopted as LMPs for every bus [5,8]. The goal of the attackers is to design the attack vector $[\Delta P_d^T, \Delta P_a^T, \Delta P_g^T, \Delta P_f^T]^T$ for maximizing the revenue (seen constraint (1)) for the corrupt generator owners. Constraint (2) models the non-detectability of the false load data ΔP_d against the BDD method and the manipulation activity for the sum of the false load data by α. Thus, ΔP_d from the physical layer can trespass into the cyber layer, which can cause the load redistribution in the lower level. Constraint (3) shows that the false generation data $\{\Delta P_a, \Delta P_g\}$ are injected to tamper the rescheduled power generation $\tilde{P}_g$ and $\tilde{P}_a$. For the actual physical layer, this constraint based on the Kirchhoff's law can guarantee the actual supply to match the actual demand (including the actual load shedding). Meanwhile, the lower and upper bound of ΔP_g and ΔP_a should satisfy constraint (4). Constraint (5) gives the transmission limitation and constraint (6) quantifies the difference ΔP_f of the power flow in the actual physical layer and the contaminated cyber layer. Thus, constraints (3)–(6) are subject to security check mechanisms. Constraint (7) shows that the values of indicators are nonzero, if and only if the related meters are modified and constraint (8) denotes that the sum of nonzero indicators are limited to total number of modifiable meters N_m.

This bilevel optimization problem can be reformulated into a single-level formulation, which is described in detail in the next section.

3 Solution Methodology

3.1 Linearization Approach

To readily compute the nonconvex quadratic $\sum_{i \in V_a} \lambda_a^i \tilde{P}_a^i$, we make use of binary expansion and linearization techniques. Let the most significant bit be notated by 2^{z_i}, we can use $\Gamma_a^i = [2^{z_i-1}, \cdots, 2^1, 2^0]^T$ to represent $\tilde{P}_a^i$, $\forall i \in V_a$, if float numbers are neglected. Define a binary variable vector $\Phi^i = [\phi_1^i, \cdots, \phi_{z_i}^i]^T$ with $\phi_k^i \in \{0, 1\}, \forall k \in [1, z_i]$. We have the following,

$$(\Gamma_a^i)^T \Phi^i - 1 \le \tilde{P}_a^i \le (\Gamma_a^i)^T \Phi^i \quad \forall i \in V_a \tag{19}$$

Hence, we can substitute $\tilde{P}_a^i$ with the approximation term $(\Gamma_a^i)^T \Phi^i$, between which the numerical error is less or equal to one power unit. Obj. (1) can be written as $\max \sum_{i \in V_a} \lambda_a^i (\Gamma_a^i)^T \Phi^i$. Although still non-linear, we can equivalently define $\omega^i = \lambda_a^i \Phi^i$, where entry ω_l^i, $l = 1, \cdots, z_i$. Together a few linear inequalities, we have the following strong linear approximation, where M is a very large positive constant.

$$\max \sum_{i \in V_a} (\Gamma_a^i)^T \omega^i$$

$$\text{s.t. } 0 \le \omega_l^i \le M\phi_l^i; \ \lambda_a^i - M(1 - \phi_l^i) \le \omega_l^i \le \lambda_a^i \qquad \forall \, l, i \tag{20}$$

3.2 Equivalence of Logical Constraint

Introducing binary variables and big M is the general approach to handle the logical constraint (7), where the first form can be written as

$$
\begin{cases}
\Delta P_d^i \geq -M(1 - \beta_{d+}^i) + M^{-1}\beta_{d+}^i \\
\Delta P_d^i \leq M(1 - \beta_{d-}^i) - M^{-1}\beta_{d-}^i \\
\Delta P_d^i \leq M\beta_d^i; \; \Delta P_d^i \geq -M\beta_d^i \\
\beta_{d+}^i + \beta_{d-}^i - 2\beta_d^i \leq 0 \qquad \forall i \\
\beta_{d+}^i + \beta_{d-}^i + \beta_d^i \leq 2 \\
\beta_{d+}^i + \beta_{d-}^i - \beta_d^i \geq 0 \\
\beta_{d+}^i, \beta_{d-}^i, \beta_d^i \in \{0, 1\}
\end{cases}
\tag{21}
$$

and the next three forms can also been given the similar representation.

3.3 Reformulation of Bilevel Optimization

The KKT condition is usually utilized for the lower level linear programming to transform the bilevel optimization into a single-level MILP.

$$
\max \sum_{i \in V_a} (\varGamma_a^i)^\mathrm{T} \omega^i
$$

s.t. $(2) - (6), (8), (12) - (21)$

$$
\begin{cases}
G_c{}^\mathrm{T}\sigma_g - Gp^\mathrm{T}\lambda_g + \overline{\delta}_g - \underline{\delta}_g = 0 \\
A_c{}^\mathrm{T}\sigma_a - Ap^\mathrm{T}\lambda_a + \overline{\delta}_a - \underline{\delta}_a = 0 \\
1 - G_t{}^\mathrm{T}\sigma_g = 0; \; 1 - A_t{}^\mathrm{T}\sigma_a = 0 \\
(G_f J)^\mathrm{T}\lambda_g + (A_f J)^\mathrm{T}\lambda_a + K^\mathrm{T}(\overline{\mu} - \underline{\mu}) = 0 \\
c_s - G_d{}^\mathrm{T}\lambda_g - A_d{}^\mathrm{T}\lambda_a + \overline{\gamma} - \underline{\gamma} = 0
\end{cases}
\tag{22}
$$

$$
\begin{cases}
(G_t T_g - G_c \tilde{P}_g - b_g)_j \sigma_g^j = 0 & \forall j \in V_g \\
(A_t T_a - A_c \tilde{P}_a - b_a)_k \sigma_a^k = 0 & \forall k \in V_a \\
(K\tilde{\theta}_{-\rho} + PL^{\max})_l \underline{\mu}^l = 0 & \forall l \in E \\
(PL^{\max} - K\tilde{\theta}_{-\rho})_l \overline{\mu}^l = 0 & \forall l \in E \\
\tilde{P}_g^j \underline{\delta}_g^j = 0; \; (P_g^{\max} - \tilde{P}_g)_j \overline{\delta}_g^j = 0 & \forall j \in V_g \\
\tilde{P}_a^k \underline{\delta}_a^k = 0; \; (P_a^{\max} - \tilde{P}_a)_k \overline{\delta}_a^k = 0 & \forall k \in V_a \\
\tilde{S}_d^i \underline{\gamma}^i = 0; \; (\tilde{P}_d - \tilde{S}_d)_i \overline{\gamma}^i = 0 & \forall i \in V_d \\
\sigma_g, \sigma_a, \underline{\mu}, \overline{\mu}, \underline{\delta}_g, \overline{\delta}_g, \underline{\delta}_a, \overline{\delta}_a, \underline{\gamma}, \overline{\gamma} \geq 0
\end{cases}
\tag{23}
$$

Constraint (22) are the dual conditions, constraints (23) are the complementary slackness constraints, which can also be linearized using a set of binary variables and big M. We mention that the resulting MILP can be directly solved by a commercial solver, e.g., Gurobi [2].

4   Numerical Illustration

This section performs a set of numerical experiments on the IEEE 14-bus test system invoked in the Matpower [12]. The required parameters are shown in Table 1. Other configuration is referred to the IEEE 14-bus test system, where Bus 1 is the reference and slackness bus and the total actual demand is 259MW. There are 56 meters used for the real power measurements of generators, loads and transmission lines. Suppose that the generator owners at Bus 2 and Bus 6 are coordinated as the attackers.

Table 1. Simulation configuration

Gen. Bus No.	1	2	3	6	8	Line No.	max.cap. (MW)
min.cap. (MW)	0	0	0	0	0	1	160
max.cap. (MW)	300	50	30	50	20	2~20	60
marg.cost ($/MWh)	15	25	35	45	30	$\tau = 0.2$	$N_m = 20$
	20	30	40	50	35	$M = 10^6$	$c_s = 100(\$/MWh)$
	25	35	45	55	40	$H = I_{N_d}$	
intercept($/h)	0	0	0	0	0		
	−500	−50	−50	−50	−25		
	−1500	−200	−150	−200	−100		

This case illustrates the trending of actual and nominal power generation, LMPs, and total illegal profit at Bus 2 and Bus 6 when the load redistribution is triggered under the economic-driven FDI attacks. The total false load injection gradually increases as the injection rate α increases by 0.02 from 0 to 0.12, which is shown in the horizontal axes of four figures. The left and right vertical axes of Figs. 2 and 3 denote the power generation, the LMPs, the illegal profit and the increment percentage of the attackers' revenue, respectively. The right vertical axes of Figs. 4 and 5 denotes the actual and nominal power generation at Bus 1, respectively.

When $\alpha = 0$, i.e., $\sum_{i \in V_d} \Delta P_d^i = 0$, the total actual demands remain unchanged at 259 MW but $\Delta P_d \neq 0$ will cause the load redistribution. Figure 2 shows that the attacked LMPs are consistent with the normal LMPs but the total attacked power generation at Bus 2 and Bus 6 exceed the total normal generation. Figure 3 illustrates that the total actual profit under attacks slightly increase by 5% upto 1940 ($/h) from 1856 ($/h), the total profit without attack but the total nominal profit under attack just is 1802 ($/h), which is displayed in the central operation center.

When α raises below 0.12, this means that the total corrupt demand gradually increases in the cyber layer. Figure 2 draws that the attacked LMPs at Bus 2 and Bus 6 gradually rise up and the attacked power generation at Bus 2 equals to the normal power generation, but that at Bus 6 always keep increasing. As a result, the trending of total actual illegal profit is rising until 54%, shown in

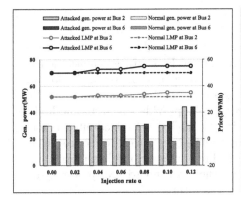

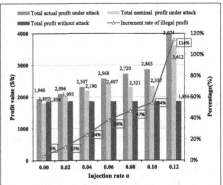

Fig. 2. Power generation and LMPs

Fig. 3. Total illegal profit

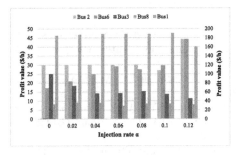

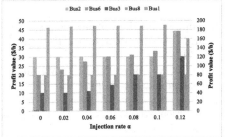

Fig. 4. Actual power generation

Fig. 5. Nominal power generation

Fig. 3, while the nominal profit will grow upto 2337 ($/h), which is still less than total actual profit so that such illegal profit might remain to misguide the central operation center. These experimental results conform with the consequence of the load redistribution.

When $\alpha = 0.12$, the attacked power generation at Bus 2 and Bus 6 get rapidly large while the attacked LMPs nearly have no growth, which can lead to the attackers' revenue upto 144%. Nevertheless, when $\alpha > 0.12$, the attacked LMPs become sharply increasing under the case that the SCED model does not consider the common scenario of the load shedding. Here, it is worthwhile to note that the drastic increased profit may trigger the detection alarm, but the existing works almost ignore this class of the detection risk.

In Figs. 4 and 5, we can also see that the actual power generation gradually decrease but the nominal power generation almost increase at Bus 1, 3 and 8. Nevertheless, the actual and nominal power generation almost keep consistent at Bus 2 and 6. That implies that the illegal profit obtained by the corrupted generator actually comes from that generated by the normal generator but the central operation control can not discover such anomaly due to the misguidance of nominal power generation tampered by the attacker.

5   Conclusion

In this paper, we reveal the impact of a potential misconduct of the corrupt generator owners who can launch the economic-driven FDI attack against the electricity market. From attackers' perspective, we develop a bilevel leader-follower game theoretical model to derive a false data injection based load redistribution attack that maximizes the attacker's revenue. We provide a solution method to reformulate the bilevel nonlinear model into a single-level mixed-integer linear program that is readily computable by any professional solver. Numerical results show that such type of FDI attack is stealthy but with a serious disruption power. Hence, our work is significant for securing the data integrity of power system against the economic-driven FDI attack in the future.

References

1. Cintuglu, M.H., Mohammed, O.A., Akkaya, K., Uluagac, A.S.: A survey on smart grid cyber-physical system testbeds. IEEE Commun. Surv. Tutor. **19**(1), 446–464 (2017)
2. Grant, M., Boyd, S.: CVX: Matlab software for disciplined convex programming, version 2.1, March 2014. http://cvxr.com/cvx
3. Liang, G., Zhao, J., Luo, F., Weller, S.R., Dong, Z.Y.: A review of false data injection attacks against modern power systems. IEEE Trans. Smart Grid **8**(4), 1630–1638 (2017)
4. Liu, C., Zhou, M., Wu, J., Long, C., Kundur, D.: Financially motivated FDI on SCED in real-time electricity markets: attacks and mitigation. IEEE Trans. Smart Grid (2017)
5. Liu, H., Tesfatsion, L., Chowdhury, A.: Locational marginal pricing basics for restructured wholesale power markets. In: Power and Energy Society General Meeting, PES 2009, pp. 1–8. IEEE (2009)
6. Liu, X., Li, Z., Shuai, Z., Wen, Y.: Cyber attacks against the economic operation of power systems: a fast solution. IEEE Trans. Smart Grid **8**(2), 1023–1025 (2017)
7. Liu, Y., Ning, P., Reiter, M.K.: False data injection attacks against state estimation in electric power grids. ACM Trans. Inf. Syst. Secur. (TISSEC) **14**(1), 1–13 (2011)
8. Orfanogianni, T., Gross, G.: A general formulation for lmp evaluation. IEEE Trans. Power Syst. **22**(3), 1163–1173 (2007)
9. Tan, S., De, D., Song, W.Z., Yang, J., Das, S.K.: Survey of security advances in smart grid: a data driven approach. IEEE Commun. Surv. Tutor. **19**(1), 397–422 (2017)
10. Xie, L., Mo, Y., Sinopoli, B.: Integrity data attacks in power market operations. IEEE Trans. Smart Grid **2**(4), 659–666 (2011)
11. Yuan, Y., Li, Z., Ren, K.: Modeling load redistribution attacks in power systems. IEEE Trans. Smart Grid **2**(2), 382–390 (2011)
12. Zimmerman, R.D., Murillo-Sánchez, C.E., Thomas, R.J.: MATPOWER: steady-state operations, planning, and analysis tools for power systems research and education. IEEE Trans. Power Syst. **26**(1), 12–19 (2011)

Author Index

Printed in the United States
By Bookmasters